COMPUTER METHODS
IN
OPERATIONS RESEARCH

OPERATIONS RESEARCH
AND INDUSTRIAL ENGINEERING

Consulting Editor: J. William Schmidt

CBM, Inc., Cleveland, Ohio

Applied Statistical Methods
I. W. Burr

Mathematical Foundations of Management Science
and Systems Analysis
J. William Schmidt

Urban Systems Models
Walter Helly

Introduction to Discrete Linear Controls: Theory and Application
Albert B. Bishop

Integer Programming: Theory, Applications, and Computations
Hamdy A. Taha

Transform Techniques for Probability Modeling
Walter C. Giffin

Analysis of Queueing Systems
J. A. White, J. W. Schmidt, and G. K. Bennett

Models for Public Systems Analysis
Edward J. Beltrami

Computer Methods in Operations Research
Arne Thesen

In preparation:

Cost-Benefit Analysis: A Handbook
Peter G. Sassone and William A. Schaffer

Modeling of Complex Systems
V. Vemuri

COMPUTER METHODS
IN
OPERATIONS RESEARCH

ARNE THESEN

DEPARTMENT OF INDUSTRIAL ENGINEERING
UNIVERSITY OF WISCONSIN
MADISON, WISCONSIN

ACADEMIC PRESS   New York   San Francisco   London   1978

A Subsidiary of Harcourt Brace Jovanovich, Publishers

ACADEMIC PRESS, INC.
111 Fifth Avenue, New York, New York 10003

United Kingdom Edition published by
ACADEMIC PRESS, INC. (LONDON) LTD.
24/28 Oval Road, London NW1

Library of Congress Cataloging in Publication Data

Thesen, Arne.
    Computer methods in operations research.

    (Operations research and industrial engineering
series)
    Includes bibliographies.
    1.   Operations research—Data processing.
I.   Title.
T57.6.T47   001.4$'$24$'$02854   77-74063
ISBN 0−12−686150−1

CONTENTS

v

PREFACE

This text is designed to fill the growing gap between the computational requirements emerging in modern industrial engineering and operations research (IE/OR) applications and the algorithmic and computational methods commonly available to the IE/OR student and practitioner.

As an illustration of this gap, consider the conventional labeling or "scratch pad" approaches to shortest or longest (i.e., critical path method) path network problems discussed in introductory OR texts. These techniques work well for hand calculation where a visual representation of the network is available. They also work in computer programs designed to handle small problems where manual procedures can be mimicked in an exact manner. However, substantial additional considerations enter when programs are to be written that handle larger than illustrative problems.

These considerations include issues such as: (1) What errors are likely to occur in the input phase? How can they be avoided, detected, or corrected? (2) What are the different ways available to represent the network in the computer? (3) What is the most efficient algorithm for the problem at hand? (4) What errors are likely to occur during the analysis phase? How can they be avoided or detected and possibly corrected? (5) How should the performance of the resulting program be evaluated? While these issues are rightfully ignored both in introductory level computer programming courses and in introductory level OR courses, they are important issues of substantial economic significance that the practicing systems analyst cannot afford to ignore.

The academic level of a course based on this book would be suitable for a senior or first-year graduate student in engineering or business. Prerequisites for this course would include a course in FORTRAN programming and a course in deterministic OR models (including linear programming (LP) and network analysis). The course itself could be useful as a corequisite for more advanced courses in graph theory or network analysis as well as a useful prerequisite for a thorough course in simulation techniques.

In Chapter I we provide a review of some of the basic principles that make a software development effort successful. Throughout this chapter the need to keep things simple and understandable is stressed. The computer is a servant, not a master. The development of a code that is not used because the potential user does not believe or understand it is a wasted effort. Considerable attention is also devoted in Chapter I to the subject of software evaluation.

Chapters II and III cover the basic principles of list processing, searching, and sorting. Such subjects are normally included in second or third level computer science courses. However, these courses are usually too specialized and have too many prerequisites to be available to the anticipated audience of this textbook.

In Chapter IV the concept of networks is introduced and several matrix and list oriented methods for representing networks in the computer are discussed. Techniques for spanning all nodes and/or links in a network are then developed.

The critical path method (CPM) is discussed in Chapter V. We show how to develop efficient CPM algorithms. We also investigate the problem of designing CPM packages as computer-based management tools. Guidelines are developed for handling the detection of input errors and for the design of reports. The needs of the user (rather than the computer or the analyst) are the major concern here.

Chapter VI presents more complex programs and algorithms to handle scheduling of activities under precedence and resource restrictions. To illustrate these approaches, the resource-constrained scheduling problem is formulated both in an exact (using integer programming) and in a heuristic manner. The difficulties of implementing these approaches in a computer are discussed. Finally, a complete commercial scheduling package for managerial use is reviewed in detail. This chapter also serves as a vehicle for an in-depth discussion of many aspects of program evaluation.

The design of algorithms for the solution of large linear programming problems is discussed in Chapter VII. A simple review is given of the formulation and solution of LP problems, using the revised simplex method. This discussion is followed by a review of how various algorithmic aspects, such as the handling of sparse matrices, pricing, and the updating of the inverse, are implemented so that the resulting usage of computer resources is minimized. This chapter also contains a brief overview of available mathematical programming systems, and the mathematical programming systems data input format is reviewed in detail. Finally, the chapter contains a discussion of the concepts of generalized upper bounds as implemented in the MPSIII system designed by Management Science Systems, Inc. (Permission to reprint their discussion on this subject is greatly appreciated.)

The application of list processing concepts to the development of branch and bound algorithms for solution of combinatorial optimization problems is discussed in Chapter VIII. Design considerations for branch and bound algorithms are given. An illustration is presented to demonstrate how sorting and list processing can be used as the two basic techniques to solve multidimensional knapsack problems efficiently.

The design of pseudorandom number generators is discussed in Chapter IX. We first show how uniformly distributed pseudorandom numbers can be generated, using multiplicative congruential methods. Values of appropriate constants for several different computers are given. This discussion is followed by a review of four different tests for checking the acceptability of pseudorandom number generators. Finally, the generation of random deviates from the exponential, Erlang, normal, chi-square, and Poisson distributions is discussed.

Chapters X and XI are concerned with discrete event simulation studies. The discussion of fundamental modeling and programming aspects in Chapter X is centered around a simple data structure and a few rudimentary subroutines designed to carry out the essential steps in any discrete event simulation program. Chapter XI is concerned with simulation modeling, using formal simulation languages. Discussions are presented here on two widely different languages. GPSS (the main simulation language in use in the United States today) and WIDES (a much simpler language especially designed for inexperienced users).

ACKNOWLEDGMENTS

I wish to acknowledge the labors and influences of a few friends and colleagues without whom this text would not have materialized. Dr. E. L. Murphree of Sage, a consulting cooperative in Champaign, Illinois, introduced me to many of the subjects in the text, and, more notably, his contagious curiosity and ability to kindle creative thinking have had a monumental impact on my professional growth. The present form of this manuscript is the result of many hundreds of hours of stimulating interaction with students using several earlier drafts of this text. In particular, I wish to acknowledge the efforts of S. Miller, E. Hobbs, F. Cheung, and L. Strauss for weeding out many annoying errors in earlier drafts. The assistance of Ms. Lynda Parker in editing an early draft of the text is also appreciated. Finally, Mrs. Doreen Marquart is to be thanked for a patient and highly competent job in typing all drafts as well as the final manuscript.

CHAPTER I

CONSIDERATIONS IN PROGRAM DESIGN AND EVALUATION

A. INTRODUCTION

Although the code in a FORTRAN program must follow very strict syntactic rules, the act of designing such a program is a very creative process subject to few if any formal rules. This has resulted in the development of highly individualistic styles of program development and design. Some of these styles are effective; others are not. Some do not work at all.

Our intent in this chapter is to identify the key attributes of "good" programs and "good" programming practices. In addition, we will suggest several programming procedures and guidelines that may reduce the time and effort required to write a program and may also improve the quality of the end product. However, we are dealing with empirical guidelines; what works for us, may or may not work for you.

The process of writing complex programs requires many considerations and decisions. Of primary concern is the reduction of the time and effort to be expended in the programming task so as to release time for the design and development of the algorithms which your program represents.

B.   PROGRAM DEVELOPMENT PROCESS

As shown in Fig. I-1, the program development process starts with the user recognizing a problem and ends with his interpreting a computer printout that may provide relevant information and/or answers. The success or failure of a particular programming effort is primarily determined by the degree to which this printout assists the user in resolving his problem.

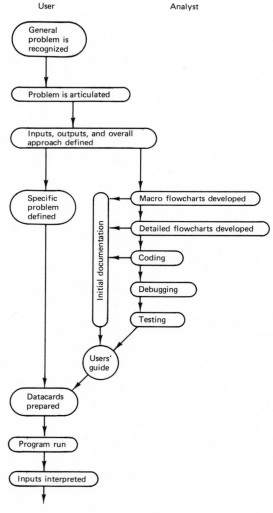

FIG. I-1   Program development process.

All program development activities should be geared toward the goal of maximum user impact. Activities that have little or no bearing on this impact (such as the development of a superefficient code that reduces the number of statements or execution time by 10%) should be omitted or abandoned. Activities that do have great user impact, such as documentation and output design, should be given in-depth attention.

In order to achieve maximum user impact, the program should possess the following attributes and features:

(1) adequate documentation,
(2) user oriented input requirements,
(3) outputs designed to fit user needs,
(4) validity checking of user inputs,
(5) meaningful error messages if necessary,
(6) reasonable turn around time.

These features must be incorporated as integral program elements from the start of the program design process and cannot be added as an afterthought.

The following guidelines have proved effective in developing reasonably efficient, error-free code in a relatively short time:

(1) Spend considerable time planning the programming effort.
(2) Use a standardized program organization.
(3) Write simple code.
(4) Write self-documented code.
(5) Be general whenever possible.
(6) Do not punch a single card until the program design is completed.

To breach this last guideline can at times be most tempting. However, to do so will almost certainly result in failure and loss of precious time. Detailed discussion of all six guidelines will occur in the following sections.

C. PROGRAM ORGANIZATION

Simplicity is the key to good program organization. The goal is to achieve a modularized program wherein two things occur: (1) the different logical functions are separated in different sections of the program, and (2) these separate sections are integrated in as simple a manner as possible.

A good test for adequacy of organization is to show the program to a competent programmer. If after some study he is able to determine what the program is supposed to do, then the program structure is probably sufficient.

One way to achieve a well-structured modular program design is to use a hierarchical approach in drawing the program flowchart. An initial one page flowchart is drawn showing the major steps in the program. On successive flowcharts, the functions in individual flowchart "boxes" are "blown up" in more and more detail. Whenever possible, do not extend a flowchart to a continuation page. Keeping the flowchart on one page increases its readability and allows the programmer to focus on program details relevant to a given module without being distracted by other programming concerns. In Fig. I-2 we show a hierarchical flowchart of a program designed to multiply two matrices together. This flowchart also incorporates the following two key flowcharting conventions:

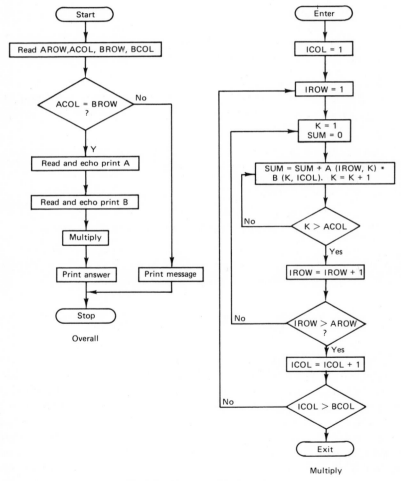

FIG. I-2   Hierarchical flowchart.

(1) Always draw flowcharts such that the longest chain of logic appears as a straight line down the middle of the page.

(2) Do not cram too much information into one flowchart.

The layout of the computer code can be determined as soon as the flowchart has been completed and all issues regarding method and program design have been resolved. We advocate the use of a consistent layout for all programs. The following sequence of major program blocks may serve as an illustration of how a large number of computer codes can be structured:

(1) comment cards describing program purpose, outputs, input card preparation,

(2) additional comment cards describing the method and key variables (if necessary),

(3) declarative statements in the following order:

```
IMPLICIT
REAL
INTEGER
DIMENSION
COMMON
LABELED COMMON
DATA
```

(4) program initialization section,

(5) data input section,

(6) method,

(7) output.

While you may choose a different layout than the one suggested here, it is important that you consistently use the same layout every time you write a program.

D. PROGRAMMING DETAILS

A standardized approach to programming results in a semiautomatic execution of trivial tasks (such as program layout, choice of variable names, assignment of statement labels). Thus, it reduces the likelihood of errors in these tasks and frees time and attention for more important tasks. A standardized approach also pays off in maintenance and debugging since the resulting standardized format renders the programs very easy to read and understand.

The following rules will assist in achieving a consistent and self-documenting style in the production of programs:

TABLE I-1

KEY FEATURES OF USA FORTRAN IV

Identifier	Abbrev.	Definition	Example
Constant	a	Real number	$2.735, -0.153$
	i	Integer	$73, 8321, -43$
	—	Logical variable	.TRUE., .FALSE.
	d	Double precision	2.2357682173
Expression	e	Composite of operators and variables and/or constants of a single mode	$(A * B - Q)/2.738$
Label	l	Unsigned integer constant	1000, 100, 2730
List	—	List of variables separated by commas	A, B, C
Name	—	Identifier of functions, subroutines, and common areas	WIDES, A100
Variable	a, i, v	Identifier of storage areas containing constants	A, B, C, I, KONT

Executable statement	General form	Example
Assignment	variable = expression	A = 2.2 * AVG − STDV
BLOCK DATA	BLOCK DATA	BLOCK DATA
	COMMON/name/list	COMMON/LOC/A, B, C
	DATA list/constants/	DATA A, BC/2.2, 2 * 7.01
	END	END
CALL	CALL name (list)	CALL BILL(CREDIT)

	General form	Example
CONTINUE	label CONTINUE	1000 CONTINUE
DO	DO label $i_1 = i_2, i_3, i_4$	DO 1000 I = 1, N
GO TO, unconditional	GO TO label	GO TO 1000
GO TO, computed	GO TO (label$_1$,...,label$_n$),i	GO TO (1,2,3), I
IF, arithmetic	IF (e) l_1, l_2, l_3	IF (A−B) 1,2,3
IF, logical	IF (e) executable stmt	IF (A.EQ.B) B = C
READ, formatted	READ (unit, label) list	READ(6,100)A,B,C
READ, unformatted	READ (unit) list	READ(TAPE)LIST
RETURN	RETURN	RETURN
RETURN, alternate	RETURN i	RETURN 2
STOP	STOP	STOP
WRITE, formatted	WRITE (unit, label) list	WRITE (IPT, 100) A,B,C
WRITE, unformatted	WRITE (unit) list	WRITE (DISK), A,B,C

Nonexecutable statements	General form	Example
COMMON, labeled	COMMON/name/list	COMMON/BILL/A,B,C
COMMON, unlabeled	COMMON LIST	COMMON A,B,C
DATA	DATA list/constants/	DATA A,B,C/2.4,2*7/
DIMENSION	DIMENSION $v_1(i_1,...,i_n), v_2( ),...$	DIMENSION A(10,10), B(10)
EQUIVALENCE	EQUIVALENCE (list$_1$) ... (list$_n$)	EQUIVALENCE (A(1,10), B(1))
END	END	END
FORMAT	Label FORMAT (specifications)	100 FORMAT (2F3.2, 2HHH)
FUNCTION	FUNCTION name (list)	FUNCTION MAX (LIST)
SUBROUTINE	SUBROUTINE name (lists)	SUBROUTINE MAX (LIST)

(1) Use about as many comment cards as FORTRAN cards.

(2) Precede and follow each comment by a blank card.

(3) Clearly delimit each section of the code with a "C————————" card.

(4) Almost always use self-explanatory variable names.

(5) Almost always use self-explanatory subscript names (exception: short or implied DO loop).

(6) Use a consistent label assignment scheme:

    (a) $1000 + 10 * i$ for the ith statement number,

    (b) $100 + i$ for the ith FORMAT statement.

(7) Terminate all DO loops in CONTINUE statement.

(8) Indent all code between the DO and the corresponding CONTINUE by two columns.

(9) Immediately follow an input–output (I/O) statement by the appropriate FORMAT statement.

(10) Avoid use of unlabeled common; use labeled common instead.

(11) Avoid use of numeric constants. Replace these by variables initialized at the head of the program.

(12) Use free format input whenever possible.

Most FORTRAN installations provide a slightly different instruction set. However, almost all FORTRAN installations incorporate as a subset a standardized version of FORTRAN IV that has been approved by the United States of America Standards Institute. Key features of this FORTRAN are shown in Table I-1. Many extensions of FORTRAN IV are available. These provide many nice features not available in standard FORTRAN. However, even though we are enthusiastic about many of these features, we caution against their use because programs using them are seriously restricted in portability and generality.

E. THE USER INTERFACE

The user interacts with the program through three different channels. The *program documentation* tells him whether or not the program is suitable for his needs. If it is, the documentation then tells him how to prepare *inputs* (the second channel) and how to interpret the *outputs* (the last channel). Murphy's law (if something can go wrong, it will) applies with certainty in the user interface. To avoid embarrassment and misunderstanding, the programmer is therefore well advised to design a user interface that minimizes the likelihood that errors will be made there. In this section, we shall suggest several systems design practices that will assist in reaching this goal.

1. Documentation

Adequate program documentation provides for a number of time and money saving advantages: (1) versatility—clear documentation will render the program accessible to any programmer, not just the initial programmer; (2) continuity—details of the program will be accessible to the user regardless of the time lapsed since the start of the program; and (3) accuracy—the user will work with clear indicators of the problems and answers to be considered in this program.

It is difficult to formulate standards for good program documentation. A program that will be widely used by a large number of relatively unsophisticated users clearly requires a different quality of documentation than a one-shot "quick-and-dirty" program written by the user himself. There is a clear tradeoff between the time and effort spent documenting a program and the difficulty experienced by the user in attempting to use it.

The level of documentation is in some cases determined by contract or federal or military specification. If so, such specifications must be followed to the letter. Otherwise, a document containing at least the following information should be generated:

(1) Program title   short but descriptive,
(2) Author   include address and phone number,
(3) Date   initial date and date of all revisions,
(4) Purpose   in general terms,
(5) Algorithm   be specific, give references,
(6) Limitations   *important*,
(7) Method of use   problem definition, card preparation, deck setup, outputs and error messages,
(8) Sample problem   problem description, data cards, outputs, discussion.

In many cases a program listing and/or a flowchart may also be indicated.

It is extremely difficult to write unambiguous documentation. For important programs, or programs receiving a widespread distribution, it may be a good idea to debug the documentation by testing it on a few users with about the same training and background as the intended final audience.

2. User Inputs

The program should be designed such that the probability of errors in user inputs is minimized. This means that the choice of input format should be dictated by what is convenient for the user, not by what is easy to program.

If data is available in a certain format, this format should be used. The data can then be easily converted to whatever internal format is required for subsequent internal processing.

In Fig. I-3 we summarize the most likely sources of errors in the data input section. Errors are of at least two fundamentally different kinds. The first class contains user modeling errors. Here the data is correctly transmitted to the computer; however, the situation described by the data is one that cannot be handled by the program. Examples of such errors include an attempt to compute the square root of a negative number or an attempt to generate an Erlang random variable (Chapter IX) with a noninteger k. A well-designed program will usually check all input parameters for validity and generate appropriate error messages when required. The programmer should always make sure that no program (well-designed or not) is able to successfully compute an "answer" to an impossible problem. In some cases, it may suffice to ensure that the program aborts on some random error condition

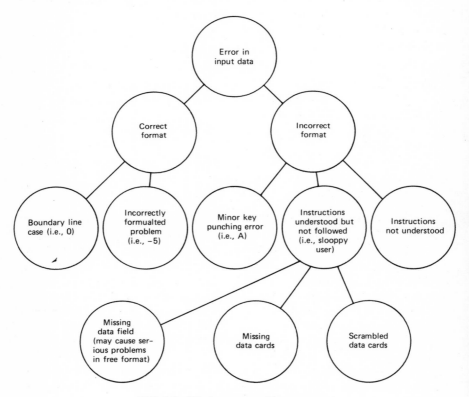

FIG. I-3   Likely sources of input errors.

prior to obtaining the answer (but without a meaningful error message). This approach may, however, lead to considerable expenditure of time in finding some assumed programming error that really is caused by erroneous user inputs.

The second class of errors contains those cases where cards are not prepared in accordance with user instructions. Such errors usually result in an input format error and an automatic program abort. These errors are normally easy to locate if an echo of the input cards is provided.

Certain of the input parameters for most programs or subroutines are usually restricted to a limited range. For example, a matrix multiplication program may require the number of rows and/or columns to be between 1 and 100. A program intended for widespread use should always check input data for such validity. If invalid parameter values are encountered, a message should be written for a main program, and execution should be terminated. The action taken in a subroutine should reflect the severity of the error and the type of the subroutine. Execution could either be terminated, or control could be returned to the main program to the regular or an alternate location.

The golden rule to follow is that input requirements should be designed such that the easiest method for the user is also the correct method. As an added precaution, the validity of the input parameters should be ascertained so that any errors can be found and corrected at their source.

3. Outputs

A computer printout should (1) identify the output case and (2) contain only information relevant to that case. A one or two page summary of conclusions has much more impact than stacks of computer printouts.

We have found it effective to spend substantial time in designing the format of our output reports. In fact, we usually do this in the planning stage before any of the program is written. Whenever possible, we try to lay out the printout so that we can cut the 11×14 printout to get a neat looking $8\frac{1}{2} \times 11$ page that slips readily into the final report.

To facilitate the design of such a report, we present in Table I-2 the available columns and lines for $11 \times 8\frac{1}{2}$ and $8\frac{1}{2} \times 11$ reports with different sized margins. The line counts offered here may differ from the one at your installation since the first and last line on a page is determined by a paper tape in the printer and not by the computer itself.

When the program in question is a subroutine, care should be taken to avoid changing the value of any of the input parameters. This kind of unexpected output will win few friends and influence many people—the wrong way.

TABLE I-2

Available Lines and Columns for $8\frac{1}{2} \times 11$ and $11 \times 8\frac{1}{2}$ Reports with Different Margins

Paper size		Margins				Columns (10 per in.)				Lines[a] (6 per in.)			
Width	Height	Left	Right	Top	Bottom	First	Center	Last	Total	First	Center	Last	Total
$8\frac{1}{2}$	11	$\frac{1}{2}$	0	$\frac{1}{2}$	$\frac{5}{8}$	1	48	80	80	1	30	60	60
		1	$\frac{1}{2}$	$\frac{1}{2}$	$\frac{5}{8}$	6	40	75	70	1	30	60	60
		1	1	1	1	6	38	70	65	5	30	56	52
		$1\frac{1}{2}$	1	1	1	10	40	70	61	5	30	56	52
11	$8\frac{1}{2}$	$\frac{1}{2}$	0	$\frac{1}{2}$	0	1	50	105	105	1	25	49	48
		$\frac{1}{2}$	$\frac{1}{2}$	1	$\frac{1}{2}$	2	50	100	99	5	26	46	42
		1	1	1	1	6	50	95	90	5	24	43	39
		1	1	$1\frac{1}{2}$	1	6	50	95	90	11	27	43	33

[a] Slightly installation dependent.

12

F. PROGRAM EVALUATION

All programs of the complex nature discussed in this text should be thoroughly tested and evaluated prior to a release to potential users. Failure to do so may have catastrophic consequences when ill-conceived or erroneous code is released. Unfortunately, we are only able to specify empirical guidelines or loose rules for how a program is to be evaluated or tested. In fact, the evaluation and testing of computer programs is even more of an art than is the design of such programs.

To put some structure on the problem of testing and evaluation, we will recognize four different levels of evaluation criteria:

(1) program correctness,
(2) computational efficiency,
(3) analytic effectiveness,
(4) systems efficiency.

The first of these evaluation levels is concerned with program testing or debugging. The other three levels are concerned with performance evaluation of how efficient the program is, of how "good" the answers are, and of how well the program assist in solving the problem at hand. In this chapter we shall discuss program testing, computational efficiency, and analytic efficiency. These topics will also be discussed and illustrated throughout the text. The problem of systems efficiency will not be discussed. This is because (a) systems efficiency draws upon many concerns outside this text, and (b) the state of the art is even less formally developed here than in the other fields of program evaluation.

1. Program Correctness

All computer programs should at least be checked to ascertain that they do what they were intended to do. This is usually done by solving one or a few small test problems with known or obvious answers. While this practice may be sufficient in the development stages of a computer program, such a cursory evaluation does in no way guarantee the integrity of a program. To do this, the test problems must be of a complexity and size identical to those for which the program was designed; and a sufficient number of different test problems must be solved in order to test all the various branches in the program. However, the difficulty of this task is easily underestimated since the number of required test problems becomes prohibitively large even for only moderately complex problems. Thus, while the main chains of logic can be tested prior to release, it is unreasonable to expect that the more obscure or infrequently traversed combinations of program branches can be adequately evaluated prior to a field test where the program is used under actual conditions. Thus, the program testing phase of any new piece of software should either include a formal field test or a close supervision of the program's performance until its integrity has been actually established.

A body of literature on automatic or formalistic approaches to program testing is slowly emerging. Many of these approaches entail the design of programs or languages containing substantial redundancies such that logical inconsistencies can be detected. The interested reader is referred to the review article by Huang (1975) or to the conference proceedings edited by Hetzel (1973).

It is not sufficient to determine that the program works correctly with valid data. Tests should also be made to ascertain that the program responds appropriately to invalid data. The appropriate response could range from having the program ignore invalid data for minor errors to aborting the program run for more serious mistakes.

2. Computational Efficiency

In addition to ascertaining the integrity of the code and the corresponding documentation, it is desirable to evaluate the performance of the computer code under various conditions. Such evaluations are performed both to provide potential users with sufficient data to determine the suitability of a particular code in a given context and to show the superiority of a newly developed code over the existing ones. Computational efficiency can be measured in terms of the computer resources (primarily time and core) required to solve certain problems or in terms of computer independent measures such as the number of iterations or pivots required to solve a given problem. While the former approach is fairly easily implemented, it does raise the question of how data can be translated from one machine to another.

Prime measures among the machine independent measures are variables such as the number of moves, comparisons, or iterations. These measures can either be analytically derived (see, e.g., Knuth, 1975) or empirically measured by solving test problems. This approach works reasonably well and yields reasonably meaningful answers when relatively simple algorithms such as sorts or numerical integration methods are analyzed. Machine independent measures are less meaningful when complex algorithms such as integer programming or location–allocation algorithms are analyzed. This is because the steps in the algorithms can be fairly complex and/or because the fundamental steps are substantially different in the different algorithm. For example, the knapsack algorithm in Chapter VIII is designed to evaluate a large number of alternatives in an extremely short time; however, each individual evaluation involves only a few computer instructions. Geoffrion's RIP30C integer programming code (Geoffrion and Nelson, 1968), on the other hand, evaluates extremely few alternatives but each evaluation is fairly lengthy and involves the solution of a large linear program. If an iteration is defined as the evaluation of an alternative solution, then it is clear that an iteration count will not yield meaningful comparison data in this case.

However, even in this case machine independent measures are useful in comparing the performance of algorithms as problem attributes (such as size and constraint tightness) change.

The prime machine-dependent efficiency measures are central processing unit (CPU) time and core storage. In time sharing and other computers utilizing virtual memory in a paging system, the amount of I/O time will also be important. Most computer installations provide a timing function that returns the elapsed time in milliseconds either since the last call or since the start of the program. For example, the University of Wisconsin Harris Datacraft 6024/3 minicomputer provides the FORTRAN function MILSEC that returns elapsed time in tens of milliseconds since the start of the program. To use this function to measure the amount of time required to perform a sort using the Quicksort routine presented in Chapter III, we would write

```
      TIME = MILSEC(X)
      CALL QSORT(RANDOM,NVAR)
      TIME = ( MILSEC(X)-TIME)/10.0
      WRITE (6,100) TIME,NVAR
100 FORMAT(F8.2,' MILLISECONDS WAS NEEDED TO SORT A LIST OF SIZE',I5)
```

Many timing routines give distorted measurements when a program segment containing I/O is measured. Therefore, either all CPU time measurements should be taken of code that is void of I/O statements, or the clock should be stopped whenever I/O requests are encountered.

The CPU time required to execute a program solving a given problem on a given computer depends upon several important factors such as programmer skill, operating system efficiency, compiler design, and the intrinsic machine efficiency. Thus, it is usually not possible to estimate how fast the program

TABLE I-3

AVERAGE SPEED (IN MSEC) OF BASIC OPERATIONS ON DIFFERENT COMPUTERS

	Integer			Floating point		
	Add	Mply	Divide	Add	Mply	Divide
IBM 370/158	0.5	1.6	9.4	2.0	1.8	8.6
UNIVAC 1108	0.8	2.4	10.1	1.9	2.6	8.3
DATACRAFT 6024/3	2.0	8.0	15.0	14.0	14.0	23.0

would run on another machine. To illustrate one aspect of this difficulty, we present in Table I-3 the amount of CPU time to perform six basic operations on several different computers. It is seen that while the IBM 370 performs a floating point multiplication faster than the Univac 1108, its floating point division is slightly slower than that of the Univac.

However, even with these difficulties machine time measurements remain one of the most meaningful efficiency measures in use today.

3. Analytic Effectiveness

Souder (1972) defines analytic effectiveness as the ability of a model to prescribe higher valued courses of action than those prescribed by alternate methods. For example, in the context of resource constrained scheduling algorithms, analytic effectiveness refers to the ability of heuristic algorithms to produce schedules of the same quality as those produced by optimal algorithms solving the same problem. In this case, parameters such as additional cost or tardiness (in percent over the optimal solution) may be used as measures of analytic effectiveness. When optimal solutions are unavailable, an evaluation measure such as the "solution quality" (calculated cost over some lower bound of cost) introduced by Ritzman (1972) may be used. Unfortunately this measure does not lend itself well to comparisons between problems since the quality of the bound is both variable and unknown. An alternative to this approach would be to measure and compare the effectiveness of several different approaches to each other rather than to some exact norm.

The analytic effectiveness can be obtained through theoretical analysis or through empirical measurement. The field of numerical analysis contains many examples of theoretical approaches to the computation of the expected errors in certain well-defined algorithms.

G. TEST PROBLEMS

Most evaluations are performed by solving specific test problems under controlled conditions. Three different classes of test problems can be identified. First, we have relatively small and simple problems with known solutions primarily designed to assist in the development and primary debugging of the code. Second, we have larger more realistic problems, usually with known answers. These problems are used both to test the integrity of the code and to test the amount of resources required by the code to solve specific problems. To facilitate comparisons between different codes, standardized or published test problems should be used if at all possible. Such problems are frequently in circulation among experts in various fields. For example, the Mathematical Programming Society has established a Working Committee on Algorithms that, among other things, is charged with the collection and distribution of test problems. Test problems or references to test problems are also frequently published in the open literature. For example, Patterson and Huber (1974) identify twelve standard resource constrained scheduling problems, and Geoffrion and Marsten (1972) identify a large number of standard integer programming problems.

The third and last class of problems contains randomly generated problems. Such problems differ from the problems in the previous two classes for the following reasons:

(a)   their solutions are usually not known in advance,

(b)   specific problems may not be reproducible on different computers, and

(c)   comparison between the efforts required to solve single randomly generated problems is usually difficult or meaningless.

However, these disadvantages may be substantially outweighed by the following potential advantages:

(a)   a random problem generator is easily portable,

(b)   a well-designed generator allows for the generation of problems of widely different but controlled attributes, and

(c)   statistical methods may be used to study how the algorithm responds to problems with a spectrum of different attributes.

Small test problems are easily constructed by the analyst himself. Standard test problems should be obtained from the literature or from sources such as the Mathematical Programming Society. Random problem generations may also, in certain circumstances, be obtained from the literature (Chapters IV and VIII; Rardin and Lin, 1975). However, it is frequently necessary or convenient to develop problem generators locally.

BIBLIOGRAPHY

Carnaham, B., and J. O. Wilkes, *Digital Computing and Numerical Method.* Wiley, New York, 1973.

Dahl, O. J., E. W. Dijkstra, and C. A. R. Hoare, *Structured Programming.* Academic Press, New York, 1972.

Dijkstra, E. W., "Go to Statement Considered Meaningful" (letter to editor), *Comm. ACM* **11**, No. 3 (March 1968), 147–148.

Geoffrion, A. M., and R. E. Marsten, "Integer Programming: A Framework and State-of-the-Art Survey," *Management Sci.* **18**, No. 9 (May 1972), 465–491.

Geoffrion, A. M., and **A. B. Nelson,** "Users Instructions for Integer Linear Programming Code RIP30C," RM–5627. The Rand Corp., Santa Monica, California, 1968.

Gottfried, B. S., *Programming with FORTRAN IV.* Quantum Publ., New York, 1972.

Hetzel, W. C., ed., *Program Test Methods.* Prentice-Hall, Englewood Cliffs, New Jersey, 1973.

Huang, T. C., "Program Testing," *Comput. Rev.* (1975).

Inmon, B., "An Example of Structured Design," *Datamation* (March 1976), 82–86.

Knuth, D. E., *The Art of Computer Programming*, Vol. 3, Sorting and Searching, second printing. Addison-Wesley, Reading, Massachusetts, 1975.

Loeser, Rudolf, "Some Performance Tests of 'Quicksort' and Decendents," *Comm. ACM* **17,** No. 3 (March 1974), 143–52.

Kuester, J. L., and **J. H. Mize,** *Optimization Techniques with Fortran.* McGraw-Hill, New York, 1973.

Maynard,. J., *Modular Programming.* Auerbach, 1972.

Meeber, R. E., and **C. V. Ramamoorty,** "A Study in Software Reliability and Evaluation," Tech. Memo. Univ. of Texas, Austin, February 1973.

Mills, H., "Top Down Programming in Large System," in *Debugging Techniques on Large Scale System* (R. Rustin, ed.). Prentice-Hall, Englewood Cliffs, New Jersey, 1971.

Patterson, J. H., and **W. D. Huber,** "A Horizon-Varying-Zero-One Approach to Project Scheduling," *Management Sci.* **20,** No. 6 (February 1974), 990–998.

Rardin, R. L., and **B. W. Y. Lin,** "Development of a Parametric Generating Procedure for Integer Programming Test Problems," Paper presented at the *1975 Fall Joint ORSA/ TIMS Meeting, Las Vagas, Nevada.*

Ritzman, L. B., "The Efficiency of Computer Algorithms for Plant Layout," *Management Sci.* **18,** No. 5, Part I (January 1972), 24–248.

Sass, C. J., *FORTRAN IV Programming and Applications.* Holden-Day, San Francisco, 1974.

Souder, W. E., "Analytical Effectiveness of Mathematical Models for R & D Project Selection," *Management Sci.* **19,** No. 8 (April 1973).

Walsh, D., "A Guide for Software Documentation." Advanced Computer Techniques Corp., New York, 1969.

Wooldridge, S., *Computer Output Design.* Petrocelli/Charter, New York, 1975.

CHAPTER II

LIST PROCESSING

A. BASIC CONCEPTS

1. Simple Lists

A list consists of a set of elements. Each element contains a (possibly empty) set of *data* and at least one relational *pointer* to other elements. These pointers may imply that the items belong to the same set or that some sequence relationship exists. The first element in a list is called the HEAD and the last element in the list is called the TAIL (Fig. II-1a).

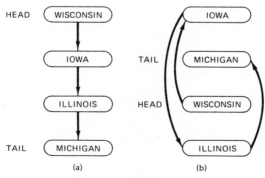

FIG. II-1

The ordering of elements in this list is uniquely defined by the relational pointers. (Some lists may have several sets of pointers.) The physical location of items in the list is of no significance; thus, the list shown in Fig. II-1b is identical to the list in Fig. II-1a. Simple lists are readily stored as two-dimensional arrays in the computer using the following data declarations:

```
      INTEGER HEAD
      INTEGER POINTR
      DIMENSION LIST(100,2)
C
C     LIST(I,1) CONTAINS THE LOCATION OF THE NEXT ITEM IN THE LIST
C     LIST(I,2) CONTAINS THE VALUE OF THE I*TH DATA ITEM
C     HEAD      POINTS TO THE FIRST ENTRY IN THE LIST
```

In this case, the list is dimensioned to 100 items, and it will, of course, be necessary to initialize both LIST and HEAD before items are removed from the list.

2.   Accessing Data Items

To investigate the data item at the head of the list, we set

```
      IDATA = LIST(HEAD,2)
```

This assumes that we have at least one item of data in the list. If the list were empty, HEAD would most probably have a value of zero, and the previous statement would result in an execution error. The following approach prevents such errors:

```
      IDATA = -99999
      IF(HEAD.GT.0) IDATA=LIST(HEAD,2)
      IF (IDATA.EQ.-99999) GOTO 1000
```

where statement number 1000 contains the code designed to handle the case of an empty list. This, of course, assumes that -99999 is not a valid data item and that this value is a sufficient flag to signify the absence of valid data. The careful programmer may also wish to protect himself against some invalid value stored in the variable HEAD:

```
      IDATA = -99999
      IF (HEAD.GT.0.AND.HEAD.LE.MAX)IDATA = LIST(HEAD,2)
      IF (IDATA.EQ.-99999) GOTO 1010
```

where statement number 1010 handles the error condition and MAX is the maximum size of the list. Without such protection, the program may process invalid data for some time before a random error (normally, overflow or illegal subscript) occurs at a later point in a different section of the program. Tracing such an error back to the absence of valid data in a list is usually difficult. It is even possible for the program to run "successfully" to completion without any visible errors—even though only garbage is being processed.

To investigate the second item in the ordered list (remember that this item need not be the item in the second physical location), we would like to execute the following statements:

```
POINTR = LIST (HEAD,1)
IDATA = LIST(POINTR,2)
```

This approach will work only if both the first and the second data items exist. A subscript error will result if the list is empty (and HEAD is zero) or if it contains only one item (such that POINTR is zero or undefined).

The following code will prevent such errors:

```
      IF (HEAD.LE.0) GOTO 2000
      POINTR = LIST(HEAD,1)
      IF (POINTR.LE.0.OR.POINTR.GT.MAX) GOTO 2000
      IDATA = LIST(POINTR,2)
      .
      .
      .
 2000 CONTINUE
C
C  ANY APPROPRIATE ERROR STATEMENT
```

The third item could be developed by similar logic as

```
IDATA = LIST(LIST(LIST(HEAD,1),1),2)
```

However, we would again encounter problems if the list were too short. Instead let us therefore explore the more general case—how we may go from the Ith to the $(i+1)$th item:

```
      POINTR = location of the Ith item
      IF(POINTR.LT.1.OR.POINTR.GT.MAX) GOTO 2000
      POINTR = LIST(POINTR,1)
      IDATA = LIST(POINTR,2)
      .
      .
      .
 2000 CONTINUE
C
C  ANY APPROPRIATE ERROR CONDITIONS
```

We can now use this code segment to write a general code to find the Nth item in a list:

```
C  LOOK AT THE FIRST ITEM
C
      POINTR = HEAD
      ICOUNT = 1
C
C  DOES THE ITEM EXIST
C
 1000 IF (POINTR.LE.0.OR.POINTR.GT.MAX) GOTO 2000
C
C  ITEM EXISTS, IS IT THE N*TH ITEM
C
      IF (ICOUNT.EQ.N) GOTO 1010
C
C  NO  LOOK AT THE NEXT ITEM
C
```

```
      ICOUNT = ICOUNT + 1
      POINTR=LIST(POINTR,1)
      GOTO 1000
C
C  ITEM FOUND
C
 1010 IDATA = LIST(POINTR,2)
         .
         .
         .
      RETURN
 2000 CONTINUE
C
C  ANY SUITABLE ERROR CONDITION
```

3. Example

The array representing a particular linked list is given in Table II-1. (We will later discuss how this array was generated.) The HEAD of the list is given to be at location 7, and it is apparent that the TAIL is at location 10 since this is the first item with a zero in column one.

Observe that list items appear in no particular order in the array and that not all storage locations are utilized. This particular list could be presented graphically as shown in Fig. II-2. To find the third item in the list, the code

TABLE II-1

Row	Column 1	2
1	10	1478
2	0	0
3	5	973
4	0	0
5	11	13
6	3	−14
7	6	−86
8	0	0
9	0	0
10	0	23
11	1	74
12	0	0
⋮	⋮	⋮
MAX	0	0

FIG. II-2

developed in the previous section would generate the following trace:

	POINTR = 7	point to the head of the list
	ICOUNT = 1	initialize the location counter
1000	FALSE	POINTR has a valid value
	FALSE	third item not found yet
	ICOUNT = 2	update location counter
	POINTR = LIST(7, 1) = 6	location of second item
1000	FALSE	POINTR has a valid value
	FALSE	third item not found yet
	ICOUNT = 3	update location counter
	POINTR = LIST(6, 1) = 3	location of third counter
1000	FALSE	POINTR has a valid value
	TRUE	third item is found
1010	IDATA = LIST(3, 2) = 973	data in third item is found

4. Backward Pointers

It is easy to search the list from front to back by use of the previously discussed organization. Frequently, however, it is necessary to step *backward* into a list. For this process, we use backward pointers. As the name implies, they start at the TAIL of the list and end up at the HEAD. A three-dimensional array is required to store a list with both forward and backward pointers and one data item.

```
      DIMENSION LIST(100,3)
      INTEGER BWDPTR
      INTEGER FWDPTR
      INTEGER HEAD
      INTEGER TAIL
c
c  VARIABLES
c      BWDPTR     POINTER TO PREVIOUS ELEMENT
c      FWDPTR     POINTER TO NEXT ELEMENT
c      HEAD       PHYSICAL LOCATION OF FIRST ELEMENT
c      IDATA      VALUE OF PARTICULAR DATA ELEMENT
c      LIST(I,1)  FORWARD POINTER FROM ITEM IN I*TH LOCATION
c      LIST(I,2)  BACHWARD POINTER FROM ITEM IN I*TH LCCATION
c      LIST(I,3)  VALUE OF DATA ITEM
c      TAIL       POINTER TO LAST ENTRY IN LIST
c
```

Again, we remind you that the list structure must be properly initialized before items can be found in the list.

B. FUNDAMENTAL OPERATIONS

We have already seen how an item of a particular value or relative position can be located in the list. In this section, we will look at three other fundamental list operations. These are: (1) modifying a given element, (2) deleting an element, and (3) inserting an element.

1. Modifying a Data Element

In most cases, the act of modifying a particular data item, after the pointer to its location has been found, is simple:

LIST$(I, 3)$ = new value.

However, the value stored in LIST$(I, 3)$ may not be the data item itself but rather a pointer to the data item. (This approach has many advantages when the data item is bulky.) Assuming that the actual data item is stored in the one-dimensional REAL array, ARRAY, the following will work if ARRAY is dimensioned to 100:

```
      INDEX = LIST(I,3)
      IF(INDEX.LE.0.OR.INDEX.GT.100) GOTO 2000
      ARRAY(INDEX) =
         .
         .
         .
 2000 CONTINUE
    C
    C  ANY SUITABLE ERROR CONDITION
```

Note that in this case no modification has taken place in the LIST itself. A similar approach is used when the actual data is stored on random access storage devices such as disc files.

2. Deleting an Element

It is significantly more complex to delete an element from a list than it is to alter the value of the element. The reason for this is that we need to alter several pointers in order to completely remove (delete) the element from the list. On the other hand, data items do not need to be altered because they will no longer be accessible, and their values become irrelevant.

Let us look at the example shown in Fig. II-3a. We wish to remove ILLINOIS from the list. To accomplish this, we need to replace the forward pointer from IOWA to ILLINOIS by a pointer from IOWA to MICHIGAN. We also need to replace the backward pointer from MICHIGAN to ILLINOIS by a pointer from MICHIGAN to IOWA. This results in the list given in Fig. II-3b.

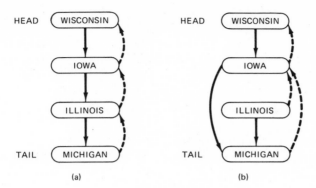

FIG. II-3

Note that we have not removed ILLINOIS or changed any of its data items or pointers. We have only pointed around ILLINOIS. Changing the information in the ILLINOIS element was not necessary since we are not able to reach this element any more.

To delete ILLINOIS from the list, the following two operations were performed:

(1) The forward pointer from the element preceding ILLINOIS was linked to the one following it.

(2) The backward pointer from the element following ILLINOIS was linked to the element preceding it.

It is clear that it would be extremely difficult to perform either of these operations without the use of *both* the forward and the backward pointers. To change the forward pointer from ILLINOIS, we need the backward pointer from ILLINOIS to locate the new origin of the pointer. To change the backward pointer, we need the forward pointer from ILLINOIS to tell us the new value of this pointer.

The procedure to remove an item from a linked list is summarized in flow-chart form in Fig. II-4. A subroutine to remove items from linked lists will be presented somewhat later in this chapter. This subroutine is slightly more complex than the present flowchart since it incorporates features that render released storage locations accessible for newly inserted items at a later time.

3. Inserting a New Element

Adding MINNESOTA in the third logical location in our list between IOWA and MICHIGAN will result in the list given in Fig. II-5. To do this, we need to know two things: (1) the location of the elements between which

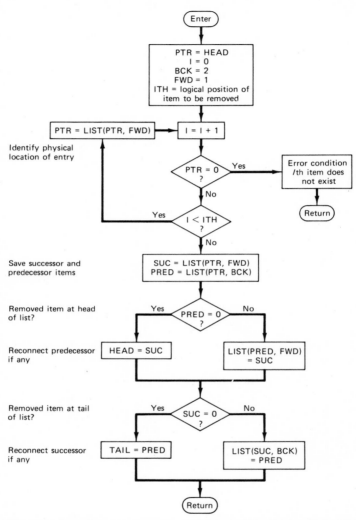

FIG. II-4   Procedure to remove item in *I*th logical location in a linked list.

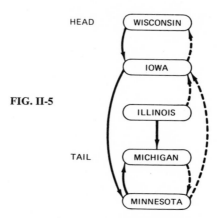

FIG. II-5

the new element is to logically reside and (2) the physical location of the new element. Introducing the new element will require the following operations:

(1) Replace forward pointer from IOWA to MICHIGAN by pointers from IOWA to MINNESOTA and MINNESOTA to MICHIGAN.

(2) Replace backward pointer from MICHIGAN to IOWA by pointers from MICHIGAN to MINNESOTA and from MINNESOTA to IOWA.

Again, it is easy to see that it would be difficult to perform either of these operations without the use of both the forward and backward pointers.

The procedure followed to insert an item into a specific logical and physical location in a linked list is summarized in flowchart form in Fig. II-6. Note that this flowchart appends the new item to the end of the list whenever the list is too short for the specific position. A subroutine performing this task will be presented somewhat later in this chapter (Fig. II-10). This subroutine is somewhat more complex than the present flowchart as it automatically identifies and assigns an unused physical location for the new item.

4. Examples

Consider the list given in Table II-2 (again we do not discuss how the list was generated, nor are we concerned with the values of the blank entries in the array). This list may be presented graphically as in Fig. II-7. We first wish to remove the entry in the sixth row as listed in Table II-2. In order to do this, the backward pointer from row six ($= 10$) must be determined. We then change the forward pointer in row $10 (= 6)$ to be equal to the forward pointer in row 6 (i.e., $LIST(10, 1) = 8$).

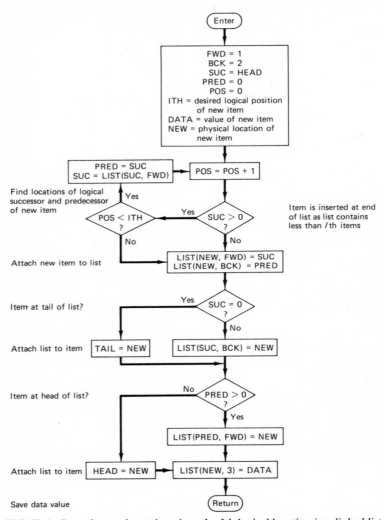

FIG. II-6　Procedure to insert item into the *I*th logical location in a linked list.

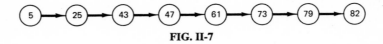

FIG. II-7

TABLE II-2

Column / Row	Forward 1	Backward 2	Value 3
1	10	15	25
2	13	8	73
3			
4 TAIL	0	13	82
5			
6	8	10	47
7			
8	2	6	61
9			
10	6	1	43
11			
12			
13	4	2	79
14			
15 HEAD	1	0	5

The backward pointers are handled in the same way. The current backward pointer in row 8 (equal to 6) is changed to be equal to the backward pointer in row six (i.e., = 10). These operations result in the list presented in Table II-3 (all changed elements are circled).

If a new element of value 74 is to be inserted in row 5, as listed in Table III-3, and is to be linked to follow the element in row 2, the following steps should be executed: The forward pointer in row 5 is set equal to the forward pointer in row 2. The forward pointer in row 2 (13) is then set equal to 5. (It has been established that the element in row 13 used to follow the element in row 2.) The backward pointer in row 13 is therefore altered to point to row 5. At the same time, the backward pointer in row 5 is set equal to 2. Finally, the data item 74 is inserted into LIST(5, 3). These operations result in the list given in Table II-4 (all modified items are circled).

5. Garbage List

When we discussed insertion of new entities, it was assumed that we knew the location of a vacant row in our list. The easiest way to obtain this knowledge is to maintain *two* lists in the array LIST. One list would contain the list of interest and the other would contain a list of all unused elements (frequently called a "garbage list"). The garbage list would initially contain all the entries in the array. As locations are needed for entries in the list of entries, locations are removed from this list and assigned to the other list. As the order of elements in the garbage list would be of no significance, elements could both be inserted and removed at the head (HEADG) of the list. Using the garbage list, the initial array LIST for the previous example (Figure II-2) would read as shown in Table II-5. Following the insertion of the new item

TABLE II-3

Column Row	1	2	3
1	10	15	25
2	13	8	73
3			
4	0	13	82
5			
6	8	⑩	47
7			
8	2	10	61
9			
10	⑧	1	43
11			
12			
13	4	2	79
14			
15	1	0	5

TABLE II-4

Column Row	1	2	3
1	10	15	25
2	⑤	8	73
3			
4	0	13	82
5	⑬	②	㊲
6	8	10	47
7			
8	2	6	61
9			
10	6	1	43
11			
12			
13	4	⑤	79
14			
15	1	0	5

in row 5 (note that row 5 is at the head of the garbage list) the list is modified as shown in Table II-6. When a garbage list is used, the fundamental removal operation must be revised to include an operation to insert the released row into the garbage list. Likewise, the insert operation should be revised to obtain a vacant row from the garbage list. The storage arrays for linked lists must always be initialized before they are used.

TABLE II-5

Column Row	Forward 1	Backward 2	3
1	10	15	25
2	13	8	73
3	7	5	0
4	0	13	82
5	3	0	0
6	8	10	47
7	9	3	0
8	2	6	61
9	11	7	0
10	6	1	43
11	12	9	0
12	14	11	0
13	4	2	79
14	0	12	0
15	1	0	5

HEAD = 15
TAIL = 4
HEADG = 5
GTAIL = 14

TABLE II-6

Column Row	1	2	3
1	10	15	25
2	⑤	8	73
3	7	⓪	0
4	0	13	82
5	⑬	②	㊲
6	8	10	47
7	9	3	0
8	1	6	61
9	11	7	0
10	6	1	43
11	12	9	0
12	14	11	0
13	4	⑤	79
14	0	12	0
15	1	0	5

HEAD = 15
TAIL = 4
HEADG = ③
GTAIL = 14

C. AN IMPLEMENTATION

In this section we will first introduce three subroutines designed to perform simple list processing tasks, then we will show how these routines may be used to perform a sort on randomly organized data. The first subroutine (INIT) is designed to initialize the data storage area. The second subroutine (INSERT) is designed to insert an item into a linked list. Finally, the last subroutine (REMOVE) is used to remove an item in a particular logical position from the list.

The organization of the data for this implementation is documented in subroutine INIT (Fig. II-8). Pointers for both the desired linked list and the garbage list are stored in the first 99 rows of the array LIST. The corresponding data item is stored in a separate real array ALIST. The last (one hundredth) row of LIST contains the head and tail pointers for the linked list. A separate

```
      SUBROUTINE INIT
C
C THIS SUBROUTINE INITIALIZED A STORAGE AREA FOR SUBSEQUENT INSERTIONS
C AND REMOVALS OF ITEMS IN A LINKED  LIST.
C
C LIST ORGANIZATION
C     IFWD                      = 1
C     IBCK                      = 2
C     LIST(I,IFWD)              = FORWARD POINTER
C     LIST(I,IBCK)              = BACKWARD POINTER
C     ALIST(I)                  = DATA ITEM
C     LIST(1,IFWD)              = POINTER TO HEAD OF LINKED LIST
C     LIST(1,IBCK)              = POINTER TO TAIL OF LINKED LIST
C     HEADG                     = POINTER TO HEAD OF LIST CONTAINING ALL
C                                 CURRENTLY UNASSIGNED LOCATIONS IN THE
C                                 STORAGE AREA.
C
      INTEGER HEADG
      COMMON /LIST/ LIST(100,2),IFWD,IBCK,IDATA,HEADG,ALIST(100)
      IFWD = 1
      IBCK = 2
C
C INITIALIZE HEAD AND TAIL POINTER TO INDICATE AN EMPTY LIST
C
      LIST(1,IFWD) = 1
      LIST(1,IBCK) = 1
C
C PLACE REMAINDER ITEMS IN THE GARBAGE LIST
C
      HEADG = 2
      DO 1000 I = 2,100
         LIST(I,IFWD) = I+1
         LIST(I,IBCK) = 1
 1000 CONTINUE
      LIST(100,IFWD) = 1
      RETURN
      END
```

FIG. II-8   Subroutine to initialize storage area for linked list.

variable HEADG is used to identify the head of the garbage list. The head item in a list is flagged by a backward pointer to location one. Likewise the tail of a list is flagged by a forward pointer to location one. We will see that the use of location one instead of the more logical location 0 for this purpose has several advantages since a subscript of one is legal in FORTRAN while a subscript of zero is not. Subroutine INIT initializes the empty list storage area by using forward pointers to link together the entire storage area into a single garbage list and by indicating that the head of the garbage list is at location two. Finally INIT indicates that the list is empty by setting the forward and backward pointers in row one (i.e., the head and tail pointers) equal to one. This results in a list with the organization shown in Fig. II-9. Note that the backward pointers are not initialized as they are not needed in the garbage list, nor was it necessary to initialize the data storage array ALIST.

Subroutine INSERT (Fig. II-10) is used to insert an item into the list in a position such that the data items in the list are always maintained in increasing numeric order. When requested to insert an item, INSERT first checks to make sure that the garbage list is not empty so that a storage location will be available for the new item. (An empty garbage list is indicated when HEADG points to location one.) A message is printed and control is returned to the main program if no space is available. Otherwise the head of the garbage list is assigned to the new item, and the successor to the current garbage head is made the head of the list. Because of the way the garbage list was initialized, a pointer to one indicates that the garbage list is empty when HEADG is assigned this pointer value; we have thus automatically flagged the fact that our storage area is full.

INSERT now obtains the location of the head of the list from LIST (IFWD, one) and then proceeds to successively scan the items in the list until either the first item with a value higher than DATA or the end of the list is found. (The end of the list is found when the indicated next item resides in location one) The pointers of the appropriate items in the list as then adjusted to reflect the new organization of the list, and control is returned to the main program

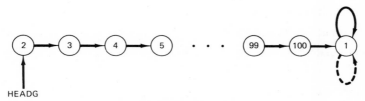

FIG. II-9

```
      SUBROUTINE INSERT(DATA)
C
C SUBROUTINE TO INSERT 'DATA' IN INCREASING ORDER IN A LINKED LIST
C THE PHYSICAL LOCATION OF THE NEW ITEM IS ASSIGNED FROM A GARBAGE LIST
C OF AVAILABLE UNUSED STORAGE LOCATIONS.
C THE LIST MUST FIRST BE INITIALIZED BY SUBROUTINE INIT
C
      INTEGER HEADG
      COMMON /LIST/ LIST(100,2),IFWD,IBCK,IDATA,HEADG,ALIST(100)
C
C IS LOGICAL LOCATION VALID
C
      IF(0.LT.ITH.OR.99.GE.ITH) GO TO 1000
      WRITE(6,100) ITH
  100 FORMAT(' CALL INSERT(DATA,ITH),  ITH IS OUT OF RANGE( =',I6,')')
      RETURN
C
C IS LIST FULL
C
 1000 IF(HEADG.GT.1) GO TO 1010
      IF(DATA.LE.ALIST(ISUC))GOTO 1030
      WRITE(6,101)
  101 FORMAT(' CALL INSERT(DATA,ITH),LIST IS FULL!')
      RETURN
C
C FIND PHYSICAL LOCATION OF NEW ENTRY, REMOVE FROM GARBAGE LIST
C
 1010 NEW = HEADG
      HEADG = LIST(HEADG,IFWD)
C
C SEARCH FOR LOCATIONS OF PREDECESSOR AND SUCCESSOR ITEMS
C FIRST RETRIEVE HEAD OF LIST
C
      ISUC = LIST(1,IFWD)
      IPRED = 1
      I = 0
 1020 I = I+1
C
C LIST EXHAUSTED
C
      IF(ISUC.LE.1) GO TO 1030
      IF(I.GE.ITH) GO TO 1030
C
C POINT TO NEXT PAIR OF ITEMS
C
      IPRED = ISUC
      ISUC = LIST(IPRED,IFWD)
      GO TO 1020
C
C LOGICAL LOCATION HAS BEEN FOUND, INSERT ITEM.
C
 1030 LIST(NEW,IFWD) = ISUC
      LIST(NEW,IBCK) = IPRED
C
C LINK TO SUCCESSOR ELEMENTS
C
      LIST(ISUC,IBCK) = NEW
C
C LINK TO PREDECESSOR ELEMENTS
C
      LIST(IPRED,IFWD) = NEW
C
C SAVE DATA ITEM
C
      ALIST(NEW) = DATA
      RETURN
      END
```

FIG. II-10   Subroutine to insert item into linked list.

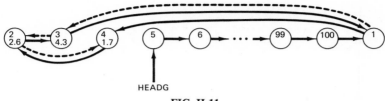

FIG. II-11

The array LIST will have the organization shown in Fig. II-11 after INSERT has been used to insert the three data items 2.6, 4.3, and 1.7 (in this order).

Subroutine REMOVE (Fig. II-12) is used to remove an item in a given logical position in the list. For example, a request to return the second item in the above list would set DATA equal to 2.6 and would move the first location in LIST to the garbage list, resulting in the organization of the array LIST given in Fig. II-13.

Subroutine REMOVE is written in a straightforward manner and need not be explained in detail. However, we should draw your attention to the fact that to save time, REMOVE does not alter the backward pointer from the item newly assigned to the garbage list nor does it erase the value of the removed data item.

These three subroutines may now be combined to form a crude program capable of sorting up to 99 data items:

```
      I=0
1000  READ(5,100,END=1010)A
      I = I+1
      CALL INSERT(A)
      GOTO 1000
1010  DO 1020 J=1,I
         CALL REMOVE(A,1)
         WRITE(6,100)A
1020  CONTINUE
 100  FORMAT(F10.2)
      STOP
      END
```

Data items are read, counted, and inserted one by one into the list. When the end of the input stream is reached, items are removed from the head of the list and printed one by one until the list is exhausted. Since the list is maintained in increasing order, it is clear that a continuing "peeling off" of the head item of the list will indeed ensure that items are printed in increasing order.

This particular sort method (called a straight insertion sort) is not very efficient and is not recommended for extensive sort applications.

More efficient methods of sorting are introduced in Chapter III.

```
      SUBROUTINE REMOVE(DATA,ITH)
C
C  SUBROUTINE TO RETRIEVE 'DATA' IN THE ITH LOGICAL LOCATION IN A
C  PREVIOUSLY  DEFINED LINKED LIST. RELEASED LOCATIONS ARE ASSIGNED TO A
C  GARBAGE LIST FOR FUTURE USE WHEN NEW ITEMS ARE INSERTED.
C
      INTEGER HEADG
      COMMON /LIST/ LIST(100,2),IFWD,IBCK,IDATA,HEADG,ALIST(100)
C
C  IS LOCATION VALID
C
      IF(ITH.GT.0.AND.ITH.LE.99) GO TO 1010
 1000 WRITE(6,100) ITH
  100 FORMAT(' CALL REMOVE(DATA,ITH)  ITH  IS OUT OF RANGE (= ',I6,')')
      RETURN
C
C  IDENTIFY PHYSICAL LOCATION OF THE ITH LOGICAL ITEM
C
 1010 IPTR = LIST(1,IFWD)
      I = 0
 1020 I = I+1
C
C  DOES LIST EXTEND THIS FAR
C
      IF(IPTR.LE.1) GO TO 1000
      IF(I.GE.ITH) GO TO 1030
      IPTR = LIST(IPTR,IFWD)
      GO TO 1020
C
C  PHYSICAL LOCATION IS FOUND
C  IDENTIFY SUCCESSOR AND PREDECESSOR
C
 1030 ISUC = LIST(IPTR,IFWD)
      IPRED = LIST(IPTR,IBCK)
C
C  CHANGE POINTER FROM PREDECESSOR
C
      LIST(IPRED,IFWD) = ISUC
C
C  CHANGE POINTER FROM SUCCESSOR
C
      LIST(ISUC,IBCK) = IPRED
C
C  RETRIEVE DATA ITEM
C
      DATA =ALIST(IPTR)
C
C  ASSIGN RELEASED LOCATION TO HEAD OF GARBAGE LIST
C
      LIST(IPTR,IFWD) = HEADG
      LIST(IPTR,IBCK) = 1
      HEADG = IPTR
      RETURN
      END
```

FIG. II-12   Subroutine to remove item from a linked list.

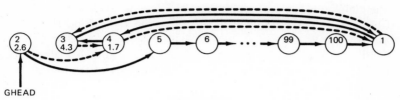

GHEAD

FIG. II-13

PROBLEMS

1. For the list given in Fig. II-14, modify the pointers in the following ways:
   (a) delete *B*,
   (b) have *B* follow *S*,
   (c) introduce *W* to follow *T*,
   (d) reverse the order of the items in the list.

2. A particular computer is capable of simultaneously executing 15 programs. To facilitate this, each program is handled by logical units called initiators. Thus, the computer has 15 initiators.

The computer operates on a priority scheme based on the relative core use of different active programs. Thus, an ordered list of the programs managed by the computer is maintained at all times.

At a given instance the computer executes eight programs:

Initiator:	1	2	3	4	5	6	7	8	9	10	11	12	13	14	15
Core:	25	73	—	82	—	47	—	61	—	43	—	—	79	—	5

   (a) What does the ordered list look like?
   (b) Remove the 47K job.
   (c) Add a 74K job.

3. A payroll system is to include a data file containing records for several hundred employees. Design a list structure that renders it possible to access these records both in alphabetical order and in order of increasing employee number. (How many chains are required?)

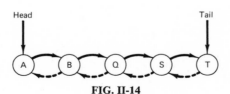

FIG. II-14

For the following four programming assignments assume that the list in question already has been created by subroutine INIT (Fig. II-8). The list may or may not be empty.

4. Write a subroutine that lists the items in the list in their logical order.

5. Write a subroutine that switches the logical order of the logical Ith and Jth items in the list.

6. Write a subroutine that changes the organization of the lists to one where items are ranked in decreasing order on the value of the data items.

7. Write a subroutine that reverses the order of the items in the list without changing the value of any of the pointers in the list.

8. Write a subroutine that inserts an item into its proper logical place when the list is ranked in decreasing order on the value of the data items.

9. Show how the data structure and program in Figs. II-8, II-10, and II-12 can be modified to hold up to 10 interwoven lists in a single array.

BIBLIOGRAPHY

Berztiss, A. T., *Data Structures: Theory and Practice*, 2nd ed.. Academic Press, New York, 1975.

Brillinger, P. C., and **D. J. Cohon,** *Introduction to Data Structures and Non-Numeric Computations.* Prentice-Hall, Englewood Cliffs, New Jersey, 1972.

Dahl, O. J., and **Belsnes, D.,** *Algorithmer og Datastructurer.* Student Literatur, Lund, Sweden, 1973.

Deo, N., *Graph Theory with Applications to Engineering and Computer Science.* Prentice-Hall, Englewood Cliffs, New Jersey, 1974.

Foster, J. M., *List Processing.* Macdonald, London, 1967.

CHAPTER III

SORTING AND SEARCHING

A. SORTING

1. Why Sort?

Sorting of data is frequently an extremely useful activity. As we will observe later, optimization algorithms often work most efficiently (i.e., obtain answers in a shorter time) when data is sorted in certain ways; plotting becomes easier with sorted data, and sorting results in a certain order will often increase the legibility of outputs. Updating of data on disc storage is often not even possible if the data is not sorted. For example, if you have a program stored as a source module on either the Harris-Datacraft or the Univac, your update cards must appear in order of increasing line number for the FORTRAN preprocessor to work.

In general, it is faster and safer to sort data *first* and *then* process it, with the knowledge that items will appear in a given, predefined order, than it is to process data that may appear in any order.

For these and other reasons, business data processing languages such as COBOL (which is designed to process large masses of data) incorporate sort functions in the same manner that FORTRAN has sine and cosine functions. Most business data processing sorts incorporate large masses of data, and their sorts are designed to utilize offline storage devices such as tapes or discs. On the other hand, in most systems analysis applications we are usually not handling more than a few hundred to a thousand data points, and in-core sorts are usually feasible and desirable. Thus, we will restrict ourselves in this development to a discussion of *internal* sorts only.

2. Approaches to Sorting

The sorting problem can be generalized as follows:

(a)   A file F of N records is given.

(b)   Each record R_i may contain any number of data items.

(c)   A portion of each record contains a *key* item K_i.

(d)   An ordering relationship between any two records R_i and R_j is uniquely defined by the values of the two keys K_i and K_j.

(e)   Three ordering relationships are available. These are equality ($=$), superiority ($>$), and inferiority ($<$).

(f)   It is desired to rearrange the records in F (or to construct a new file F') such that $K_1 \leqslant K_2 \leqslant \cdots \leqslant K_N$.

Sorting techniques differ in the manner in which the new sequencing relationships are established and in the manner in which the file is physically rearranged. Three different approaches to file rearrangements are available:

(a)   physical move of records,

(b)   use of address tables,

(c)   use of linked lists.

A physical move of records is both the most obvious approach and the approach that is the easiest to program. However, this approach usually results in fairly inefficient computer programs since a large number of records may have to be moved. This approach also requires in some cases that two complete files, F (the unsorted) and F' (the sorted), be maintained in core. This may result in unnecessarily large computer storage requirements.

When an address table is used, an array ADDR is developed such that ADDR(I) contains a pointer to the Ith ranked record. The additional storage required by this array is usually not excessive. Unfortunately, the method has limited applicability as the intermediate information provided by several different sort algorithms is not conveniently handled in this format.

An example of the use of linked lists in sorting was presented in Chapter II. More elaborate applications of linked lists in sorting that involve the use of several linked lists will be studied later in this chapter. As a rule, sort programs utilizing linked lists may be harder to write than those utilizing physical moves or address tables. However, they tend to result in more efficient programs.

A large number of different approaches to the development of new sequencing relationships is available. Knuth (1975) classifies these as sorting by

(a)   enumeration,
(b)   insertion,
(c)   selection,
(d)   exchange,
(e)   merging,
(f)   distribution.

The *enumeration* approach is based on the premise that the sorted position of record R_i can be uniquely determined by counting the number of records in F that have keys inferior to K_i. Using this approach, it is necessary to fully scan the file once for each of the N items in the file. Thus, the effort required in this case will be proportional to N^2. The enumeration approach is a natural candidate for the use of address tables. Two complete files (F and F') must be accommodated if address tables are not used.

In the *insertion* approach records are selected sequentially from the unsorted file and inserted into their correct relative position in the growing sorted file. In the previous chapter we utilized an insertion sort to illustrate the application of simple list processing techniques. We present a flowchart of a relatively simple but somewhat inefficient straight insertion sort in Fig. III-1.

Sorting by *selection* resembles the insertion method. Items are now carefully selected from the unsorted list such that they can be inserted one by one at the tail of the sorted list. The simplest such method is the straight selection sort:

(1)   Find the location i of the lowest valued key K_i in F.
(2)   Assign K_i to the first unassigned location is F'.
(3)   Replace K_i by ∞ in F.
(4)   Go to 1 unless F is exhausted.

The expected effort required to execute such a sort is of the order of magnitude N^2. Thus, this method cannot be recommended for anything but very short sorts.

Sorting by *exchanging* is based on a sequence of pairwise comparisons of items on the partially sorted list. Compared items are left unmoved if they appear in the right order. They are interchanged if they do not.

Two different exchange based sort algorithms, the *bubble sort* and the *Quicksort* will be presented in the next section.

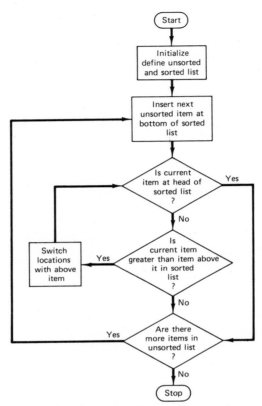

FIG. III-1   Straight insertion sort.

When we sort by *merging*, we first partition the list into smaller lists and then reassemble the list by successively moving the smallest (or largest) item at the head of the sublists to the head of the new (merged) list. Merge sorts are frequently used in conjunction with tape storage devices when files larger than those that fit in core are to be sorted. As an illustration of the merge approach to sorting, we will discuss in the following section the *n-bucket* sort–merge algorithm.

A *distribution* sort is illustrated by the old fashioned unit record mechanical approach to sorting. Ten bins are available, and items are assigned to bins such that items with identical last digits fall in the same bin. The items are then assembled in order of increasing last digit and redistributed according to the value of the second to the last digit, etc. Eventually the items will be assembled in increasing numeric order. (Note that if a sufficient number of bins were available, a distribution sort could be performed in one pass.)

3. Specific Methods

a. Bubble Sort

The bubble sort is an illustration of a simple but inefficient exchange based sort method. As illustrated in the flowchart in Fig. III-2, the method is based on a sequence of pairwise comparisons. Item 1 is compared with item 2. If they are out of order, they are interchanged. Item 2 is then compared with item 3 and so on until the end of the list is reached. The highest valued item will now have reached the end of the list. However, other items will be out of order. Additional passes are, therefore, required until complete order is restored. To illustrate the bubble sort, consider a sort of the following list:

$$2, \quad 27, \quad 11, \quad 23, \quad 13, \quad 12, \quad 18, \quad 3.$$

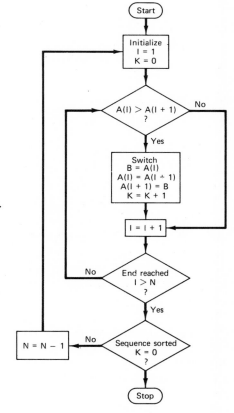

FIG. III-2 Bubble sort.

In the first pass the following comparisons and switches are performed:

$$2, \quad 27, \quad 11, \quad 23, \quad 13, \quad 12, \quad 18, \quad 3$$
$$11, \quad 27$$
$$23, \quad 27$$
$$13, \quad 27$$
$$12, \quad 27$$
$$18, \quad 27$$
$$3, \quad 27.$$

This results in the following list:

$$2, \quad 11, \quad 23, \quad 13, \quad 12, \quad 18, \quad 3, \quad 27.$$

Here the largest number has "trickled" like a bubble up to the top position (thus the name). In the second pass, the following operations are performed:

$$2, \quad 11, \quad 23, \quad 13, \quad 12, \quad 18, \quad 3, \quad 27$$
$$13, \quad 23$$
$$12, \quad 23$$
$$18, \quad 23$$
$$3, \quad 23.$$

The third pass yields:

$$2, \quad 11, \quad 13, \quad 12, \quad 18, \quad 3, \quad 23, \quad 27$$
$$12, \quad 13, \quad 3, \quad 18.$$

And eventually the sixth pass yields the sorted sequence:

$$2, \quad 3, \quad 11, \quad 12, \quad 13, \quad 18, \quad 23, \quad 27.$$

b. Quicksort

The bubble sort is easy to program and easy to understand. Unfortunately, it is usually an inefficient method that cannot be recommended for extensive sorting work. However, another exchange sort method, the Quicksort method, has proven to be a reasonably efficient approach to sorting. This efficiency is unfortunately gained at the cost of having a substantially more complex program.

As illustrated in the flowchart in Fig. III-3, the Quicksort algorithm works

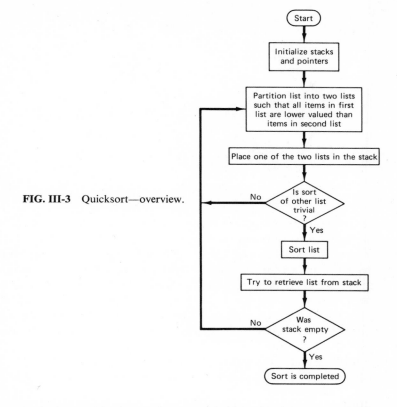

FIG. III-3 Quicksort—overview.

by recursively partitioning and rearranging the list into successively smaller lists such that strict ordering relationships exists between items in different lists. Items within a list remain unordered. However, this partitioning will eventually be carried so far that it becomes trivial to order items in sublists. To illustrate this partitioning concept, consider a sort on the list used for the bubble sort example. Through successive partitioning and rearrangements the tree shown in Fig. III-4 is developed. The bottom row in this tree is indeed a sorted representation of the initial list. Many different implementations of Quicksort algorithms have been suggested. The first problem to be tackled in any implementation is how to find the median value of items in a list such that items with a higher value can be moved to the right and items with a lower value can be moved to the left.

To compute the exact value of the median (12.500 for the initial list) requires too much effort to be feasible. Thus, the median is estimated by calculating the average value of a few (very few, usually 1, 2, or 3) sample keys. Such estimates will be inexact, and the symmetry of the above tree will be

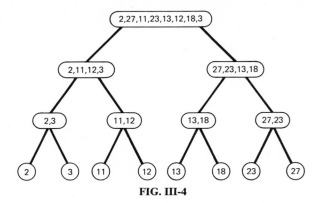

FIG. III-4

lost. For example, if the median of the ordered list were estimated from the average of the first two values in the initial unordered list $((2+27)/2 = 14.5)$, the tree shown in Fig. III-5 would be developed for the preceding example. The second problem faced in designing a quicksort algorithm is to determine how to handle the large number of lists that may be generated. This is less of a problem than it may appear to be since all lists may be developed and stored within the space used to contain the initial list. All we need to store in addition to this list is a set of pointers to the first and last item in each sublist.

To minimize the number of partially sorted lists (and thus to reduce pointer storage requirements) we always select the shortest of two newly created sub-

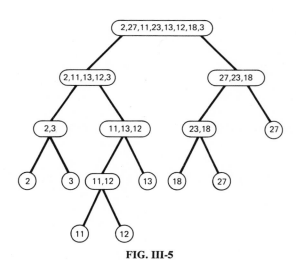

FIG. III-5

lists for immediate further partitioning. The other list is placed in a stack for later partitioning.

To partition a specific list, the list is simultaneously scanned from the left until an item belonging in the right list is found and from the right until an item belonging in the left list is found. These items are then switched and the scan is continued until the pointers eventually cross at the point of partitioning.

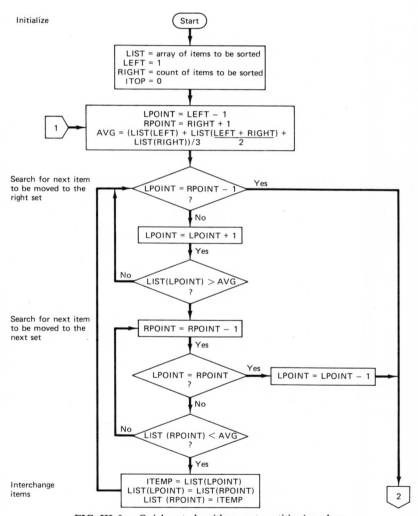

FIG. III-6a Quicksort algorithm—set partitioning phase.

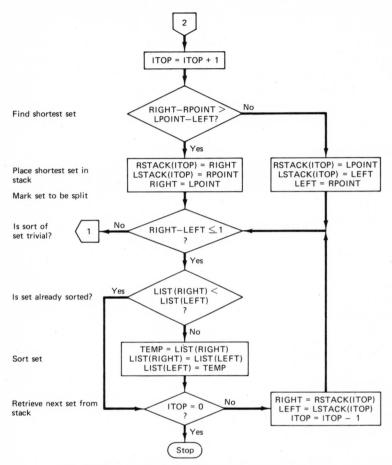

FIG. III-6b   Quicksort algorithm—set management phase.

In Figs. III-6a and III-6b we present a detailed flowchart of a Quicksort program implementing the ideas presented here. The sort is being performed on the items in the array LIST (note that the initial organization of LIST is lost as the sort progresses). The left-most location of the sublist to be partitioned is marked by the pointer LEFT while the right-most location is marked by the pointer RIGHT. The pointers LPOINT and RPOINT are used to scan this sublist from the left and right, respectively. Items with a value less than or equal to the average value (AVG) of the left-most, the center, and the right-most items are retained in or moved to the left list. All other items are retained in or moved to the right list.

The scan starts from the left with the pointer LPOINT being moved to the right until either an item belonging to the right list is found or until the left pointer is about to hit the right pointer. The latter will happen when there are no more items to interchange. If an item to be moved was found, then a scan is made from the right for an item such that these may be interchanged. This scan is performed by moving RPOINT from the right to the left until either an item is found or RPOINT is equal to LPOINT. In the latter case, no interchange is possible and the out-of-place item in the last location in the left list is assigned to the right list by moving LPOINT one location to the left (thus excluding this item). In the former case, the interchange is carried out and the scans of the list are continued.

Upon completion, this scan–interchange procedure has rearranged the list bounded by LIST(LEFT) and LIST(RIGHT) such that the items found in location LEFT through location LPOINT are of lower value than those found in locations RPOINT through RIGHT.

The right and left pointers of the longer of these two sublists is now placed in the stack arrays RSTACK and LSTACK, and if the shorter list contains three or more items, it is again partitioned. Lists containing two or fewer items are, if necessary, sorted by a simple interchange, and the leftmost and rightmost location of the next list to be split is obtained from the stacks LSTACK and RSTACK. The sort is completed when these stacks are empty.

This particular algorithm will sort the previously discussed list in the manner shown in Fig. III-7.

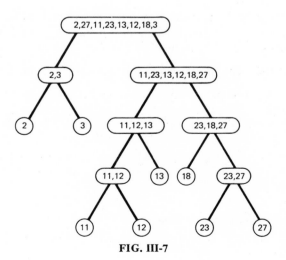

FIG. III-7

An evaluation of a Quicksort program based on these flowcharts is presented in Section A.3.d. It is seen that this algorithm is the most efficient of the algorithms discussed in this text.

c.   n-bucket Sort–Merge

In this approach, the data are split in each pass into n different arrays (buckets) in such a way that the $n-1$ first arrays contain data in increasing order while the last array contains randomly ordered data that could not be placed in the first $n-1$ arrays. Following each pass, the data is merged from each array back into the initial array. The splitting operation is repeated on this merged array; the new split arrays (buckets) are merged; and so on until data in the merged array appear in the proper sequence. A completed sort is guaranteed when the nth bucket is empty when the merge is performed.

Example Use a four-bucket sort to order the following 10 items in increasing sequence:

$$56 \quad 81 \quad 71 \quad 87 \quad 50 \quad 04 \quad 83 \quad 59 \quad 79 \quad 80.$$

After sequentially assigning each item to the first bucket where it is larger than the previous entry, the following buckets are formed:

Bucket 1	Bucket 2	Bucket 3	Bucket 4
56	71	50	04
81	83	59	
87		79	
		80	

The data in these buckets are now merged by consecutively removing the lowest valued item from four buckets and assigning it back to the initial array. This yields a perfectly ordered array:

$$04 \quad 50 \quad 56 \quad 59 \quad 71 \quad 79 \quad 80 \quad 81 \quad 83 \quad 87.$$

A similar sort could be performed using three buckets:

Bucket 1	Bucket 2	Bucket 3
56	71	50
81	83	04
87		59
		79
		80

After the merge we get the sequence

$$50 \quad 04 \quad 56 \quad 59 \quad 71 \quad 79 \quad 80 \quad 81 \quad 83 \quad 87.$$

This sequence is not in increasing order and a second pass is required. This pass yields the following results:

	Pass 2:	Bucket 1	Bucket 2	Bucket 3
		50	04	
		56		
		59		
		71		
		79		
		80		
		81		
		83		
		87		

A merge of these will, of course, yield a properly ordered sequence.
Finally, this sort may be attempted using two buckets.

	Pass 1:	Bucket 1	Bucket 2
		56	71
		81	50
		87	04
			83
			59
			79
			80

A merge yields the sequence

56   71   50   04   81   83   59   79   80   87.

A second pass is necessary:

	Pass 2:	Bucket 1	Bucket 2
		56	50
		71	04
		81	59
		83	79
		87	80

The merge yields the sequence

50   04   56   59   71   79   80   81   83   87.

The third pass is necessary:

Pass 3:   Bucket 1   Bucket 2

50   04
56
59
71
79
80
81
83
87

A merge will now yield the sorted sequence.

The algorithm followed in these sorts is documented in the flowcharts in Figs. III-8, III-9, and III-10. In this formulation, since we do not know how data will be distributed between the buckets, it is necessary to dimension each bucket to accept the complete sort array. It is unrealistic to assume that sufficient core storage will be available to accommodate such excessive requirements for sort buckets. Another possibly undesirable feature of the present algorithm is the fact that it performs sorting by moving data rather than by manipulating pointers to data. Both of these deficiencies can be corrected through the use of list processing techniques.

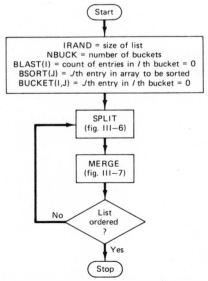

FIG. III-8   n-bucket sort—overview.

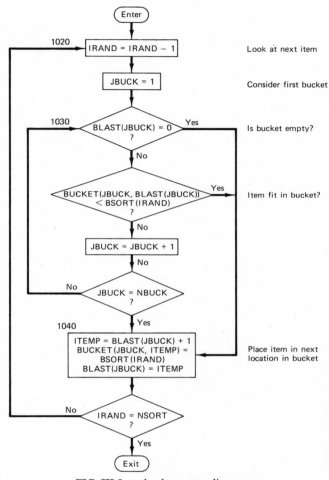

FIG. III-9 n-bucket sort–split segment.

In this case, the program maintains $n+1$ ordered chains of variables. The first chain contains the variables yet to be sorted, while the remaining chains contain the data in the n buckets. Items are moved from the head of the unsorted list to the head of the bucket lists by pointer manipulation. When the unsorted list is completely dispersed, a new merged list is developed by selectively moving items from the head of the bucket lists to the head of the merged list. With this pattern of movement, each list functions as a stack and only one pointer per item is required.

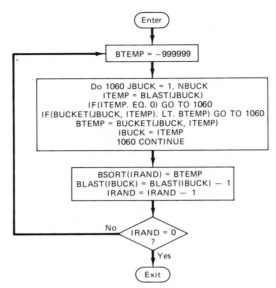

FIG. III-10   n-bucket sort–merge segment.

d.   A Comparison of Different Methods

It is often difficult to decide which of the many different approaches to sorting should be used for a particular application. The dominant criteria for making such a selection usually are core space, execution time, and availability. Since considerable time and effort is expended in writing and testing a new sort code, availability is probably the prime criteria for short, one-shot applications.

Time and core requirements become the overriding concerns for extensive or repeated applications. The same is true if several different tested codes are available to choose from. Since the methods presented here are designed for in-core sorts and each use about the same amount of core, storage requirements are not really a factor in selecting among these methods. However, computer time requirements differ extensively from method to method.

To facilitate an educated choice, we have conducted a comparative study of the execution times required to sort randomly organized lists using four of the methods presented here. The results are shown in Figure III-11 where we present the average execution time for four separate sorts of lists using the bubble, n-bucket, straight insertion, and Quicksort sort algorithms.

From this figure it is clear that the Quicksort method should be chosen when data appearing in random order is to be sorted. However, we frequently perform sorts on partially ordered lists as well. We must, therefore, also

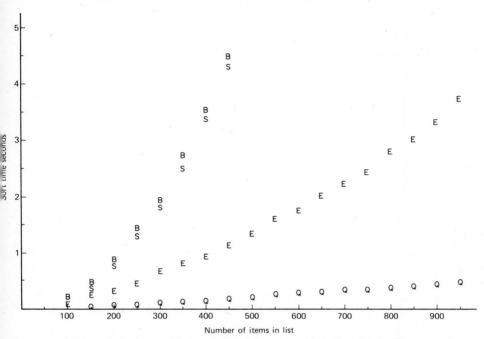

FIG. III-11 Efficiency of different sort programs—random lists. B: bubble sort; S: straight insertion sort; E: eight bucket sort; Q: Quicksort.

determine the performance of the algorithms under such conditions. Thus, we present performance data in Fig. III-12 for the extreme conditions of perfectly ordered and reverse ordered lists. The Quicksort method is again found to be superior and we can now unequivocally recommend this method as the preferred choice among the methods tested here.

4. Sorts on Nonnumeric Data

To understand the effect of sorts on nonnumeric data, it is necessary to first review some of the different ways that data may be internally represented in the computer. Let us first consider INTEGER data. Here, the data appears in binary notation in one word (normally 24, 32, or 36 bits depending upon the computer). For example, in a 24 bit machine, the number 12 appears as the binary string

$$000000000000000000001100.$$

The largest integer number that can be represented in this machine is $2^{24} - 1$

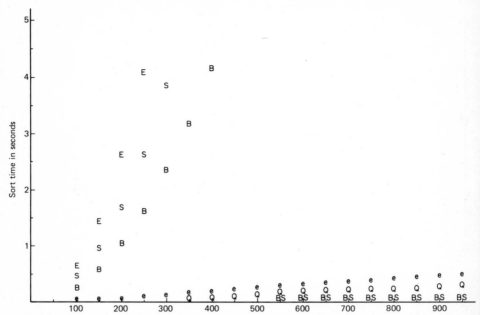

FIG. III-12   Efficiency of different sort programs—ordered lists. E: eight bucket sort; S: straight insertion reverse order; B: bubble sort reverse order; e: eight bucket perfect order; Q: Quicksort perfect and reverse order; BS: bubble sort and straight sort perfect order.

represented by the binary string

$$0111111111111111111111111.$$

Negative numbers are represented by replacing all zeros by one and vice versa. Thus, all negative numbers have a binary 1 in their first position, while all positive numbers have a leading zero. A negative 12 would be represented by

$$1111111111111111111110011.$$

To simplify the writing of such long binary strings, octal (or hexadecimal) notation is frequently used. Here strings of three (or six) bits are combined and written in their octal (hexadecimal) notation. Thus, an integer 12 would be represented in octal by 00000014 and a minus 12 would be represented by 77777763.

Numeric data are also frequently represented in a REAL format. Here the number is broken up into two binary strings. The first string represents the order of magnitude, and the second represents the significant digits of the number. A comparison between REAL and INTEGER data is therefore meaningless without prior conversion.

TABLE 3-1 REPRESENTATION OF CHARACTER DATA IN VARIOUS CODES

| | | UNIVAC | | |
Dec.	Octal	Fieldcode	ASCII	BCD
0	00	@		&
1	01	[		1
2	02	]		2
3	03	#		3
4	04	Δ		4
5	05	(Space)		5
6	06	A		6
7	07	B		7
8	10	C		8
9	11	D		9
10	12	E		0
11	13	F		=
12	14	G		,
13	15	H		:
14	16	I		>
15	17	J		@
16	20	K		Blank
17	21	L		/
18	22	M		S
19	23	N		T
20	24	O		U
21	25	P		V
22	26	Q		W
23	27	R		X
24	30	S		Y
25	31	T		Z
26	32	U		,
27	33	V		(
28	34	W		%
29	35	X		/
30	36	Y		□
31	37	Z		
32	40	)	Blank	-
33	41	-	!	J
34	42	+	"	K
35	43	<	#	L
36	44	=	$	M
37	45	>	%	N
38	46	&	&	O
39	47	$	'	P
40	50	*	(	Q
41	51	(	)	R
42	52	%	*	!
43	53	:	+	$
44	54	?	,	*
45	55	!	-	]
46	56	,	.	;
47	57	/	/	Δ
48	60	0	0	+
49	61	1	1	A
50	62	2	2	B
51	63	3	3	C
52	64	4	4	D
53	65	5	5	E
54	66	6	6	F
55	67	7	7	G
56	70	8	8	H
57	71	9	9	I
58	72	'	:	?
59	73	;	;	.
60	74	/	<	)
61	75	.	=	[
62	76	□	>	<
63	77	≠	?	#
64	100		@	
65	101		A	
66	102		B	
67	103		C	
68	104		D	
69	105		E	
70	106		F	
71	107		G	
72	110		H	
73	111		I	
74	112		J	
75	113		K	
76	114		L	
77	115		M	
78	116		N	
79	117		O	
80	120		P	
81	121		Q	
82	122		R	
83	123		S	
84	124		T	
85	125		U	
86	126		V	
87	127		W	
88	130		X	
89	131		Y	
90	132		Z	
91	133		[	
92	134		—	
93	135		]	
94	136		□	
95	137		Print	

The third internal representation mode is the character mode. Here the word is broken into substrings of (usually) eight bits. Each substring represents a single character. Thus, a 24 bit word may contain three characters while a 32 bit word may contain four characters. The particular binary representations used to represent different characters is established by industry conventions. Three such standards are presented in Table III-1. Here, the octal representation is given. Thus, an ASCII X is represented as 130 octal or 001011000 binary. Observe that the first two bits will always be zero. The first of these bits is omitted in the 8 bit character representation scheme.

The internal representation of a character depends upon the location of the character in the word. By convention, characters are left justified and padded with blanks if less than three characters are present. Thus, a single ASCII X is represented as

$$\underbrace{01011000}_{x} \qquad \underbrace{00100000}_{\text{blank}} \qquad \underbrace{00100000}_{\text{blank}}$$

and "blank, blank, X" is represented as

$$\underbrace{00100000}_{\text{blank}} \qquad \underbrace{000100000}_{\text{blank}} \qquad \underbrace{0101100}_{x}$$

Since the computer is unaware of the conventions used to insert data in different storage locations, INTEGER sorts can be readily performed in character data. In this case, the characters will be treated as integer numbers with the equivalent binary representation. For example, a left justified X will be treated as a 23068672. While this may sound complicated, the effect of such sorts will be a sorting of the characters from left to right in the order in which they appear in Table III-1. Thus, three blanks will be first on the sorting sequence for an ASCII sort.

B. LIST SEARCHES

The problem of searching occurs when it is necessary to retrieve an item of a particular value or property such that other data affiliated with this item can be examined. For example, such a search is executed when you consult the telephone book for a friend's phone number.

A large number of different approaches to searches are available. When the lists become very long or are ordered on several different keys, a search can become rather complex and proprietary data systems are frequently called for. In this section, we will discuss those search methods that can be used when the data is organized in a single long list (such as the telephone book). In the following section we shall discuss searches where the data has a more complex structure. With this in mind, we shall now consider searches in lists with the following organizations:

(1) Items appear in random order—no links provided.
(2) Items appear in increasing order—no links provided.
(3) Items appear in random order—chain in increasing order provided.
(4) Position of items in list is calculated from value of item.

1. Random Order—No Links

When items appear in a list without any particular organization, it is not possible to develop a search method more efficient than the brute force method. That is, we must investigate sequentially each item in the list until we find the item we want. The complete list must be searched before we can say with certainty that a particular item is not in the list.

2. Increasing Order—No Links

Substantial improvements in search efficiency are obtained if the items are ordered in such a way that they physically appear in increasing (or decreasing) order. The most common approach to a search in such a list would be the binary search.

Here, instead of starting at the top of the list, we start the search by investigating the item closest to the middle of the list. If this is the item we are looking for, we stop. If not, we check to see if this item is higher or lower valued than the item we are looking for. If the center item is of higher value, then the item in question must reside in the top half of the list. If the center item is of lower value, then the reverse is true. Thus, having eliminated half the list from consideration, we investigate the center of the remaining list. We eliminate half of this list. We will continue in this manner until the desired item is found or until we have ascertained that the item is not a resident of the list. Since each check eliminates half of the remaining list, the search efficiency is greatly improved over the brute force method.

To illustrate this search, consider a search for Kholait in the list in Figure III-13. This list has 15 entries (randomly chosen from the Madison, Wisconsin, telephone book). Entry number 8 is in the center of the list. The name in this location (Khelladi) is inferior to Kholait in the collating sequence. Thus, we must search the bottom 7 entries of the list. The center of this portion of the list is in location $\frac{9}{2} + \frac{15}{2} = 12$. The name in this location (Khoribut) is superior to Kholait, and this time we must continue our search in the upper half (9 through 11). The center of this list is location 10. Kholait resides in this location; thus, the search is successfully completed. In this instance, we

Line	Entry	Search Order	Binary tree representation of search
1	Key	4	
2	Keyes	3	
3	Keys	4	
4	Keyser	2	
5	Khajezaden	4	
6	Khan	3	
7	Khazai	4	
8	Khelladi	1	
9	Khleif	4	
10	Kholait	3	
11	Khorana	4	
12	Kharibut	2	
13	Kiang	4	
14	Kibbutz	3	
15	Kibby	4	

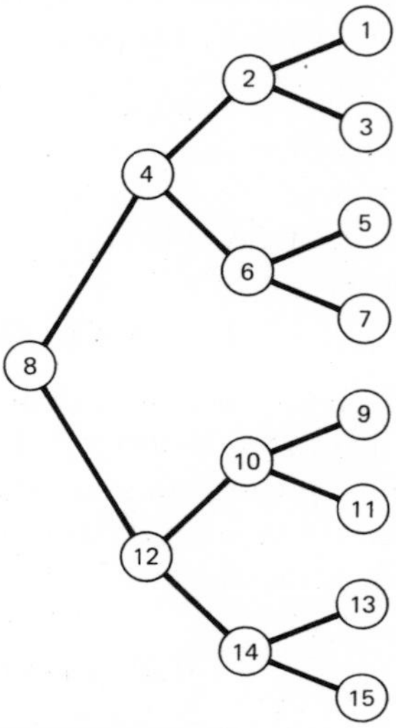

FIG. III-13   Binary search tree.

only investigated two other entries prior to finding the right one. A brute
force search would have required nine checks.

A search for a nonexisting entry, say Keynes, would require four checks
using a binary search while 15 checks would be required with the brute force
method.

The average number of items that must be checked before a particular item
is found in a binary search is computed by first adding up the actual number
of items investigated to find each item in the list and then by dividing this
sum by the number of items in the list. The total number of searches required
to find all items in the list is found by observing that one item (Khelladi) can
be found in one step. Two items (Keyser, Kharibut) can be found in two
steps; four items can be found in three steps; and, in general, 2^{n-1} items are
found in exactly n steps.

Thus, if the list contains exactly $2^n - 1$ items (which is the case when a
binary tree with n levels is searched) a total of

$$1 + 2 \cdot 2^1 + 3 \cdot 2^2 + \cdots + n \cdot 2^{n-1} = (n-1)2^n - 1$$

searches are required to find all elements. Or, on the average,

$$\frac{(n-1)2^n - 1}{2^n - 1} \doteq n - 1$$

searches are to be expected to find an element residing in a list of size $2^n - 1$.

Thus, the expected number of searches increases with the log of the number of items in the list.

It is fairly straightforward to program a search algorithm. However, to write a successful program, care must be taken to accomplish the following:

(1)   Round indices properly if list is of odd size (truncating will always work).

(2)   Terminate search if item is not found.

(3)   Avoid searching any single element more than once.

The actual programming of a binary search subroutine is left as an exercise.

3.   Random Order—Links Provided

In many cases, the items appear in random order with links being provided to generate an ordered chain of items. We show in the list processing section how a sequential search starting at the HEAD of the chain could be written for such a list. Unfortunately, such a sequential search is not any more efficient than a brute force search of a randomly organized list. To gain efficiency in searching a list organized this way, we need additional pointers identifying several intermediate items in the list. Such an approach may be used in designing large mass storage files for off-line use. This approach is, however, of little relevance to the practicing systems analyst utilizing the computer primarily as a problem solving tool.

4.   Hash Coding

Hash coding differs significantly in concept from the other search methods which we have explored. The sequence of elements in a hash coded list is of no significance, and no pointers are provided to indicate any implied order. Instead, when an item is inserted into the list, the key (on which we later will search for the item) is converted into an address for a location in the list. If this particular location is not occupied, the item is inserted here. Should this position be occupied by another item, a conventional sequential search is made of the following positions until a vacant position is found.

This approach is frequently used in compilers and in business data processing. The top line of your magazine subscription label is probably a (hash) coded composite of your name and address providing the computer with a unique description of your subscription. Hash coding is useful in systems analysis when we have a small to medium amount of data and speed is important. The main drawback of the use of hash coding for in-core searches lies in the fact that this method does not utilize available memory very efficiently.

For a hash coding application to work in a satisfactory manner, the computed codes for most items should indicate *unique positions* within the list. Ideally, we would also like the system to be able to *utilize all* positions in the list. Clearly there are two decisions the hash code designer must make:

(1) How many positions should the list contain?
(2) How should the hash code be computed?

In the interest of computational speed, it is desirable to have the number of positions in the list substantially exceed the expected number of entries. This not only minimizes the probability that a location is already occupied (by another item with the same hash code or by a spillover from a previous entry), it also reduces the length of the search for a vacant location should a conflict occur. A rule of thumb for systems analysis applications would be to make the list at least two to five times as long as the expected number of entries.

Many different schemes for computation of hash codes have been suggested (see, e.g., Knuth, 1975; Lum *et al.*, 1971; Morris, 1968; Villers and Wilson, 1974). For large data processing applications, the choice of scheme is a significant one as the degree to which it allows data to be packed on storage media may have a significant economic implication. In most systems analysis situations, it is more important that the scheme be simple and easy to use while yielding reasonably "conflict free" addresses. A frequently used technique that fits this bill is to divide the search key (the social security number) by the largest prime number n less than the size of the storage area using the remainder i as the indicated location. Since i will be in the range of $0 - (n - 1)$, $i + 1$ must be used as the index in FORTRAN to avoid the subscripting error that would result from a subscript of zero.

To illustrate how this technique is implemented, let us consider the design of a grade information system for a class with 16 students. We will use an array DATA to store student grades and an array LIST to store the identification numbers of the students who have received a particular grade. To indicate that a particular storage location is not used, LIST is initialized in all locations with -999999's. It is not necessary to initialize DATA. In accordance with the recommended guidelines, we dimension both arrays to 37.

The students are identified by their identification numbers as

1	5254	2	2875	3	0305	4	3672
5	8236	6	0264	7	4866	8	4287
9	2757	10	5078	11	1571	12	4747
13	6782	14	8765	15	8614	16	5780

The grade (an A) for 5254 is stored first. The desired storage location i for this grade is computed as $i = 5254 \bmod (37) + 1$ or, since $5254/37 = 142$,

$i = 1$. A check is made to see if this location is available, and it is. Thus we set $DATA(1) = A$ and $LIST(1) = 5254$. The remaining grades are inserted in a similar manner with conflicts being resolved by inserting the second claimant to a storage location into the first available subsequent storage location. After all items have been inserted in this manner, the data shown in Table III-2 are available. In constructing this list, competing demands for a

```
      SUBROUTINE INSERT(KEY,ADATA)
C
C SUBROUTINE TO INSERT A  'KEY' AND AFFILIATED 'DATA' INTO THE
C POSITION IN A LIST INDICATED BY A COMPUTED HASHCODE.
C SHOULD THIS PARTICULAR LOCATION BE OCCUPIED, DATA IS PLACED
C IN FIRST SUBSEQUENTLY AVAILABLE POSITION. ITEM IS NOT INSERTED IF
C LIST IS FULL.
C THIS PROGRAM IS DIMENSIONED TO 300. THUS, IT MAY CONTAIN 50-100
C ITEMS
C
      INTEGER HASH
      DIMENSION LIST(300),DATA(300)
      COMMON LIST,DATA,ICOUNT
C
C IT IS ASSUMED THAT 'LIST' IS INITIALIZED ALSEWHERE TO
C CONTAIN -999999 IN ALL LOCATIONS. IT IS ALSO ASSUMED THAT
C THIS PARTICULAR VALUE WILL NEVER BE INSERTED. FURTHERMORE
C ICOUNT IS ASSUMED TO BE INITIALIZED TO 0.
C
C IF EXTENSIVE DATA IS TO BE STORED IT WILL BE MORE
C EFFICIENT TO STORE A POINTER TO THE DATA RATHER
C THAN THE DATA ITSELF IN THE HASHCODED LOCATION.
C
C
C IS THE LIST FULL?
C
      IF(ICOUNT.GE.300) GO TO 2000
C
C NO, COMPUTE HASHCODE AS REMAINDER OF ITEM/293+1
C
      HASH = MOD(KEY,293)+1
 1000 IF(LIST(HASH).NE.-999999) GO TO 1010
C
C VACANT POSITION IS FOUND. INSERT KEY AND AFFILIATED DATA
C
      LIST(HASH) = KEY
      DATA(HASH) = ADATA
      ICOUNT = ICOUNT+1
      RETURN
C
C POSITION IS OCCUPIED INVESTIGATE SUBSEQUENT POSITIONS
C
 1010 HASH = HASH+1
C
C HAS END OF LIST BEEN REACHED, IF SO, ROLLOVER TO BEGINNING
      IF(HASH.GT.300) HASH = 1
      GO TO 1000
 2000 WRITE(6,200) KEY
  200 FORMAT(' LIST IS FULL, KEY',I6,'COULD NOT BE INSERTED.')
      RETURN
      END
```

FIG. III-14 Subroutine to insert item into a hash coded list.

TABLE III-2

i	DATA (i)	LIST (i)	i	DATA (i)	LIST (i)	i	DATA (i)	LIST (i)
1	A	5254	14	C	6782	27	F	2875
2	—	−999999	15	—	−999999	28	—	−999999
3	—	−999999	16	—	−999999	29	—	−999999
4	—	−999999	17	—	−999999	30	—	−999999
5	—	−999999	18	A	1571	31	A	8614
6	B	0264	19	—	−999999	32	B	−999999
7	—	−999999	20	A	4866	33	B	4287
8	—	−999999	21	C	2757	34	A	8765
9	B	5780	22	—	−999999	35	—	−999999
10	B	3672	23	F+	8326	36	—	−999999
11	A	5078	24	—	−999999	37	—	−999999
12	B	4747	25	—	−999999			
13	B	0308	26	—	−999999			

```
      SUBROUTINE RETRIV(KEY,ADATA,ITEST)
      INTEGER HASH
      DIMENSION LIST(300),DATA(300)
      COMMON LIST,DATA,ICOUNT
C
C SET FLAG OFF
C
      ITEST = 0
      K = 0
      IF(ICOUNT.EQ.0) RETURN
C
C RECOMPUTE THE HASHCODE
C
      HASH = MOD(KEY,293)+1
 1000 IF(LIST(HASH).NE.KEY) GO TO 1010
C
C RETRIEVE THE DATA, SET FLAG OFF
C
      ADATA = DATA(HASH)
      ITEST = 1
      RETURN
C
C LOOK AT NEXT LOCATION
C
 1010 HASH = HASH+1
      IF(HASH.GT.300) HASH = 1
      IF(LIST(HASH).EQ.-999999) RETURN
      K = K+1
      IF(K.GE.301) RETURN
      GO TO 1000
      END
```

FIG. III-15 Subroutine to remove item from a hash coded list.

storage location occurred three times. 5078 has a hash code of 10. However, since 10 was occupied, 5078 was assigned to location 11. 6782 had $i = 12$; however, since 12 and 13 both were occupied, 6782 was stored in location 14. Finally, 2752 was stored in 21 instead of 20.

When items are retrieved from this data file, we first compute the proper hash code i (9 for 5780); then we consult LIST(i) (LIST(9) = 5780) to see if the location contains data for the proper student (it does). Finally, when the proper storage location is verified, we retrieve the grade (B). If LIST(9) had contained a -999999, the search would be terminated as the data record would not be in the system. If LIST(9) contained somebody else's identification number, then subsequent rows would be searched until the proper identification or -999999 were found. In Figs. III-14 and III-15 we present programs implementing these ideas.

C. TREE SEARCHES

A tree is represented graphically by a collection of *nodes* interconnected by a set of *links*. These links establish one and only one path from one node to any other node. The example tree given in Fig. III-16 will be used to illustrate several key points in tree searches. Trees are used in a wide range of different applications. In most applications of tree structures, information is affiliated with nodes only, while the links reflect relationships between nodes. An organization chart is a good example of such a tree. A map of a sewerage pipe system is an example of a situation where links, in addition to relational data, contain substantive information. Fig. III-17 contains another intriguing application of a tree structure. Here each node represents a letter. The path from the *root* to a letter represents the morse code for that letter. This representation is achieved by interpreting each left pointing arc as a *dot* and each right pointing arc as a *dash*. This particular tree is referred to as a *binary tree* since each node has exactly two successors (if any).

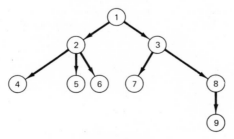

FIG. III-16

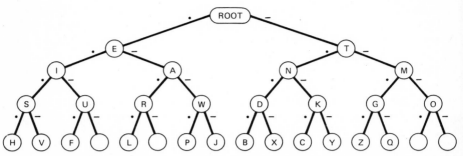

FIG. III-17   Binary representation of the international Morse code. Each step to the left is a *dot*; each step to the right is a *dash*.

Trees are also used to represent different, mutually exclusive solutions to complex problems. For example, in Chapter VIII we will explore how tree structures are used in the solution of combinatorial optimization problems. Searches in trees are of intrinsic interest to computer scientists. However, our interest in trees and tree searches is also caused by the fact that tree searches form a convenient vehicle for introduction of important concepts that later will be used when more general networks are explored.

1.   List Representation of Trees in the Computer

Trees form a special class of more general networks, and as such any of the representational methods that we will later suggest for networks will work for trees. However, certain unique features of the structure of a tree make it possible to develop an alternative pointer-oriented representation resulting both in reduced storage requirements and improved computational efficiency.

Consider the tree structure presented above. Here a node has (at most)

TABLE III-3

Node	Successors	Predecessor
1	2, 3	—
2	4, 5, 6	1
3	7, 8	1
4	—	2
5	—	5
6	—	2
7	—	3
8	9	3
9	—	9

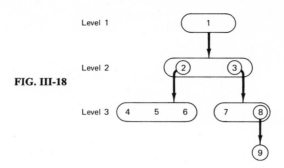

FIG. III-18

one predecessor while it may have any number of successors. To describe the structure for this tree, Table III-3 is presented. (In fact, this table contains too much information since the tree may be redrawn even after the successor or predecessor column is discarded.)

It is an intrinsic property of tree structures that a node appears exactly once in the successor column. Observe that individual nodes are linked to mutually exclusive sets of nodes as shown in Fig. III-18.

This notation clearly is isomorphic to the previous one since we can generate either one from the other one. An alternative way of describing a tree is now emerging. With each node, affiliate pointers to

(1)   the first node on the lext level (the first-on-next (FON) pointer),
(2)   the next node on the same level at the node (the next-on-same (NOS) pointer).

Using a conventional arrow for the first FON pointer and a double arrow for the second NOS, the tree can now be drawn as a binary tree (Fig. III-19).

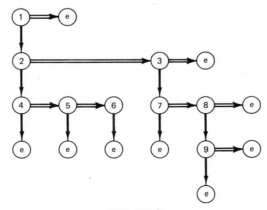

FIG. III-19

We have now reached a point where we are able to represent any tree network by affiliating exactly two pointers with each node. In this context the absence of a pointer (e for empty) in a location is also relevant information.

Using these pointers, Table III-4 can be developed for our example tree.

Again, this representation is isomorphic to the previous notations. Any one representation can be created from any other one.

There are two main reasons why the FON–NOS concept is useful when trees are analyzed on the computer:

(1)   We now need only two words (pointers) per node to store a tree of any structure.

(2)   These two pointers are readily exploited in the development of efficient tree search algorithms.

2.   Considerations for Spanning of Trees

The act of systematically considering the information stored in and between each node of the tree is called spanning. Most of us can do this visually without the use of a formal algorithm. However, to do this on the computer, we need both a memory and an algorithm. Two approaches to spanning are available. First we may span branches left to right, fully exhausting a branch before the next branch is considered. This approach will search the nodes in our example tree in the order shown in Fig. III-20 (note that the numbers in the nodes reflect the *order* not the node labels). Second, we may span all nodes on a given level before nodes on the next level are considered. The search order of this algorithm is represented by the node labels in our example tree.

Both approaches require the following basic operations to be performed:

(1)   Step down: the node pointed to by the FON pointer is considered.
(2)   Step to the right: the node pointed to by the NOS pointer is considered.
(3)   Step up: the node considered on the previous (higher) level is retrieved.

TABLE III-4

Node	FON	NOS
1	2	—
2	4	3
3	7	—
4	—	5
5	—	6
6	—	—
7	—	8
8	9	—
9	—	—

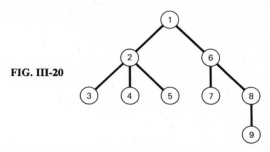

FIG. III-20

In addition to these operations, we need a memory to identify those nodes which we have searched and those which we still need to search. Fortunately, since we may consistently search from left to right, the set of unsearched nodes is uniquely identified by the index of the last node searched on each level. This information is conveniently stored in a *stack*. A stack (sometimes referred to as a push down list) is an extremely important concept in many computer languages. In the operation of a stack, items are inserted on the top of the stack, causing all remaining items in the list to pop down one position. Items are also removed from the top of the stack, causing all remaining items to pop back up one level. Thus a stack operates as a last-in-first-out (LIFO) queue. Computer languages such as PL/1 with recursive abilities incorporate automatic operation of stack memories. In the more primitive FORTRAN language we can only emulate such stack logic.

3. A Tree Search Algorithm

A flowchart for a tree search algorithm is presented in Fig. III-21. To illustrate how this algorithm works, consider how a search for the data affiliated with item U in the morse code binary tree in Fig. III-17 is conducted.

TABLE III-5

Location	1	2	3	4	5	6	7	8	9	10	11	12	13	14
FON	18	—	—	2	9	—	26	—	19	—	3	—	7	4
NOS	—	24	25	11	20	—	15	22	1	—	—	—	—	13
DATA	A	B	C	D	E	F	G	H	I	J	K	L	M	N

Location	15	16	17	18	19	20	21	22	23	24	25	26	27
FON	—	—	—	12	8	—	6	—	16	—	—	—	5
NOS	—	10	—	23	21	14	—	—	—	—	—	17	—
DATA	O	P	Q	R	S	T	U	V	W	X	Y	Z	ROOT

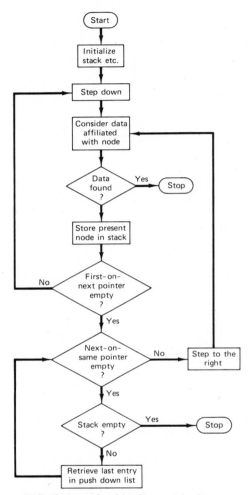

FIG. III-21   Algorithm for search of a tree.

The search is initialized by defining the list representation of the tree (Table III-5). The search starts by stepping down from the root to location 5. The E is stored in this location. Since this is not the desired item, place location 5 in the stack and explore the location indicated by FON(5). This is location 9. The I resides here. Since I is not the desired letter, 9 is placed on top of 5 in the stack and we proceed to location 19 (since FON(9) = 19). The S resides here. Since S is not the desired letter, 19 is placed on top of 9 in the stack. We then proceed to location 8 (since FON(19) = 8). The H resides in this location. This is not the desired item either. At this point we are unable to step down any further. We therefore step sideways to the next location on the same level. This is location 22 since $NOS(8) = 22$. The V resides here.

At this point we are both unable to step down and unable to step sideways. Thus, we must step back up to the previous level. The last visited location on the previous level is retrieved from the top of the stack. This is location 19 corresponding to S. The search is now resumed by stepping sidewise to location 21 as indicated by $NOS(19)$. The U resides at this location. This is the desired item and the search can now be terminated.

PROBLEMS

1. Write a subroutine to perform a bubble sort on up to 100 real numbers.

2. You are given a subroutine ISORT (IRAND, NVAR, IORD). This routine returns the NVAR elements in IRAND sorted in increasing order in array IORD. Using this subroutine, write a program that reads up to 100 17-character Hollerith strings, sorts these strings in increasing order, and then prints them out.

3. Which of the sort methods discussed here can sort the longest list within a fixed amount of core space?

4. How can the n-bucket sort procedure be modified to capitalize on random access storage space?

5. Determine the sort sequence of alphanumeric data by identifying the internal representation of alphanumeric characters in your computer. To do this, read in 20 different characters (both right and left justified) using an A format, and print out the corresponding variable using I, A, and O format. Convert one or more of these to binary. Compare with data given in text.

6. Write a program for n-bucket sorts using linked lists and a user specified number of buckets. Test for the optimal number of buckets for 50–100 and 200 item lists.

7. Write a sort program that:

  (a)   partitions the unsorted list into two lists A and B such that the first half of the original list is in A and the second half is in B, then

  (b)   calls another sort program to sort the halved lists, and finally

  (c)   merges the two sorted lists into a sorted version of the original list.

Evaluate this program by timing sorts of 24, 50, and 100 items using both a bubble sort and a Quicksort sort bubble.

8. Perform a comparative evaluation of the performance of three different sort routines by determining the time required to perform sorts on random lists with 50, 100, 200, and 400 items. For each size list determine the sort time as the average time required to sort four different lists.

9. Write a subroutine for a binary search for an item in an ordered list of size 200 or less.

10. Write a subroutine that works like a binary search except that the pointer partitions the list such that $\frac{1}{3}$ of the list falls into the left list and $\frac{2}{3}$ falls into the right list.

11. Determine empirically the average amount of time required by the previous two subroutines to locate an item in a 10, 50, 150, and 200 item ordered list. Compare your results with the estimates of effort developed in the text and with using the brute force method.

12. Generate or obtain a list of 25 random four-digit numbers. Determine the amount of duplicate storage assignments resulting from an attempt to hash these items into lists of size 29, 37, 51, and 73.

13. Determine the average amount of computer time required to insert 100, 200, 300, and 400 items into an empty hash coded list of length 503.

14. Develop a method for ascertaining that an item is not in a list when hash codes are used.

15. Develop a tree structure similar to the one used in Fig. III-17 to represent the characters in the Univac Fieldcode. (The Univac Fieldcode is given in Table III-1.)

16. Develop a tabular representation of the tree developed in Problem 15.

17. Write a program that performs a tree search to determine the alphanumeric equivalence of a 6 bit string coded in Univac Fieldcode. (*Hint*: solve Problems 15 and 16 first.)

18. Write a computer program that, when initialized with the tree in Fig. III-17, is capable of reading in an alphabetical character and generating a four-digit code describing the morse code symbol corresponding to the character. (*Hint*: Use the code $0 = $ no symbol, $1 = $ dot, and $2 = $ dash. Thus

$$E = 1\ 0\ 0\ 0, \qquad D = 2\ 1\ 1\ 0.)$$

19. Use the experience gained in Problem 18 to develop a program that determines the letter corresponding to a given morse code.

20. A university maintains three separate data files: one for students, one for courses, and one for faculty. Determine the organization and content of these files, and provide proper linkages between them if the following questions are to be answered:

    (a)   Who takes IE 423?
    (b)   Who in IE 423 is a graduate student?
    (c)   Does Smith, Robert E. audit IE 423?
    (d)   What other courses does Smith, Robert E. take?
    (e)   Who teaches CS 417?
    (f)   What else does he teach?
    (g)   What is the home address of Jones, Sara?
    (h)   When does Engr 817 meet?

BIBLIOGRAPHY

Hoare, C. A. R., "Quicksort", *Comp. J.* **5** (1962), 10–15.

Hoare, C. A. R., "Algorithm 64 Quicksort," *Comm. ACM.* **4**, No. 4 (July 1961), 321.

Knuth, Donald E., *The Art of Computer Programming, Vol. 3, Sorting and Searching*, second printing, Addison-Wesley, Reading, Massachusetts, 1975.

Loeser, Rudolf, "Some Performance Tests of 'Quicksort' and Decentants," *Comm. ACM.* **17**, No. 3 (March 1974), 143–152.

Lum, V. Y., P. S. T. Yuen, and M. Dodd, "Key-to-Address Transform Techniques: A Fundamental Performance Study on Large Existing Files," *Comm. ACM.* **14**, No. 4 (April 1971), 222–239.

Morris, R., "Scatter Storage Techniques," *Comm. ACM.*, **11**, No. 1 (January 1968), 38–44.

Villers, E. V. D. S. de, and L. B. Wilson, "Hashing the Subscripts of a Sprace Matrix," *Nordisk Tidskr. Informationsbehandling (BIT)* **14** (1974), 347–358.

CHAPTER IV

NETWORKS—FUNDAMENTAL CONCEPTS

A. USES OF NETWORKS

The theory of networks forms the basis for a wide range of different systems analysis tools and techniques. The power of these tools and techniques stems in part from their flexibility and ability to represent widely different entities (such as those physical relationships present in electrical networks or building structures) as well as many logical relationships (such as those present in flowcharts or sequencing problems).

One of the first and most famous applications of a graph as a problem solving tool was performed by Leonhard Euler in 1736. He used graph theory to solve the long standing Koenigsberg Bridge problem. As illustrated in Fig. IV-1, this problem involved a river flowing through the city of Koenigsberg and the two islands formed by this river in the middle of the city. Seven bridges connected the islands to each other and to either bank. The problem which Euler had to solve involved the route of the bridge guard whose duty entailed lighting the lights on the bridges each night and putting out the lights each morning. Specifically, Euler had to design a route for the guard such that he could leave the guard house, cross all the bridges *once*, and then return to the guard post without having to cross any of the bridges more than once.

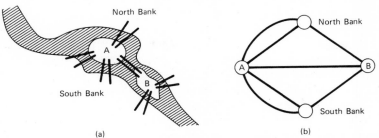

North Bank

South Bank

A

B

North Bank

A   B

South Bank

(a)   (b)

FIG. IV-1 (a) Illustration of Koenigsberg's bridges. (b) Euler's graph representing Koenigsberg bridge problem.

Euler drew a graph of the situation (Fig. IV-1), and used *nodes* to represent the land areas and *edges* to represent the different bridges. He then proved that in order for a solution to the problem to exist, each node would have to have an even number of edges connected to it (if not, you would eventually have to depart from a node on a previously crossed edge as no untraversed edge would be available). Since this was not the case for the Koenigsberg bridge problem, the problem did not have a solution.

In this text, we will encounter other more modern applications of networks to assist in the solution of such problems as those dealing with scheduling and optimization. However, we first need to develop a fundamental understanding of graphs, networks, and their representation and analysis on the computer. This is the purpose of this chapter.

B.   REPRESENTATION OF NETWORKS

1.   Introduction

The words "network" and "graph" are frequently interchanged and confused. A graph is a well-defined abstract entity with many nice mathematical properties. A network, on the other hand, usually has physical interpretations (such as an electric network or a water distribution network) in addition to its abstract properties.

In this text we are primarily concerned with networks as opposed to graphs. However, to be able to use networks intelligently we first need to review and understand the basic concepts of graphs since they form the logical foundation of any network that we may encounter.

2.   Basic Properties of Graphs

A linear graph is defined to contain

(a)   a set of objects $V = v_1, v_2, v_3, \ldots$ (frequently called vertices or nodes),

(b)   a possibly empty set of relations or edges $E = e_1, e_2, \ldots,$

(c)   a mapping $M(v_l, v_j, e_k), (v_l, v_m, e_n), \ldots$ such that each edge is affiliated with exactly two vertices.

The most common representation of a graph is in the form of a diagram where vertices are shown as points and edges as lines as shown in Fig. IV-2. While this method is suitable for visual analysis, other techniques must be used for algorithmic processing of the information contained in the network.

In general, a graph may have parallel edges as well as edges originating and terminating in the same vertex (self-loop). Furthermore, it is not necessary for all vertices in the graph to be connected. However, the graphs studied in this text will be loop-free *connected* graphs. In addition, many graphs will be *simple* in the sense that they are void of parallel edges.

In many cases, the mapping of vertices onto edges may be ordered. This will be the case whenever the two ends of an edge have different properties (such as "in" and "out"). Such graphs are called directed graphs (Fig. IV-2c). The edges in a directed network are frequently called *arcs*. They are usually represented by affiliating an arrowhead with one end of the edges. Directed graphs frequently exhibit *circuits*. This happens whenever the arcs are ordered such that it is possible to follow a succession of arcs (all pointing in the same direction) from a vertex back to the same vertex. In Fig. IV-2c, $e_3-e_2-e_4$ form a circuit. Connected directed graphs without any circuits are called *acyclic graphs*.

Directed graphs are useful because they can easily be used as models of real life situations (such as electrical circuits, sewer systems, precedence diagrams). When directed graphs are used in this applied context, they are usually referred to as *networks*. The vertices are called *nodes*, and the arcs are referred to as *links* or *branches*.

A *chain* is a progression of links or branches (Fig. IV-3a). A chain may terminate in itself, forming a circuit.

A connected network can be partitioned into two separate networks by

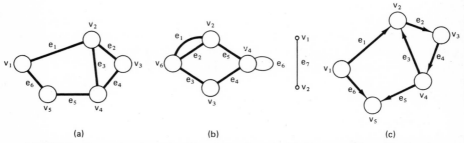

FIG. IV-2   Properties of graphs: (a) connected graph, (b) disconnected graph with a loop and parallel edges, (c) direct graph.

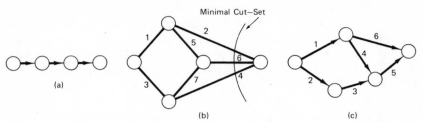

FIG. IV-3   Properties of graphs: (a) chain, (b) graph with a cut-set, (c) connected directed network.

removing certain links (Fig. IV-3b). (Removal of links 2, 5, 6, and 4 in the connected network will partition the network.) The set of arcs used to partition the network is called a *cut-set*. A cut-set may contain any arc whether or not it is essential to the partitioning of the network (such as edge 5). A cut-set containing only those arcs essential to the partitioning (2, 4, and 6) is called a *minimal cut-set*.

Circuits may be present in connected networks. This distinguishes such networks from *trees* where no circuits exist and where there is only one possible route by which you can traverse from a node to any other node. The concept of trees is frequently useful in network analysis and trees are often developed by removing arcs from richer networks. The result is called a *spanning tree* (so called since it spans all nodes in the network). Many different spanning trees can usually be developed for a network. Two different spanning trees for the connected directed network in Fig. IV-3c are given in Fig. IV-4.

3.   Incidence Matrices

For any useful network processing to take place in the computer, the network structure must be represented in some machine understandable form. A wide spectrum of different representation methods are available. Most of these are based either on an incidence matrix scheme or on a linked list format.

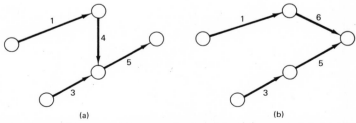

FIG. IV-4   Two different spanning trees developed from the connected directed network of Fig. IV-3c.

All methods are capable of representing virtually any network and straightforward algorithms can be developed to convert between most methods. Thus, the choice of method does not depend so much upon the structure of the network as upon the nature of the problem and the intended processing. For example, a matrix format is convenient for the analysis of electrical circuits since the resulting matrices are in a format suitable for mathematical analysis. On the other hand, linked lists are more efficient for the analysis of the logical relationships in large critical path method (CPM) networks.

In the following sections we will discuss four different notational methods. In each case, the same reference network (Fig. IV-5) will be used to illustrate the method. In addition, the following notation and conversion will be used: N, number of nodes; L, number of links; positive direction of arc is into node: $\overset{-}{\underset{}{\longrightarrow}}\,\overset{+}{}$.

a. Node-to-Node Matrices

The node-to-node incidence matrix A describes the adjacency of two nodes such that

$$A(i,j) = \begin{cases} 1 & \text{if there is a link from } i \text{ to } j, \\ 0 & \text{if there is no link between } i \text{ and } j, \\ -1 & \text{if there is a link from } j \text{ to } i. \end{cases}$$

For example, since the reference network (Fig. IV-5) has a link from 1 to 2, $A(1,2) = 1$ and $A(2,1) = -1$, and the complete matrix for the reference network is

$$A = \begin{vmatrix} 0 & 1 & 0 & 1 & 1 & 0 \\ -1 & 0 & 1 & -1 & 0 & 0 \\ 0 & -1 & 0 & 0 & 0 & 1 \\ -1 & 1 & 0 & 0 & 0 & -1 \\ -1 & 0 & 0 & 0 & 0 & 1 \\ 0 & 0 & -1 & 1 & -1 & 0 \end{vmatrix}.$$

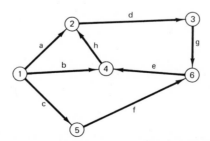

FIG. IV-5   Reference network to illustrate different notational methods.

It is clear from the definition of the matrix that $A(i,j) = -A(j,i)$ for any $i \neq j$. Thus, the node-to-node matrix is negatively symmetric and $A - A^T = 0$.

Note that since ones are used to represent links, when the nodal incidence matrix is used, the identity of the links is lost. Also note that this method must be modified to allow for more than one link between two nodes.

It is possible to reconstruct the original network even after a complete row or column is removed from A. This is because information about any link is stored in two independent rows and columns. Thus it is also possible to construct the last column in A if the first (or any) $N-1$ columns are given. This indicates that the columns in A are linearly dependent and thus that A^{-1} does not exist.

To avoid redundancy, one column must therefore be removed before the node-to-node incidence matrix is used for computational purposes. Modified node-to-node incidence matrices have diverse applications such as economic input–output tables and transportation problems.

b. Node-to-Branch Incidence Matrix

The node-to-branch incidence matrix is similar to the node-to-node matrix except that it recognizes and preserves the identity of individual links:

$$B(i,j) = \begin{cases} -1 & \text{if link } i \text{ exits from node } j, \\ 0 & \text{if link } j \text{ is not connected to node } i, \\ 1 & \text{if link } i \text{ enters node } j. \end{cases}$$

For the reference network

$$B = \begin{array}{c|cccccc} & 1 & 2 & 3 & 4 & 5 & 6 \\ \hline a & -1 & 1 & & & & \\ b & -1 & & & 1 & & \\ c & -1 & & & & 1 & \\ d & & -1 & 1 & & & \\ e & & & & 1 & & -1 \\ f & & & & & -1 & 1 \\ g & & & -1 & & & 1 \\ h & & 1 & -1 & & & \end{array}.$$

One column must usually be removed from B if the column is to be used for computation (again, this is to remove redundant information).

c. *Example*

As an illustration of a case where a node-to-branch incidence matrix natural-ly emerges in the formulation and solution of a problem, consider the fol-lowing problem:

A company requires delivery of a certain commodity from its plant to four different locations. To distribute this commodity the company rents pipe-line capacity from a private vendor at a cost of $5.00 per unit/mile. If the distribution network shown in Fig. IV-6 is available and commodity demand is as follows:

Location:	A	B	C	D
Demand (units/hour):	10	50	5	35

How should the commodity flow be routed?

This problem can readily be formulated as a linear programming (LP) problem (Chapter VII). The solution should be such that flow in individual links minimizes the total distribution cost. However, LP models do not allow for variables to be negative. This means that in this case the assumed direc-tionality of the links is critical as the LP solution will not allow for flows in the opposite (i.e., negative) direction of the assumed flow. This is not a diffi-culty in the problem just discussed because the directionality is defined by physical constraints. In cases where a doubt exists regarding the direction of flow in a given link, links in both directions may be assumed. The LP algorithm will then select the direction resulting in the lowest overall cost (it is clearly never optimal to simultaneously flow in both directions at once).

Prior to formulating the LP model, we have to identify and label the in-dividual links (Table IV-1).

If x_i represents the flow in link i, we can now formulate the following LP to solve this problem:

Minimize

$$Z = 10x_1 + 80x_2 + 40x_3 + 10x_4 + 35x_5 + 70x_6 + 40x_7 + 85x_8$$

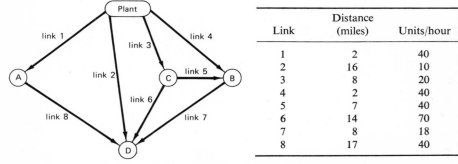

Link	Distance (miles)	Units/hour
1	2	40
2	16	10
3	8	20
4	2	40
5	7	40
6	14	70
7	8	18
8	17	40

FIG. IV-6   Distribution network for incidence matrix example.

TABLE IV-1

Link	From	To	Capacity (units/hr)	Length (miles)	Total cost per unit flow ($/unit)
1	Plant	A	40	2	10
2	Plant	D	10	16	80
3	Plant	C	20	8	40
4	Plant	B	40	2	10
5	C	B	40	7	35
6	C	D	70	14	70
7	B	D	18	8	40
8	A	D	40	17	85

subject to four conservation constraints

$$x_1 \qquad\qquad\qquad\qquad - x_8 \geqslant 10 \qquad \text{(supply A)}$$
$$x_2 \qquad\qquad + x_6 + x_7 + x_8 \geqslant 35 \qquad \text{(supply D)}$$
$$x_3 \quad - x_5 - x_6 \qquad\qquad \geqslant 5 \qquad \text{(supply C)}$$
$$x_4 + x_5 \quad - x_7 \qquad \geqslant 50 \qquad \text{(supply B)}$$
$$-x_1 - x_2 - x_3 - x_4 \qquad\qquad\qquad \geqslant -Q \qquad \text{(plant capacity)}$$

and the capacity constraints

$$x_1 \leqslant 40, \qquad x_2 \leqslant 10, \qquad x_3 \leqslant 20, \qquad x_4 \leqslant 40,$$
$$x_5 \leqslant 40, \qquad x_6 \leqslant 70, \qquad x_7 \leqslant 18, \qquad x_8 \leqslant 40.$$

It is clear that these flow conservation constraints represent nothing less than the transpose of the branch-node incidence matrix. In fact, in matrix terms, this problem could be formulated as

Minimize $Z = CX$

subject to $B^T X \geqslant b$

$$0 \leqslant X \leqslant U,$$

where C is a vector of costs for different links, b is a vector of site demands (negative for the source), U is a vector of upper bounds for individual pipe flows, and B is the branch-node incidence matrix for the distribution network.

4. Lists

Matrix notation is particularly useful when networks representing physical "forces," "flows," or "potentials" of one sort or another (electricity, structures, hydraulics, or transportation) are to be analyzed. This notation is less useful when networks representing logical relationships are analyzed. This is so since such networks usually represent many potential relationships, all of which are not necessarily valid at the same time. Thus, analysis of such networks usually involves the use of search type rather than matrix multiplication type algorithms. We will see that search algorithms are best implemented through the use of linked lists. Another reason for the use of linked lists is a resulting conservation of storage space. While incidence matrices generally are quite sparse (resulting in excessive core requirements), linked lists are normally packed (resulting in significant core savings). To facilitate our discussion, we will first explore the general concepts of lists to represent network structures. We will then procede to explore how such lists can be packed to facilitate efficient programming and storage utilization.

a. P–S *Lists*

The simplest list structure used to describe a network is an unordered list containing the ordered pairs of successor and predecessor nodes for each link. Termed a P–S list, this list thus at a minimum contains one pair of entries for each link in the system (additional entries relating to the identity or content of specific links may also be present). For example, the following list represents the example network in Fig. IV-5:

Link:	a	h	d	b	e	c	g	f
P:	1	4	2	1	6	1	3	5
S:	2	2	3	4	4	5	6	6

The fact that this is a complete description of the network structure can easily be verified by reconstructing Fig. IV-5 from this list.

Links may appear in any order in a P–S list, thus the following list is also a vaild representation of the network in Fig. IV-5:

Link:	a	b	c	d	g	h	f	e
P:	1	1	1	2	3	4	5	6
S:	2	4	5	3	6	2	6	4

P–S lists are seldom used as the main method for representing networks in a computer. This is because alternative methods lend themself better to the development of efficient analysis algorithms. However, P–S lists are useful for two reasons. First, they form a convenient starting point for the study of more complex lists. Second, P–S lists frequently appear as intermediate products when other internal representations are being developed (see, e.g., Section 4e).

b. *Sparse Lists*

In a sparse list, individual lists describing the predecessor and/or successor nodes for each node are maintained. For the reference network (Fig. IV-5), six separate lists would be maintained:

Node:	1	2	3	4	5	6
Predecessor:	—	1,4	2	1,6	1	3,5

If, for some reason, the successor relationship also needs to be recorded, another set of lists would be required. While a 6 by 6 array (36 locations) was required to store the structure of this network in a nodal incidence matrix, a 6 by 2 matrix will suffice to store this structure in a sparse list. The list contains the same information as the nodal matrix. Thus, like the matrix, the sparse list does not allow parallel links or identification of a link by other means than by its endpoints.

The main reason for *not* using sparse lists in computer programming lies in their inflexible storage requirements. This is because separate lists are required for each node. All these lists must be dimensioned to the same size. Thus, if one node can be expected to have 20 predecessors, all lists must have a size of 20.

c. *Example*

The following program reads a network structure as a sparse predecessor list. A nodal incidence matrix is generated from this input. Finally a sparse successor list is generated and printed:

```
      IMPLICIT INTEGER (A-Z)
      INTEGER PLIST(100,10)
      INTEGER SLIST(100,10)
      INTEGER PCOUNT(100)
      INTEGER SCOUNT(100)
      INTEGER NODAL(100,100)
C
C THIS PROGRAM GENERATES A SPARCE SUCCESSOR LIST FROM A
C SPARCE PREDECESSOR LIST, AS AN INTERMEDIATE
C PRODUCT THE NODAL INCIDENCE MATRIX IS GENERATED.
C
C THE PROGRAM IS DIMENSIONED FOR
C          100 NODES
C               10 PREDECESSORS FOR ANY NODE
C               10 SUCCESSORS FOR ANY NODE
C
C INPUTS : FREE FORMAT IS USED ON EACH CARD, ONE DATA CARD
C               IS USED PER NOTE, THE FOLLOWING INFORMATION MUST
C               APPEAR ON EACH CARD IN THIS ORDER :
C               1. NODE NUMBER
C               3. INDICES OF PREDECESSORS (ANY ORDER)
C               2. NUMBER OF PREDECESSORS FOR NODE
C
C               CARDS MAY APPEAR IN ANY ORDER
C               THE INPUT STREAM IS TERMINATED BY A CARD CONTAINING
C               THREE ZEROES SEPARATED BY COMMAS
C
      NODES = 0
 1000 READ,NODE,NPREDS,(PLIST(NODE,I),I=1,NPREDS)
      PRINT, NODE,NPREDS,(PLIST(NODE,I),I=1,NPREDS)
      IF(NODE.EQ.0) GO TO 1010
```

```
            NODES = NODES+1
            PCOUNT(NODE) = NPREDS
            GO TO 1000
C
C INPUT IS COMPLETED , SETUP NODAL INCIDENCE MATRIX**********************
C CLEAR INCIDENCE MATRIX
C
 1010 DO 1030 I = 1,NODES
           DO 1020 J = 1,NODES
              NODAL(I,J) = 0
 1020    CONTINUE
 1030 CONTINUE
C
C **LOAD INFORMATION INTO MATRIX***************************************
C
      DO 1050 SNODE = 1,NODES
         NPREDS = PCOUNT(SNODE)
         IF(NPREDS.EQ.0) GO TO 1050
         DO 1040 IPRED = 1,NPREDS
C
C           IDENTIFY NEXT PREDECESSOR NODE
C
            PNODE = PLIST(SNODE,IPRED)
      PRINT, NPREDS,IPRED,PNODE,SNODE
C
C           MARK EXIT OF ARC FROM PNODE
C
            NODAL(PNODE,SNODE) = +1
C
C           MARK ENTRY OF ARC INTO SNODE
C
            NODAL(SNODE,PNODE) = -1
 1040    CONTINUE
 1050 CONTINUE
      DO 9999 I = 1,NODES
      PRINT,(NODAL(I,J),J=1,NODES)
 9999 CONTINUE
C
C**GENERATE SUCCESSOR LIST********************************************
C
      DO 1070 PNODE=1,NODES
         NSUCCS = 0
         DO 1060 SNODE = 1,NODES
            I = NODAL(PNODE,SNODE)
C
C           IS 'SNODE' A SUCCESSOR OF 'PNODE'
C           I.E. IS THERE A LINK FROM PNODE TO SNODE
C
            IF(I.NE.1) GO TO 1060
            NSUCCS = NSUCCS+1
            SLIST(PNODE,NSUCCS) = SNODE
 1060    CONTINUE
         SCOUNT(PNODE) = NSUCCS
 1070 CONTINUE
C
C**PRINT LIST*********************************************************
C
      DO 1080 INODE = 1,NODES
         NSUCCS = SCOUNT(INODE)
         IF(NSUCCS.LE.0) WRITE(6,100) INODE
         IF(NSUCCS.GT.0) WRITE(6,100) INODE,(SLIST(INODE,I),I=1,NSUCCS)
 1080 CONTINUE
  100 FORMAT(1X,I3,20X,10I7)
      STOP
      END
```

d. Linked Lists

Linked lists are used to eliminate the need to reserve space for the maximum number of nodes in each individual sparse list. This is achieved by packing the individual lists into *one* list and by providing pointers to identify the location of the first entry in this list for a particular node. This arrangement is illustrated graphically in Fig. IV-7.

A computer implementation of this scheme would require the use of two one-dimensional arrays. The first array, P, would contain the packed list of predecessors (or successors). The second array, PINDEX, would contain the location in P of the first predecessors for a particular node. Thus, the first predecessor for the Ith node would be retrieved as $P(PINDEX(ITH))$, and the third predecessor of the Ith node would be retrieved as $P(PINDEX(ITH+2))$. For the reference network, P and PINDEX would be those shown in Fig. IV-8a. Here, zero is used to indicate that a node does not have any predecessors, and a pointer to the first unused position in S is inserted as the last pointer in SINDEX. A similar list is developed for a successor notation (Fig. IV-8b).

We can now retrieve the successor nodes for INODE by consulting SINDEX(INODE) for the location of the first successor node in S and by computing

$$SINDEX(INODE+1) - 1$$

to find the location of the last successor node in S. This scheme will usually

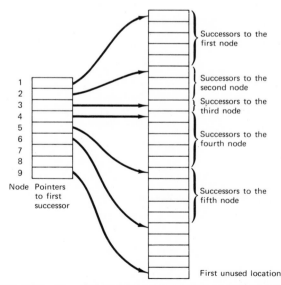

FIG. IV-7 Use of packed list to represent a network structure.

(a)

PINDEX =
0
1
3
4
6
7
9

P =	
1	node 2
4	
2	node 3
1	node 4
6	
1	node 5
3	node 6
5	
0	first unused position

(b)

SINDEX =
1
4
5
6
7
8
9

S =	
2	node 1
4	
5	
3	node 2
6	node 3
2	node 4
6	node 5
4	node 6
0	first unused position

FIG. IV-8

work. Exceptions occur when

(a) the node does not have any successors, or
(b) the subsequent node does not have any successors.

To circumvent these exceptions, we can either introduce a separate vector containing the count of successors for each node, or we can consult SINDEX of subsequent nodes until a nonzero entry is found. (The last entry will always be nonzero.) The latter requires less space, while the former may be slightly faster.

The latter approach is used in the following program that illustrates the use and handling of packed lists in a subroutine that prints the index of the successor nodes for a given node:

```
      SUBROUTINE SPRINT(INODE)
C
C  THIS SUBROUTINE PRINTS THE NAME OF ALL IMMEDIATE SUCCESSORS TO INODE
C
      COMMON /NTWRK/ S(1000),SINDEX(200),NODES
C
C  IS INODE A VALID NODE
C
      IF(INODE.GT.0.AND.INODE.LE.NODES) GOTO 1000
      WRITE(6,100) INODE
  100 FORMAT(I10,' IS AN INVALID NODE')
      RETURN
C
C  DOES INODE HAVE ANY SUCCESSORS AT ALL
C
 1000 IF (SINDEX(INODE).GT.0) GOTO 1010
      WRITE(6,101) INODE
  101 FORMAT( 'NODE',I4,' HAS NO SUCCESSORS')
      RETURN
C
C  DETERMINE LOCATION OF FIRST AND LAST SUCCESSOR IN S
C
 1010 ILO=SINDEX(INODE)
      JNODE = INODE+1
 1020 IHI = SINDEX(JNODE)
      IF(IHI.GT.0)GOTO 1030
```

```
      JNODE = JNODE+1
      GOTO 1020
C
C   PRINT SUCCESSOR NODES
C
 1030 IHI = IHI-1
      WRITE(6,102) INODE,(S(I)I=ILO,IHI)
  102 FORMAT(I4,' HAS THE FOLLOWING SUCCESSOR NODES',12I6)
      RETURN
      END
```

The relationship between a packed list and a P–S list is of interest. We observe that each node is represented once in the P-row (S-row) in the P–S list and once in the P(S) array for each time it is a predecessor (successor). Thus the only difference between P(S) and the P-row (S-row) is the *order* in which nodes appear. And, by properly ordering the links in the P–S table, the P-row can be made identical to P *or* the S-row can be made identical to S. In fact, the P-row in the first P–S list in Section 4a is identical to P, and the S-row in the second P–S list is identical to S for the example network. We also note that the S-row contains nodes in increasing numeric order when the P–S list is ordered such that the P-row is equal to P (and the same is true for the P-row when the S-row is equal to S).

e. Converting from Predecessor to Successor Lists

Conversion of lists from predecessor to successor notation is often necessary. This occurs when an algorithm requires the use of both predecessor and successor lists, or when data is available as a predecessor (successor) list while the algorithm requires a successor (predecessor) list. This conversion can be facilitated through the construction of an intermediate nodal incidence matrix. While this approach is easily understood and implemented, it is not a feasible approach for large networks where the core requirements for a nodal incidence matrix would be excessive. Instead, a more efficient and less core consuming approach is required. To develop such an approach, we capitalize on the relationship between P and the P-row and S and the S-row in suitably ordered P–S lists.

The first step is to generate the P–S list from P and PINDEX. This is readily achieved since P is identical to the P-row, and the S-row can be constructed by using PINDEX to sequentially determine the successor of each entry in P. (Nodes in the S-row will now appear in increasing order.) The second step is to sort the links in the P–S list such that nodes in the P-row appear in increasing order. Finally, S is copied from the S-row and SINDEX is constructed by noting the location of the first node of each kind in the P-row.

f. Example

(1) The S array for the reference network was shown to be

$$S = (2, 4, 5, 3, 6, 2, 6, 4).$$

(2)   By using the information in SINDEX, we are able to develop the P–S table (the identity of the links are omitted here):

$$\begin{bmatrix} 2 & 4 & 5 & 3 & 6 & 2 & 6 & 4 \\ 1 & 1 & 1 & 2 & 3 & 4 & 5 & 6 \end{bmatrix}.$$

(3)   Sort columns in order of increasing successor nodes:

$$\begin{bmatrix} 2 & 2 & 3 & 4 & 4 & 5 & 6 & 6 \\ 1 & 4 & 2 & 1 & 6 & 1 & 3 & 5 \end{bmatrix}.$$

(4)   Scan the entries in the S-row to develop the pointers to the first location in P for each node:

PINDEX = 0,   1,   3,   4,   6,   7,   9

Here PINDEX(1) was assigned a value of zero since node 1 did not appear on the sorted successor list.

The development of a subroutine for this conversion is left as an exercise. It is necessary to buffer S in this routine if the old S array is to be used after the call.

g.   Node-Link Lists

In many critical path type networks, activities are represented by branches while nodes represent discrete points in time. When this approach is used, it is necessary to uniquely identify links as well as nodes.

A space conserving way that lends itself easily to the development of efficient algorithms in this context is to affiliate pointers with *both* nodes and links such that

(a)   each node points to the *first link* originating from it,
(b)   each link points to
   (1)   the *next link* originating from the same node as it does, and
   (2)   the sink *node* of the link.

Using these pointers, a square box for links, and a round box for nodes, the sample network in Fig. IV-5 is drawn (Fig. IV-9). This representation lends itself well to the development of two lists of pointers, one for the nodes and one for the links. For the sample network these lists are:

Nodal list Node:	1	2	3	4	5	6		
First successor link:	a	d	g	h	f	e		

Link list Link:	a	b	c	d	e	f	g	h
Next successor link:	b	c	—	—	—	—	g	—
Sink:	2	4	5	3	4	6	6	2

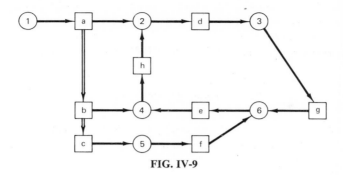

FIG. IV-9

To retrieve the successor nodes from node 1, we first find the first successor link a in the nodal list. We then move to the link list where we find that the sink node of link a is 2. Thus, the first successor node form 1 is 2. The entry for link a in the link list also tells us that b is the next link originating from node 1. Link b has 4 as sink node and c as next link. Link c terminates in node 5 and has no successor link. Thus, node 1 is followed by nodes 2, 4, and 5.

C. TRAVERSING A DIRECTED NETWORK

Two fundamentally different classes of problems trigger a need to search the nodes (and perhaps links) in a network in a systematic manner.

In the first class of problems (illustrated by a spanning tree generation problem) arcs are assumed to carry no information beyond the identity of a successor node. The purpose of the traversing algorithm is to visit each node (perhaps to perform some calculations) whenever a path from the root to the node can be developed. If a node has been reached through one path, the presence of other paths to that node becomes irrelevant and can be ignored. An efficient traversing algorithm for such a class of problems will visit each node only once and will traverse exactly one arc per visited node. Thus, the arcs traced by such an algorithm will form the branches of a spanning tree for the network.

In the second class of problems, it is assumed that not only must all nodes be reached (as in the first method) but that all arcs contain relevant information and must be searched as well. An example of such a problem is finding the longest path from the source to the sink in an acyclic network. The purpose of the traversing algorithm is to visit a node when *all paths* to the node are developed. An efficient algorithm for such problems will reach each arc exactly once and will reach each node once for each of its predecessors.

We have already explored the problem of searching or traversing all nodes in a tree. The problem of traversing all nodes and/or links in a network is quite similar to this problem and we will utilize a concept of a stack of ready-to-be (but-not-yet) searched nodes identical to the one used for a tree search.

1. A Spanning Tree Algorithm

An algorithm for generating a spanning tree for a directed network is presented in Fig. IV-10a. It is assumed that the network is described using the

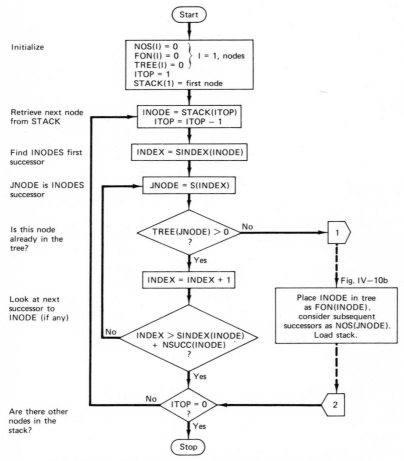

FIG. IV-10a   Algorithm to generate spanning tree node selection.

linked SINDEX and S lists as previously discussed. Furthermore, it is assumed that an array NSUCC containing the count of successors for individual nodes is available.

The resulting spanning tree will be stored in the standard next-on-same, first-on-next (NOS–FON) arrays discussed in Chapter III. The location of the root of the tree is stored in the variable IROOT. An array TREE is used to flag whether or not a node has been included in the spanning tree. A last-in-first-out (LIFO) stack of nodes eligible for consideration is maintained in the array STACK. Nodes are inserted into the tree at the same time as they become eligible for inclusion into the stack. The logic flow will now be described.

A node INODE is retrieved from the stack, and the stack is shortened by subtracting one from ITOP. The location in S of the first successor to INODE is retrieved as INDEX = SINDEX(INODE). Since the algorithm is intended for connected acyclic networks, we know that all but the last node will have a positive number of successors. Later we shall see that the last node will never be assigned to the stack. Thus, INDEX will always point to a location containing a valid node. The successor to INODE is now retrieved as JNODE = S(INDEX). This node may or may not already be included in the tree. Let us first explore the case where JNODE already belongs to the tree. Now TREE(JNODE) is positive and we increment INDEX by one in preparation to consider the next entry in S. A test is made to see if INDEX still points to a successor of INODE. If so, the new successor is retrieved and considered for inclusion in the tree. If all successors to INODE have been considered, then it is time to consider the successors to another node. Successors to any net-yet-considered node currently in the tree are eligible for considerations. These nodes are all maintained in the stack. Since ITOP points to the last entry in STACK, we know that additional nodes are available if ITOP is greater than zero. In this case we retrieve the node currently pointed to by ITOP and consider its successors. If, on the other hand, ITOP is zero, the search is terminated as all nodes have been searched.

Consider now the case where JNODE has been identified as the first successor to INODE not yet in the tree. Control is now transferred to the flowchart in Fig. IV-10b. JNODE is included in the spanning tree by setting the FON pointer from INODE equal to JNODE and by setting TREE(JNODE) equal to 1.

If JNODE has any successors, they are placed in the first unused locations in the stack, and ITOP is updated accordingly. INDEX is now incremented by one in preparation to consider the next successor to INODE. If INDEX no longer points to a successor of INODE, then control is returned to the flowchart in Fig. IV-10a where the next entry in the stack is considered.

On the other hand, if INODE has additional successors, then the identity

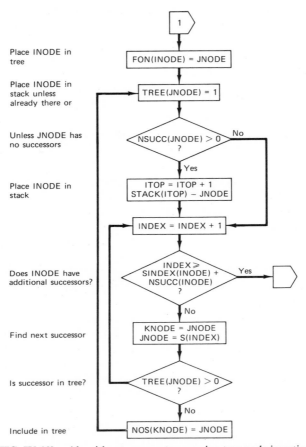

Place INODE in tree

Place INODE in stack unless already there or

Unless JNODE has no successors

Place INODE in stack

Does INODE have additional successors?

Find next successor

Is successor in tree?

Include in tree

FIG. IV-10b   Algorithm to generate spanning tree node insertion.

of the present successor is saved as KNODE, and the identity of the new successor is set equal to JNODE. If this JNODE does already belong to the tree, then the identity of subsequent successors are explored. On the other hand, if JNODE is not in the tree, then it is included in the tree as NOS (KNODE). TREE(JNODE) is then set equal to one and JNODE is included in the stack if it is not the last node in the network.

Upon completion of this algorithm, the tree shown in Fig. IV-11 has been searched for the example network in Fig. IV-5. Here the first number in the bracket over a node represents the order in which the node was *inserted* into the tree and the STACK. The second number represents the order in which the node was *removed* from the stack for further processing.

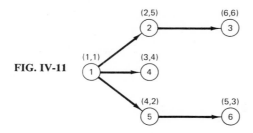

FIG. IV-11

2. A Longest Path Algorithm

The algorithm in Fig. IV-12 can be used to traverse all links in an acyclic network. A typical application of such an algorithm is to find the longest path between the source and sink. In this algorithm, a link is eligible for traversing whenever all links entering its source node have been traversed. The importance of this algorithm stems from its application in critical path type algorithms. In anticipation of this application, we take a new approach to the STACK. Items will be inserted in the first *unused* location in the STACK, and they will never be erased. Thus, items remain in the STACK even after they have been processed. At the end of the processing, the STACK contains all the nodes in the network in the order they were processed.

Again, we assume that the network is represented as a packed successor list. In addition, we introduce two additional arrays NSUCC and NPRED containing the count of successors and predecessors for each node. The information in NPRED will be modified during the processing; therefore, it will be a good practice to duplicate this array prior to any actual execution of this algorithm.

The algorithm is initialized by placing node 1 in the STACK and by initializing the two pointers SIN and SOUT to one. The first node in the STACK is then retrieved and SOUT is updated to the location of the next entry to be removed from the list. The fact that this location is empty at this point is irrelevant. A loop is now set up such that all successors (JNODES) of the current node (INODE) can in turn be investigated. For each passage in the loop, the INDEX of the successor in S is incremented by one. The loop is terminated when the value of this index exceeds the highest index for the successors of this node.

Each INODE–JNODE pair defines a unique, heretofore unexplored link. If any particular processing is to be performed on the link, it should be done at this time. Upon completion of any such processing, the count of unprocessed predecessors to JNODE is reduced by 1. Eventually, JNODE will no longer have any unprocessed predecessors. Links emerging from JNODE

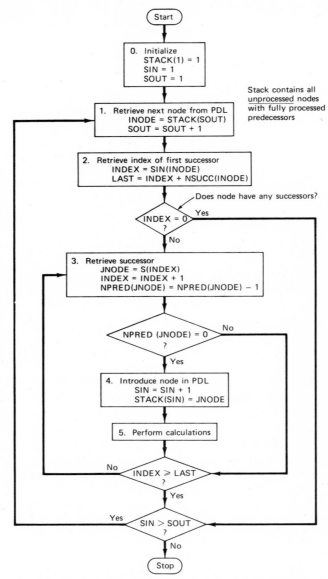

FIG. IV-12   Algorithm to traverse all links in a network.

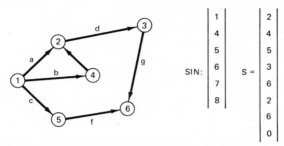

FIG. IV-13 Test problem for illustration of all links traversing algorithm.

are then eligible for processing. This is achieved by entering JNODE in the STACK as soon as the last predecessor of JNODE has been processed.

To illustrate the logic of this algorithm, we will step through a few iterations of its application to the test problem shown in Fig. IV-13 (see Table IV-2). (The algorithm only works on acyclic networks. It was therefore necessary to modify the reference network in Fig. IV-5 by removing link e.) Eventually each link in the network will be traversed once. You should verify that links

TABLE IV-2

	Step	Assignment	Comment
0.	Initialize	STACK$(1) = 1$ SIN $= 1$ SOUT $= 1$	
1.	Retrieve next node from STACK	INODE $= 1$ SOUT $= 2$	
2.	Retrieve index of first successor	INDEX $= (SIN(1)) = 1$ LAST $= 1 + 3 = 4$	Node 1 has 3 successors.
3.	Retrieve successor	JNODE $= S(1) = 2$ INDEX $= 2$ NPRED$(2) = 1$	Node 2 has two predecessors.
3.	Retrieve successor	JNODE $= S(2) = 4$ INDEX $= 3$ NPRED$(4) = 0$	Node 4 has no more predecessors.
4.	Introduce node in STACK	SIN $= $ SIN $+ 1 = 2$ STACK$(2) = 4$	Successors from node 4 are now eligible.
3.	Retrieve successor	JNODE $= S(3) = 5$ INDEX $= 4$ NPRED$(5) = 0$	This is node 1's last successor.
4.	Introduce node in STACK	SIN $= 3$ STACK$(3) = 5$	
1.	Retrieve next node from STACK	INODE $= $ STACK$(2) = 4$ SOUT $= 3$	

are traversed in the order

$$a, \quad b, \quad c, \quad n, \quad f, \quad d, \quad g.$$

How does this order differ from the one that would occur if a traditional STACK had been maintained?

3. Backward Traversing

It is frequently necessary to traverse all links in a network in two passes. First, a forward pass is made followed by a backward pass. This can be accomplished by reversing the logic of the forward spanning routine for the backward pass.

While this is a viable approach, it is time consuming and requires that we maintain a set of predecessor lists in addition to the successor lists. (This is not a restriction if the network structure is stored as an incidence matrix.) It was to overcome these problems that we modified the traditional STACK for the all-links traversing routine such that at the end of the pass it contained all nodes *in the order in which they were considered.* By considering nodes in the reverse order of their appearance in the STACK, the nodes are automatically considered in a valid sequence for a backward pass.

To illustrate this idea, consider the modified reference network presented in Fig. V-13. The STACK created after the forward pass is

$$\text{STACK} = 1, \quad 4, \quad 5, \quad 2, \quad 3, \quad 6$$

If the direction of all links were reversed, one of the following two stacks would have been created by our algorithm:

$$\text{STACK}' = 6, \quad 5, \quad 3, \quad 2, \quad 4, \quad 1$$
$$\text{STACK}'' = 6, \quad 3, \quad 5, \quad 2, \quad 4, \quad 1$$

The first would be created if $P(\text{PINDEX}(6)) = 5$, while the second would be generated if the first predecessor to six in the list were 3. Neither of these is the reverse of the list generated by the forward pass.

Let us now revise our algorithm in such a way that instead of spanning for breadth (many short paths) we span for depth (develop each path fully before proceeding to the next path). In this case one of the following two lists is developed:

$$\text{STACK}'' = 6, \quad 5, \quad 3, \quad 2, \quad 4, \quad 1$$
$$\text{STACK}' = 6, \quad 3, \quad 2, \quad 5, \quad 4, \quad 1$$

Again, the first will be developed if 5 precedes 3 on the list while the second will be developed otherwise. The latter is the reverse list of the one traced by our forward pass algorithm. In fact, the stack generated in this manner by a forward pass will always be a feasible sequence of consideration for the backward pass.

This greatly simplifies the development of a backward pass algorithm. The actual implementation of such an algorithm is deferred to Chapter V.

D. GENERATION OF RANDOM NETWORKS

Networks emerge as important elements of problems in many different settings. Thus a random network generator is frequently an integral element of a problem generator. It is easy to generate networks of a given size and density by randomly scattering plus and minus ones over a branch-node incidence matrix. However, such a procedure usually does not meet the requirements of most problem situations. Some of the constraints and considerations imposed by common problem situations include the following:

(a)   The network must be fully connected.
(b)   Parallel edges are not allowed.
(c)   The network should be acyclic.
(d)   If an indirect link exists between nodes A and B (through node C), then a direct link between A and B may not be permitted (as it is redundant).
(e)   A network connected in a certain manner (long and thin or short and fat) may be desired.

All of these objectives can be met if we use a recursive algorithm such that the ith node is generated and connected to the existing $i-1$ nodes before the $i+1$th node is generated. The following procedure implements such an algorithm:

(1)   Generate dummy start node.
(2)   Generate a node. Place the node at the bottom of the list of generated nodes.
(3)   Scan the list of previously generated nodes such that the most recently generated activity is investigated first.
   (i)   If a forward path already exists between the (old) node and the newly generated node, skip this node (this step eliminates redundant network links); otherwise,
  (ii)   Draw a random number between zero and one.
 (iii)   If the random number is less than a predefined value P, generate a predecessor link between the (old) node and the newly generated node.
 (iv)   If the node has not been successfully linked to any other nodes, link it to the dummy start node.

(4)   When the proper number of nodes is generated, append a dummy terminal node. Link all nodes without internal successor nodes to this node.

The structure of a network generated through the above algorithm can be controlled through the value of the constant P. A high value of P yields a fairly stretched out network (Fig. IV-14a). A low value of P yields a network with many short, parallel paths (Fig. IV-14b). $P = 1$ will result in a single chain (Fig. IV-14c), while $P = 0$ will result in a network with all parallel nodes (Fig. IV-14d).

In a recent paper (Thesen, 1977), we have discussed means of quantitatively measuring the information content in acyclic networks and of estimating the value of P that corresponds to a given information constant. It was shown here that the value of P used to generate a specific network could be approxi-

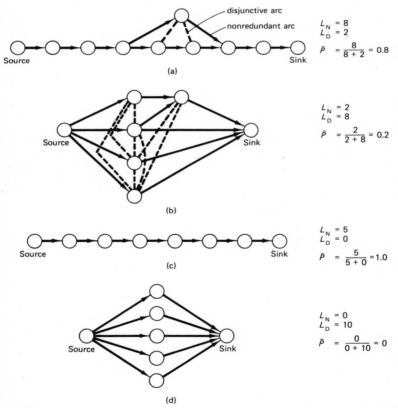

FIG. IV-14 Randomly generated networks. (a) $P = 0.8$, (b) $P = 0.2$, (c) $P = 1.0$, (d) $P = 0.0$.

mately estimated by

$$\overline{P} = \frac{L_N}{L_N + L_D}.$$

Where L_N is the number of nonredundant links not connected to the source or sink and L_D is the number of node pairs not connected by direct or indirect links. This approximation was shown to hold reasonably well for values of P in the range 0.2–0.8.

Thus when random networks are to be generated, representative real life networks could first be analyzed to determine the proper values of L_N and L_D. Similar but different networks could then be generated by using the algorithm given here with the estimated value of P.

If step $3i$ of this algorithm is to be implemented, it is necessary to determine if a path exists between any two nodes. This is easily achieved through the construction of a forward path matrix F such that F_{ij} is the number of different forward paths from node i to node j. Since nodes are generated in increasing order, F will be a matrix with nonzero elements below the diagonal only. Rows are added to the matrix as the network grows. Since the addition of a node does not alter the paths between existing nodes, there is no need to alter the content of previously generated rows as the network grows. The elements of the new row in F is determined as

$$F_{i,j} = \sum_{k=j}^{i-1} A_{i,k} * F_{k,j},$$

where $A_{i,k}$ is a modified incident matrix in which all negative entries have been eliminated.

PROBLEMS

1. Some networks can be represented in FON–NOS lists while others cannot. Under what conditions is this possible? (*Hints*: (a) It works for the network shown in Fig. IV-15a. (b) It does not work for the network shown in Fig. IV-15b.)

2. In many applications it is necessary to establish whether or not a particular network is acyclic. How can this be established within the framework of the spanning algorithms discussed here? (*Hint*: How does a loop affect the execution of a spanning algorithm?)

3. The organization of data for manual analysis is frequently different from the organization recommended for computer analysis. This is particularly true for the organization of data regarding network structures. It is therefore frequently necessary to provide front ends in network analysis programs

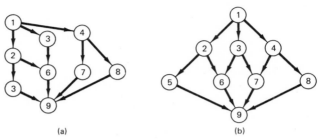

(a)   (b)

FIG. IV-15

that convert data from a "user friendly" to a "computer friendly" organization. For example, the structure of acyclic networks is most conveniently specified externally in sparse predecessor lists:

(NODE(I),   PRED(1), ..., PRED(N)

For internal processing this structure is most conveniently organized as a packed successor list.

Write a program to perform such a conversion. Allow nodes to appear in any order. This program will be used in the next chapter as an important element in a critical path analysis program.

4. A large number of different errors can be performed when the input data for the program in Problem 3 is specified. These include the following:
   (a)   successor node is undefined,
   (b)   node appears on two different cards,
   (c)   network is not connected,
   (d)   a successor is listed twice,
   (e)   network has no source,
   (f)   network has no sink,
   (g)   network has multiple sources,
   (h)   network has multiple sinks.
Additional errors may also occur depending upon the exact input requirements in this problem. Discuss how the program could be modified to catch such errors.

5. Modify the program in Problem 3 to incorporate the suggestions in Problem 4.

For the following problems, you are given the network shown in Fig. IV-16.

6. Represent this network in packed lists such that successors to a given node appear in increasing numeric order.

7. Develop spanning trees for this network using the following four methods:
   (a)   LIFO stack, place node in tree and stack at same time,

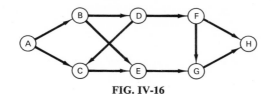

FIG. IV-16

(b) FIFO stack, place node in tree and stack at same time,

(c) LIFO stack, place node in tree when removed from stack,

(d) FIFO stack, place node in tree when removed from stack.

8. Are any of the trees developed in Problem 7 isomorphic? Why?

9. In addition to the existing labels, label nodes by the order in which they were inserted in the spanning trees. Which stack discipline resulted in a depth first search?

10. First revise the list representation of the network such that successors from the same node appear in numerically decreasing order; then redo Problem 7(a). Does the sequence in which nodes are inserted into the stack affect the resulting tree? Is there a "right" way to insert nodes?

11. Write a program that converts the representation of a network from a PINDEX and a P array to one using a SINDEX and an S array.

12. A man and a boy, bringing with them a goose, a fox, and a rabbit, are to cross a river in a small rowboat. The boy is an inexperienced rower, and, although he can row himself, he dares not bring any passengers of any kind. The man, on the other hand, may bring passengers; however, the boat only has room for one passenger (the boy *or* an animal). Thus, several trips across the river are required. Scheduling these trips is difficult since

(a) if left alone, the fox will run away,

(b) if left without human supervision, the fox will eat the rabbit,

(c) the boy is afraid of the goose unless the man is also present.

Represent this problem as a network where nodes represent the states on the two banks (one is the complement of the other) and links represent the feasible transitions (i.e., rowboat passengers) that may take place between different states. Do not forget to consider the position of the rowboat. Solve the problem by finding the shortest path between the initial state and the desired final state.

BIBLIOGRAPHY

Berge, C., *The Theory of Graphs and Its Application*. Wiley, New York. 1962.

Bondy, J. A., and U. S. R. Murty, *Graph Theory with Application*. MacMillan Press, London, 1976.

Deo, H., *Graph Theory with Applications to Engineering and Computer Science.* Prentice-Hall, Englewood Cliffs, New Jersey, 1974.

Elmaghraby, S. E., *Some Network Models in Management Science.* Springer-Verlag, New York, 1970.

Hu, T. C., *Integer Programming and Network Flows.* Addison-Wesley, Reading, Massachusetts, 1969.

Ore, O., *Graphs and Their Uses.* Random House, New York, 1963.

Thesen, A., "Measures of the Restrictiveness of Project Networks," *Networks* 7, No. 4, (1977).

CHAPTER V

CRITICAL PATH METHODS

The critical path method (CPM) is a network based method used to de-termine the earliest and latest times that activities within a project may start if that project is to be finished in the shortest possible time. CPM is of in-terest to the systems analyst for four reasons:

(1) It may be the solution to a client's problem.

(2) It may be an important element in a tailor-made system designed to solve the client's problem.

(3) It forms the basis for more elaborate algorithms, such as resource constrained scheduling methods which are presented in Chapter VI.

(4) It may be used by the systems analyst to manage his own activities.

In this section we will first review the basis of the model and the algorithm. Then, we will show how the algorithm may be programmed into a system designed to perform the day-to-day scheduling of activities.

A. PROJECT NETWORKS

CPM can be used whenever a project can be partitioned into activities with fixed durations. Included in this context would be some specifications regarding the completion of requisite (predecessor) activities prior to the start of each activity.

The project is represented as a network where nodes represent activities and links represent precedence requirements. An alternative representation associating activities with arcs and nodes with points in time is also being used. The latter method has great intuitive appeal as the lengths of the links may be proportional to activity durations. Thus, the network has some analog resemblance to the problem at hand. However, it is not always easy to model problems in this notation, nor does the resulting network lend itself as easily to computer implementation as the alternative method. We therefore recommend the activities-on-nodes approach.

To illustrate the concept of a CPM diagram, consider the simple, six-activity project presented in Table V-1.

In Fig. V-1a, we show how the resulting CPM network looks in activities-on-nodes notation. The corresponding network in an activities-on-links notation is shown in Fig. V-1b.

It is clear that the activities-on-nodes network can be stored in a simple packed link list. On the other hand, since the activities-on-links notation requires that the identity of all links be preserved, both a nodal and a link list are required to store the network structure when this notation is used.

B. THE CPM ALGORITHM

Algorithms to calculate the earliest start times for individual activities are based on the premise that an activity cannot start until all its predecessor activities have been completed. In fact, the earliest start time for an activity is the exact moment that the last of the activity's predecessor activities finishes.

Stated in network terms, this means that an activity cannot start until all activities (nodes) on all chains from the start node to that activity have been completed. (The analogy between this and the all-nodes-and-links traversing

TABLE V-1

Label	Activity	Duration (day)	Immediate predecessor
A	Start	0	None
B	Dig hole	2	A
C	Pour foundation	1/2	D, E
D	Order concrete	1	A
E	Construct forms	1	B, H
F	Remove forms	1/2	C
G	Stop	0	F
H	Order lumber	2	A

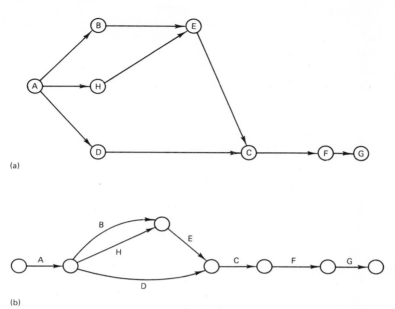

(a)

(b)

FIG. V-1 CPM Network: (a) activities-on-nodes notation; (b) activities-on-links notation.

algorithms in Chapter IV should be apparent.) Furthermore, if the lengths of these different chains are defined by the durations of the activities in the chains, then the earliets start time for an activity is defined by the longest chain from the start node to that activity.

An algorithm to calculate the *earliest start time* for all activities therefore must be able to do the following:

(1) Maintain a list of those activities whose earliest start and finish times have not been computed but whose times of predecessor activities have been computed. (Initially this list will contain the start node.)

(2) Calculate the earliest start time for activities in the list in (1) as the maximum of the finish times of its predecessors.

(3) Calculate the earliest finish times of the activities in the list as their earliest start times plus their duration.

(4) Recognize when the earliest start and finish times have been computed for *all* predecessor activities for an activity.

(5) Update the list to reflect (a) the removal of activities whose start times have been calculated, and (b) the introduction of new activities whose predecessors have been analyzed.

While these steps are conceptually simple and are easily executed by hand, their implementation in a computer program is somewhat more difficult.

This is because the sequence in which the activities are analyzed depends upon the structure of the network. (This sequence is easily established by visual inspection when the problem is manually solved.)

The listed steps clearly can be executed within the framework of an all-nodes-all-links network traversing algorithm (Chapter IV). In Fig. V-2, we

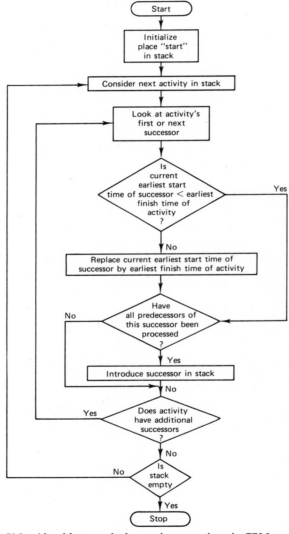

FIG. V-2 Algorithm to calculate easiest start times in CPM network.

```
      SUBROUTINE CPM
C
C SUBROUTINE FOR CALCULATION OF EARLIEST
C AND LATEST START TIME FOR ALL ACTIVITIES IN A CPM
C NETWORK
C VARIABLES:
C
C    DUR(ACT)        Activity duration
C
C    NPRED(ACT)      Count of predecessors
C
C    NSUCC(ACT)      Count of successors
C
C    S(I)            List of activity successors
C
C    SINDEX(ACT)     Location of activity's first successor in S
C
C
C                    It is assumed that the source of the network is
C                    activity 1 and that the project network is
C                    acyclic network with a single source and sink.
C
      IMPLICIT INTEGER(A−Z)
      DIMENSION LFT(100)
      DIMENSION EST(100)
      DIMENSION STACK(100)
      COMMON /CPM/ NPRED(100),NSUCC(100),
     1SINDEX(100),S(300),DUR(100),NODES,LFT,EST
C
C***FORWARD PASS
C
      STOP=1
      SBOT=0
      STACK(1)=1
      DO 999 I=1,100
        EST(I)=0
  999 CONTINUE
C
C
C
 1000 SBOT=SBOT+1
      INODE=STACK(SBOT)
      EST(INODE)=0
      INDEX=SINDEX(INODE)
      INDEXN=INDEX+NSUCC(INODE)−1
C
C    Consider the node's successors
C
```

FIG. V-3 Subroutine for CPM calculations.

```
              DO 1010 JINDEX=INDEX,INDEXN
              JNODE=S(JINDEX)
              NPRED(JNODE)=NPRED(JNODE)-1
              IF(EST(JNODE).LT.EST(INODE)+DUR(INODE))
      1            EST(JNODE)=EST(INODE)+DUR(INODE)
              IF(NPRED(JNODE).GT.O)GO TO 1010
              STOP=STOP+1
              STACK(STOP)=JNODE
   1010    CONTINUE
C
C      Return to process additional nodes if any
              IF(SBOT.LT.STOP .AND.SBOT.LT.NODES-1)GO  TO  1000 '
C      Save project duration and location of sink
C
              LAST=STACK(NODES)
              DURATN=EST(LAST)+DUR(LAST)
C
C***   BACKWARDS PASS
              DO 1030 I=1, NODES
              J=NODES-I+1

              INODE=STACK(J)
              LFT(INODE)=DURATN
C
C      Consider nodes successors
C
              LO=SINDEX(INODE)
              HI=LO+NSUCC(INODE)-1
              DO 1020 J=LO,HI
                JNODE=S(J)
                IF(LFT(INODE).GT.LFT(JNODE-DUR(JNODE))
      1            LFT(INODE)=LFT(JNODE)-DUR(JNODE)
C
C      Restore value of NPRED
C
              NPRED(JNODE)=NPRED(JNODE)+1
   1020    CONTINUE
   1030    CONTINUE
              RETURN
              END
```

FIG. V-3   (Continued).

show a conceptual flowchart of such an algorithm. After calculating all
earliest start times, the project duration is fixed as the earliest start time for
the FINISH event. The latest start time for all activities is then calculated
in a similar manner in a *backward pass*.

The backward pass is frequently performed by reversing the spanning
algorithm used in the forward pass so that the network is spanned from the

sink backward to the source. As discussed in Chapter IV, a faster approach is to utilize the observation that the stack generated by the forward pass contains the activities in the reverse order of the one that would result from a depth-first backward pass.

Utilizing these observations, the following steps will execute the backward pass:

(1)   For all activities initialize LFT = project duration.
(2)   Let I = count of activities $- 1$.
(3)   Let INODE = STACK(I).
(4)   Set up a loop to explore all the successor nodes (JNODES) of INODE.
For each successor consider an adjustment of INODE's late finish time:
$$\text{IF}(\text{LFT}(\text{INODE}).\text{GT}.\text{LFT}(\text{JNODE}) - \text{DURATION}(\text{JNODE}))$$
$$2\text{LFT}(\text{INODE}) = \text{LFT}(\text{JNODE}) - \text{DURATION}(\text{JNODE})$$
(5)   If the list is not exhausted, consider the next node:
$$\text{IF}(\text{I}.\text{GT}.\text{O})\text{GO TO 3}$$

In Fig. V-3 we show a subroutine that performs the CPM calculations in the manner described in this section. Experience has established that an upperbound on the ratios between nodes and links for most problems is 1 to 3. Thus, a CPM routine dimensioned for 100 activities should be dimensioned for about 300 precedence requirements.

C.   SYSTEMS DESIGN CONSIDERATIONS

While the CPM subroutine in Fig. V-3 will, in theory, provide the desired scheduling information for properly formulated problems, it is inadequate for use in any application oriented situation. Among the more serious discrepancies in this routine are the following:

(1)   The input data is assumed to be error free.
(2)   The clock starts at zero and works in increments of one.
(3)   The routine is only suitable as a before-the-fact scheduler. Its utility as a management tool for an ongoing project is negligible.

The following data errors can be expected in a CPM input module:

(1)   The network is not connected.
(2)   The network has loops.
(3)   The source cannot be found.
(4)   Node names are nonunique.
(5)   The stated number of nodes is incorrect.

(6) Predecessor names are invalid.

(7) Durations are negative.

(8) Activities appear in the wrong order.

(Additional errors can be expected if the user is required to identify activities by an index such that this index forms the subscript used to identify the activity in the program.)

The analyst can identify all of these errors if he provides a well designed INPUT subroutine that can (1) read the input data, (2) set up the appropriate arrays, and (3) check for errors.

The connectivity of an acyclic network can be determined by checking how many nodes have NPRED or NSUCC equal to zero. If there are more than one of each, the network is not connected. Furthermore, the network is not connected if the stack contains fewer than all nodes at the end of the forward pass. Failure to detect a nonconnected network will result in an invalid partial schedule, possibly with a significantly shorter duration than the actual schedule.

Loops in the network are caused either by a modelling error or a keypunching error. Undetected loops cause the algorithm to run out of entries in the stack prior to completion of the forward pass. This has the same effect as a disconnected network on the resulting schedule.

Writing informative error messages when a loop is detected (by not being able to complete the forward pass) is difficult. We do know that the nodes already in the stack do not belong to the loop. We also know that at least one successor to one of the nodes in the stack belongs to the loop. However, we do not have an easy way of determining which of the many unprocessed nodes belong to the loop.

Programmers frequently assume that the first activity in the input stream is the source activity. An incomplete network follows if this assumption is made and the corresponding user instructions are not followed. This is fortunately an unnecessary assumption. The source activity is easily found anywhere in the list as being the one activity without any predecessors.

It is good programming practice to let the user specify node names as alphanumeric information and to form an internal list translating these names to the internally required subscripts and indices. This can readily be accomplished through hash coding.

It is however conceivable that the user could specify several activities with the same name. (This could happen, for example, if long names are truncated.) Thus, it is necessary to check for duplication by comparing each new name with the names already supplied.

Some programs require the user to specify the number of activities to be processed while others take the philosophy that the computer can count at least as well as any human being. Either approach has merit. The first approach may cause problems if the specified number in incorrect, but this approach will save headaches if the specified number is correct and the number of datacards is incorrect.

The second approach avoids problems which might occur because the specified number is incorrect, but this approach will not avoid problems which will occur if the number of data cards is incorrect.

The lazy programmer will require the user to provide data cards ordered in such a way as to cause the predecessor to a node to be read in prior to the node itself. This approach may have some merit for quick-and-dirty solution situations. However, when this approach is taken, the likelihood of data input errors is increased many times over. At the very least, the programmer should flag those predecessor names appearing out of order and abort the run after a full analysis of all input data has occurred.

A much better approach is to allow inputs to appear in any order and then to perform an internal sort such that activities appear in the required order prior to the creation of the internal successor list. This is readily achieved by storing the network structure initially as a P–S list. It is, of course, possible that predecessor names may still be unresolved. Should this happen, these should be flagged and the run aborted.

D. SELECTION OF TIME UNITS

A clock that starts at zero and works in integer increments of one is sufficient for classroom use. However, a more meaningful time unit may be preferred for real life applications of a CPM program.

The most commonly used time unit for CPM problems is the work day, though fractions of work days do occur also. It should be noted that not all calendar days are workdays. Therefore, while work is being performed on consecutive workdays, work may not necessarily be performed on consecutive calendar days.

To overcome these difficulties, it is wise to perform all internal calculations on a continuous time scale (such as work days or a continuous hour scale), and to provide the means in the input and output routines by which to convert from/to internal time to/from external time. For example, a list can be maintained such that the calendar data corresponding to a particular work day can be retrieved. In constructing such a list, weekends, holidays, and the different length of different months can be reflected. The following list would be constructed for a project starting on July 3, 1975:

Work day:	1	2	3	4	5	6	7	8	9	10	11	12	13	⋯
Calendar date:	3	7	8	9	10	11	14	15	16	17	18	21	22	⋯

E.   CPM FOR DAY-TO-DAY CONTROL

We have assumed up to this point that CPM is a tool that is used primarily to determine the best sequence of activities and the best project duration *prior to the start of the project*. However, this is not so.

CPM is even more valuable as a tool to assist in the day-to-day management of an ongoing project. CPM in this context is however an entirely different "animal" from that which was considered in the previous context. Day-to-day control can present us with a situation where the problem is continually changing as activities are delayed or finished ahead of schedule and as precedence requirements change. This also presents a situation where the purpose of the CPM application is different from that which we discussed before. Our purpose no longer is *planning* oriented; it is *operations* oriented.

With the change in context and purpose, a revised approach to the system design is necessary. An overview of such a revised design is given in Fig. V-4.

On the input side, the original problem should be stored on mass storage for retrieval whenever necessary. Only problem revisions and updates would

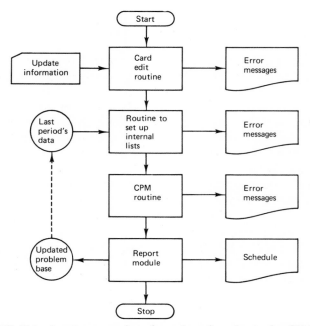

FIG. V-4   A systems overview of a package for a day-to-day CPM.

require daily inputs. These inputs should include revised durations of not-yet-started activities as well as the percentage completed of active activities not progressing according to schedule. Inputs should be of two kinds: (1) temporary changes (to allow the user to experiment), and (2) permanent updates (to reflect actual progress).

Of course, when mass storage is used, it is necessary to take conventional precautions to avoid disasters should the data set be accidently erased. This is achieved by saving input cards and (if possible) by rotating tape files in a grandfather-father-son fashion such that a data file can be reconstructed from its father file and the changes made in this file.

On the output side, the interest is shifted from total project duration to schedule slippage. The printout should flag those activities that are behind schedule. Particular attention should be drawn to those activities causing (or close to causing delays in total project duration. In cases where a large number of activities are involved, it may be a good idea to suppress printing information regarding activities not currently active or soon to be scheduled (later activities with significantly delayed start times should also be printed).

PROBLEMS

1. Determine the critical path for the following project:

Activity:	A	B	C	D	E	F	G	H	I	J
Predecessor:	—	A	A	B	B,C	C	D,E	E	F	G,H
Duration:	0	7	6	13	21	4	11	4	7	0

2. Write a program that converts a project network from an activities-on-links to an activities-on-nodes notation.

3. Write a program that converts a project network from an activities-on-nodes to an activities-on-links notation. *Note:* This is a difficult assignment since it may be necessary to introduce artificial activities with zero duration to enforce precedence relations. For example, the simple network shown in Fig. V-5a requires the use of such an artificial activity (Fig. V-5b).

4. Keypunch and test the CPM program in Fig. V-3. Determine how the computer time requirements for a CPM program increases with problem size.

5. Develop a CPM algorithm for the case where the network is stored in the form of an incidence matrix and no stacks or pushdown lists are maintained. (*Hint:* You must search the matrix each time you wish to process another node.)

6. Modify the flowchart in Fig. V-2 to allow for activities that have an external constraint on their earliest start time.

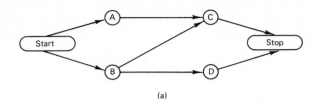

(a)

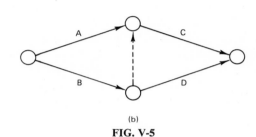

(b)

FIG. V-5

7. Refer to Problems 3 and 4 in Chapter IV and write an input subroutine for the CPM program in Fig. V-3.

8. Write an output and main program for the CPM code in Fig. V-3.

BIBLIOGRAPHY

Antill, J. M., and **R. W. Woodhead,** *Critical Path Methods in Construction Practice.* 2 ed. Wiley, New York, 1970.

Faulkner, E. E., *Project Management with CPM.* R. S. Means co., Duxbury, Massachusetts, 1973.

Horowitz, J., *Critical Path Scheduling: Management Control Through CPM and PERT.* Ronald Press Co., New York, 1967.

Kaufman, A., and **G. Desbazeille,** *The Critical Path Method; Applications of the PERT Methodology and Its Vatiants to Production and Study Programs.* Gordon and Breach, New York, 1969.

Moder, J. J., *Project Management with CPM and PERT.* Van Nostrand-Reinhold, Princeton, New Jersey, 1970.

Shaffer, L. R., J. B. Ritter, and **W. L. Meyer,** *The Critical Path Method.* McGraw-Hill, New York, 1965.

Wiest, J. D., and **F. K. Levy,** *A Management Guide to PERT/CPM.* Prentice Hall, Englewood Cliffs, New Jersey, 1969.

CHAPTER VI

RESOURCE CONSTRAINED SCHEDULING METHODS

A. THE PROBLEM

The problem of scheduling activities under limited resources and precedence constraints is a relatively common one that has received considerable attention in the literature. Unfortunately, this problem belongs to a class of problems where, at this time, optimal solution can be found only for unrealistically small problems of marginal practical value.

For larger problems, a number of heuristic algorithms are available. There is considerable conflicting evidence regarding the relative merit of the heuristics used in these algorithms, and there are few if any guidelines available regarding the choice of a heuristic algorithm. An illustrative resource constrained scheduling problem is presented in Fig. VI-1.

The problem can be described in general as follows:

(1) A set of projects is to be scheduled.
(2) Each project
    (a) consists of a set of activities,
    (b) has a schedule-dependent duration,
    (c) once started, should progress at a reasonably consistent rate.

115

Activity	Resource 1	Resource 2	Duration	Predecessors
1	0	0	0	–
2	4	2	2	1
3	3	3	1	1
4	2	3	2	2
5	1	· 5	4	2,3
6	0	0	0	4,5

Available Resources
Resource 1   6 Units
Resource 2   6 Units

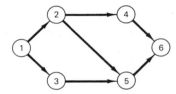

FIG. VI-1   Simple resource constrained scheduling problem.

(3) Within a project, each activity
    (a) has a known duration,
    (b) may not start until certain predecessor activities have finished,
    (c) requires a predetermined level of resources of particular kinds to be expended,
    (d) should have a constant resource level assignment,
    (e) should be interrupted only under exceptional circumstances.
(4) Limited quantities of the different resources are available.

Small problems (i.e., 50 activities or less) can be solved by an implicit enumeration approach suggested by Davis and Heidorn (1971) or by a combined CPM/zero-one programming approach suggested by Patterson and Huber (1974). Other optimization approaches to problem scheduling have been suggested by Pritsker, Watters, and Wolfe (1969), Moodie and Mandeville (1966), Mason and Moodie (1971), and others. State of the art reviews are given by Davis (1973) and Baker (1974).

For larger problems, it is necessary to use heuristic procedures to develop reasonable schedules.

B.   AN INTEGER PROGRAMMING APPROACH

In this section we shall illustrate the concepts or resource constrained scheduling by exploring how the sample problem shown in Fig. VI-1 can be modeled and solved using integer programming. In this case, the problem is formulated as

$$\text{Minimize} \quad Z = \text{finish time for last activity}$$

subject to: (1) precedence constraints
(2) resource constraints.

Unfortunately, it is difficult to find meaningful variables that allow the development of both precedence and resource constraints. We shall therefore first develop the constraints independently of each other and then introduce a new set of variables that allows both constraints to be presented by the same basic variables.

For the precedence constraints let s_i be the start time for the ith activity, and let d_i be the duration of this activity. Then, the precedence constraints become

$$
\begin{aligned}
-s_1 + s_2 &\geqslant d_1 \\
-s_1 \quad + s_3 &\geqslant d_1 \\
-s_2 \quad + s_4 &\geqslant d_2 \\
-s_2 \quad + s_5 &\geqslant d_2 \\
-s_3 + s_5 &\geqslant d_3 \\
-s_4 \quad + s_6 &\geqslant d_4 \\
-s_5 + s_6 &\geqslant d_5 .
\end{aligned}
$$

It is seen that the left side of this set of constraints is nothing more than the branch-node incidence matrix of the problem (Chapter IV). These constraints together with the objective function Minimize $Z = s_6$ form a linear program that is equivalent to the CPM formulation of the problem.

To introduce the resource constraints, it is necessary to partition the expected duration of the project into K intervals of equal length such that all activity durations are integer multiples of this basic interval length. Since the lowest common multiple of activity durations is one, and since the sum of all durations is nine, we introduce nine intervals, each of length one. Then we generate nine separate resource constraints to ensure that resource demands in all periods do not exceed the available supply. To achieve this we introduce a new variable q_{ij} equal to one if the ith activity is active in the jth period and equal to zero otherwise. The resource constraints then become

$$\sum_{i=1}^{N} a_{ik} q_{ij} \leqslant R_k \qquad \text{for all resources } k \text{ and periods } j$$

where a_{ik} is the demand for the kth resource by the ith activity, N the number of activities, and R_k the availability of the kth resource. Unfortunately, the resource constraints and the precedence constraints are not compatible in their present form. To resolve this problem, we introduce yet another variable

$$x_{ij} = \begin{cases} 1 & \text{if activity } i \text{ finishes in period } j, \\ 0 & \text{otherwise.} \end{cases}$$

The preceding variables can be developed from this variable:

$$s_i = \left(\sum_{j=1}^{T} jx_{jt} \right) - d_i, \qquad q_{ij} = \sum_{t=j}^{j+d_i} x_{it}.$$

Using this notation, the precedence constraints can be written as

$$- \sum_{j=1}^{T} jx_{1j} + \sum_{j=1}^{T} jx_{2j} \geqslant d_2$$

$$- \sum_{j=1}^{T} jx_{1j} + \sum_{j=1}^{T} jx_{3j} \geqslant d_3$$

$$- \sum_{j=1}^{T} jx_{2j} + \sum_{j=1}^{T} jx_{4j} \geqslant d_4$$

$$- \sum_{j=1}^{T} jx_{2j} + \sum_{j=1}^{T} jx_{5j} \geqslant d_5$$

$$- \sum_{j=1}^{T} jx_{3j} + \sum_{j=1}^{T} jx_{5j} \geqslant d_5$$

$$- \sum_{j=1}^{T} jx_{4j} + \sum_{j=1}^{T} jx_{6j} \geqslant d_6$$

$$- \sum_{j=1}^{T} jx_{5j} + \sum_{j=1}^{T} jx_{6j} \geqslant d_6.$$

The constraints for the resources become

$$\sum_{i=1}^{6} a_{ik} \sum_{t=j}^{j+d_i} x_{it} \leqslant R_k \qquad \text{for all } k \text{ and } j$$

and the optimization criteria is written as

$$\text{Minimize} \quad Z = \sum_{t=1}^{9} jx_{6t}.$$

Thus, to solve this apparently simple problem using an integer programming approach we need $9 \times 6 = 54$ variables, 18 resource constraints, and 7 precedence constraints. Problems of this size can be solved with existing algorithms. For problems with more activities, the resulting integer program is unfortunately too large to be solved by the existing algorithm. (See Chapter VIII for a discussion of the manner in which the effort in solving zero-one integer programming problems increases exponentially with problem size.)

C. A HEURISTIC APPROACH

A general flowchart of a scheduling algorithm utilizing "dispatching rules" or "urgency factors" is given in Fig. VI-2. The basic premise of this algorithm is the requirement that all activities are to start as early as possible. There are only two situations where an activity is *not* started at its CPM calculated earliest start time: (1) an activity is delayed if a delay of one of its predecessor activities has caused its effective earliest start time to be delayed, or (2) an activity is delayed if there are insufficient resources to start the activity at its earliest start time.

When several activities are competing for a limited amount of resources,

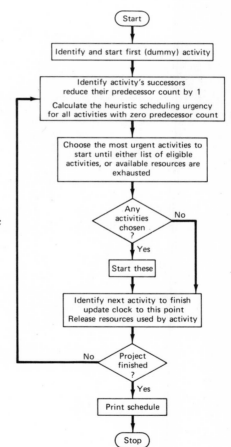

FIG. VI-2   Macro flowchart of heuristic scheduling algorithm.

activities are selected one by one to start in accordance with some priority or urgency scheme. This urgency scheme usually relates to the activity's duration, latest finish time, or slack time such that the activity with the smallest slack, earliest latest start time, etc. are selected to start first.

There are two approaches to the calculation of these urgency factors: they may either be calculated prior to the scheduling process (static scheduling), or they may be recalculated throughout the scheduling process since delays of activities have caused a change in actual slack and finish times (dynamic scheduling). We are not aware of any conclusive evidence regarding the superiority of either of these approaches. To illustrate both these approaches, we shall develop a heuristic schedule for the problem in Fig. VI-1 first using the static latest finish time as the urgency factor and then using the dynamic activity slack as a factor.

1. Static Urgency Factors

An initial CPM calculation on the project network yields the results presented in Table VI-1. By utilizing this data and the project network in Fig. VI-1, the scheduling is performed in the following stages:

TIME = 0   Activity 1 starts and finishes.

TIME = 0   Activities 2 and 3 are eligible to start. There is a tie in their latest finish time. A sophisticated algorithm would use a secondary urgency factor (such as slack) to break the tie. Most algorithms would choose whichever activity was first on the list. We use the latter approach and select activity 2 to start. Activity 2 uses 4 and 2 units of resources. Thus, there are now 2 and 4 units available for activity 3. This is insufficient, and activity 3 cannot start at this time.

TIME = 2   Activity 2 finishes. Available resources are restored to 6 and 6 units. Activity 4 is made eligible for scheduling. Activity 3 is also ready to be scheduled. Since 3 has the earliest latest finish

TABLE VI-1

Activity	Duration	Slack	EST	LFT
1	0	0	0	0
2	2	0	0	2
3	1	1	0	2
4	2	2	2	6
5	4	0	2	6
6	0	0	6	6

time, it is started first. 3 and 3 units of resources are available for activity 4. This is sufficient, and 4 is also started.

TIME = 3   Activity 3 finishes, restoring resource availability to 4 and 3. Activity 5 is eligible for scheduling, but sufficient resources are not available.

TIME = 4   Activity 4 finishes restoring resource availability to its initial level. Activity 5 can now start.

TIME = 8   Activity 5 finishes releasing all resources and rendering its successor activity 6 ready to start.

TIME = 8   Activity 6 starts and finishes.

A diagram of this schedule is shown in Fig. VI-3.

2. Dynamic Urgency Factors

Repeating the scheduling process for the case where a dynamically recalculated slack is used as the urgency factor results in the following operation:

TIME = 0   Activities 2 and 3 are eligible for scheduling. Activity 2 has the smallest slack and is selected first, thus reducing resource availability to 2 and 4. This is insufficient for activity 3 and 3 must wait.

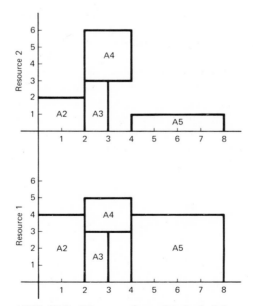

FIG. VI-3   Diagram of completed schedule.

TIME = 2   Activity 2 finishes. Slacks must be recalculated since a defacto precedence relationship between 2 and 3 now exists. Thus,

Activity	Duration	Slack	EST	LFT
3	1	0	2	3
4	2	3	2	7
5	4	0	3	7
6	0	0	7	7

Activity 2 is selected to start first. However, there are sufficient resources to allow activity 4 to start at this time as well.

TIME = 3   Activity 3 finishes releasing resources and rendering activity 5 eligible for scheduling. The slack for 5 is recalculated (=0). Sufficient resources are not available for scheduling 5 at this time.

TIME = 4   Activity 4 finishes, releasing sufficient resources to allow activity 5 to start at this time.

TIME = 8   Activity 5 finishes, rendering its successor activity 6 eligible for scheduling at this time.

TIME = 8   Activity 6 starts and finishes.

By comparing these methods, it is clear that the dynamic approach requires substantially more effort than the static approach. Since the methods frequently (as they did in this case) develop identical schedules, most algorithms use static rather than dynamic rules for urgency calculation.

3.   A Compound Scheduling Factor

In most heuristic scheduling algorithms the urgency factor is used solely to define the *order* in which eligible activities are considered for scheduling. An alternative approach is to add up the values of the urgency factors and select the feasible *combination* of eligible activities with the largest combined scheduling urgency. This means that two urgency criteria that would result in the same schedule in the sequential approach may result in different schedules in the combinatorial approach. This expands both the choices of and roles of urgency factors in heuristic scheduling. This combinatorial selection is achieved by using a zero-one (knapsack) programming routine to select starting activities.

The hybrid urgency factor U_i combining both resource and deadline consideration can be shown to be effective when this approach is used:

$$U_j = B_j + D_j,$$

where B_j is the resource utilization factor, and D_j the factor reflecting effect on delay in project duration if activity is delayed. Here

$$B_j = \sum d_j w_{ij}/W_i, \qquad D_j = ab(T-s_j)/((b-2a)s_j + Tb),$$

and d_j is the activity duration, w_{ij} the amount of resource i used by activity j, W_i the amount of resource i currently available, $s_j = \text{LFT}_j - d_j - t_{\text{now}}$ the slack time of the activity, $T = \sum d_j$ the maximum possible slack, a the constant fixing the urgency factor for an activity with zero slack ($a = 1$ works well as an initial choice), and b the constant fixing the urgency factor for an activity with maximum tardiness (i.e., $s_j = -T$) ($b = 10$ works well as an initial choice).

D_j has a negligible value for activities with large positive slack s_j. However, as the activity becomes first critical and then tardy, the value of the second term is increased at an accelerating rate until the activity is finally scheduled. The degree to which this increase takes place is defined by T and the relative value of the coefficients a and b. As with other scheduling heuristics, no single combination yields best results. However, most combinations with $b/a \geqslant 10$ yield good results. An even larger ratio (100–1000) is recommended for projects with many more (100 or more) activities.

D. AN EVALUATION OF
DIFFERENT HEURISTIC URGENCY FACTORS

The field of heuristic methods is relatively unexplored and users of such methods have few a priori guarantees about how well a particular algorithm will handle a given problem. Potential users are therefore well advised to thoroughly evaluate the proposed algorithm on representative problems before they commit themselves to its use.

Program evaluation was discussed in general in Chapter I. In this section we will show how the principles discussed there can be applied to compare the computational and analytic effectiveness of several different heuristic scheduling methods.

The subject of this evaluation is a program implementing the heuristic scheduling algorithm presented in Fig. VI-2. Algorithmic variations were introduced by using different urgency factors and by using two modes (sequentially and combinatorially—Section C.3) to select incoming activities. The following section is reprinted in part from Thesen (1976).

1. Problem Attributes

The first step in this (and any other evaluation) is to develop an appreciation for the problem to be solved. In particular, it is important to identify those attributes that affect the nature and difficulty of the problem.

Thus, a preliminary study indicated that the following problem attributes were of key importance:

(1) number of activities N,
(2) number of resources n,
(3) tightness of resource constraints t,
(4) restrictiveness of project network R.

Here the tightness of resource constraints is defined as the resource utilization that would result if the project were to be completed according to its unconstrained CPM schedule, or

$$t = \left(\sum \sum (d_i w_{ij}/W_{ij})\right)\big/ nT_{\text{CPM}},$$

where T_{CPM} is the unconstrained CPM duration of the project and n is the count of resources. Since the CPM duration for a project increases with the restrictiveness of the project network, two projects differing only in the structures of their project network may exhibit different constraint tightnesses. This difference may be substantial if one network allows for a greater amount of simultaneous activities than the other.

The restrictiveness of the project network reflects the degree to which the network restricts the number of precedence feasible activity sequences for the project. A useful definition for this measure is

$$R = 1 - \log S/\log S_{\text{max}},$$

where S is the number of precedence feasible activity sequences for the network, and S_{max} is the maximum number of sequences possible if all sequence restrictions were removed. Thus a network without precedence restrictions would have $R = 0$, and a fully connected project network allowing only one precedence feasible sequence would have $R = 1$. The concept of information content is discussed further by Thesen (1977).

2. Test Problems

Resource constrained scheduling problems appear in such a wide range of different contexts that no one class of problems can claim to be typical or representative. Thus it was decided to generate and solve test problems in a parametric sense so that, in addition to performance data on specific problems, we would be able to explore how the effectiveness of the algorithm depends on and changes with different problem parameters.

A random problem generator was used to generate the several thousand test problems used in this evaluation. The problems were generated from the following input data:

(1) number of activities,

(2) spread of activity durations,
(3) number of resource constraints,
(4) availability of each resource,
(5) spread of individual resource demands,
(6) desired information content of the project network.

Problems with from ten to two hundred activities were generated. For each problem individual activity durations were assumed to be uniformly distributed between 1 and 10 days. Problems with 1, 5, and 10 resources were generated. Resource availability was assumed to be 100 units/day for each resource. Resource demands were assumed to be evenly distributed between a lower and an upper bound. Upper bounds of 50 and 100 units/day and lower bounds of 0–50 units/day were used.

When more than one resource was considered, the bounds were assumed identical for all resources. This resulted in problems where all resource constraints were of approximately equal "tightness." Spot checks indicated that such problems were harder to solve than those where one or two constraints were considerably tighter than the other constraints.

Networks with a target restrictiveness of 0, 0.2, 0.4, 0.6, 0.8, and 1.0 were generated using the algorithm given in Chapter IV. The actual restrictiveness in the resulting networks differed slightly from this and was estimated after the problem was generated.

As a schedule for a particular problem was developed, the following items were collected:

(1) project duration,
(2) constraint tightness,
(3) actual resource utilization U,
(4) estimated restrictiveness of the project network $\hat{R}$,
(5) total computer time to develop schedule,
(6) fraction of this time spent in CPM routine,
(7) fraction of this time spent in the knapsack routine.

Core usage was not collected for individual problems as it remained constant for all problems.

The actual resource utilization was defined in a manner similar to the constraint tightness as

$$U = \left(\sum\sum d_j w_{ij}/W_i\right)/nT,$$

where T is the scheduled project duration. Since in most cases it is not possible to measure R directly, R was estimated indirectly as

$$\hat{R} = L_{\mathrm{N}}/(L_{\mathrm{D}}+L_{\mathrm{N}}),$$

where L_N is the count of nonredundant links and L_D is the count of disjunctive links in the network. A link between two nodes is nonredundant if there is no forward chain of links between the two links. A disjunctive link is an imaginary link drawn between a pair of activities without mutual precedence requirements.

3.   Computational Efficiency

The present implementation of the scheduling program requires 11.2K words of core storage to handle problems with up to 200 activities and ten resource constraints. For other problem sizes, core requirements may be estimated as $(600 + (16 + \text{resources}) \times \text{activities})$.

To determine the computer time required by this code to solve problems of different attributes, several hundred different test problems with problem attributes in the ranges discussed in the previous section were generated and solved. Each problem was solved using five different scheduling urgency factors. The problem was first solved using the combinatorial approach using knapsack routine to select incoming activities and then resolved using the sequential procedure. Thus each problem was solved 10 different ways.

As an illustration of the data obtained in this evaluation, we list in Table VI-2 test results obtained for problems with 50 activities. To save space, only the range of solution time for the 10 different solutions of each problem is included in this table.

The conclusions of an analysis of the resulting performance data may be summarized as follows:

(1) If everything else remained unchanged, execution time increased linearly with increases in

    (a)   problem size,
    (b)   number of constraints,
    (c)   constraint tightness.

(2) The rate of increase of computer time with constraint tightness was proportional to the restrictiveness of the network.

(3) The choice of urgency factor has a significant impact on computer time requirements. The spread in solution times for different urgency criteria was particularly wide for problems with tight constraints and a network with limited restrictiveness. To illustrate the range of solution times for different urgency factors we present the solution times (in seconds) for a loosely structured network ($R = 0.2$) with 50 activities and 10 constraints solved using the combinatorial method (Table VI-3). It is seen that for tight constraints

TABLE VI-2
COMPUTATIONAL EFFICIENCY OF ALGORITHM APPLIED TO RANDOM 50-ACTIVITY PROBLEM

Network number	Information content	10 resources		5 resources	
		Tightness	Solution times	Tightness	Solution times
1	0.22	0	0.33	0	0.27
		0.27	0.34	0	0.26
		0.49	0.40–0.46	0.53	0.29–0.35
		0.79	0.47–0.70	0.68	0.36–0.48
		1.09	0.48–0.85	1.11	0.41–0.62
		1.12	0.49–0.96	1.32	0.45–0.75
2	0.39	0	0.33	0	0.25
		0.21	0.33	0.18	0.26
		0.35	0.34–0.35	0.45	0.26–0.27
		0.59	0.41–0.42	0.59	0.30–0.33
		0.69	0.43–0.55	0.75	0.32–0.35
		0.88	0.41–0.53	1.11	0.34–0.45
3	0.55	0	0.33	0	0.25
		0.15	0.33	0.14	0.25
		0.26	0.34	0.27	0.26
		0.40	0.37–0.38	0.37	0.29–0.30
		0.62	0.39–0.54	0.55	0.31–0.33
		0.78	0.38–0.54	0.71	0.31–0.43
4	0	0.34	0.34	0	0.26
		0.11	0.34	0.13	0.26
		0.24	0.34	0.22	0.26
		0.35	0.34–0.35	0.37	0.27
		0.48	0.37–0.46	0.50	0.28–0.30
		0.52	0.38–0.43	0.52	0.29–0.33
5	1.0	0	0.35	0	0.27
		0.12	0.35	0.09	0.27
		0.19	0.35	0.20	0.27
		0.33	0.35	0.29	0.27
		0.40	0.35–0.38	0.41	0.27–0.30
		0.53	0.35–0.38	0.52	0.27–0.29

the wrong choice of urgency factor may double the solution time. One explanation for this phenomenon is based on the degree to which the urgency factor discriminates between different activities. The closer the individual urgencies are to each other, the more alternatives are considered for inclusion and the longer the time required for the scheduling process.

(4) The use of the knapsack routine increased solution time slightly, but in no case by more than 10%. This behavior can be explained by several factors. First, the particular knapsack routine used has exhibited an exceptionally good solution time for small problems of the kind encountered here.

TABLE VI-3

	Urgency factors				
Tightness	$99999 - LFT_i$	D_i	B_i	d_i	U_i
0	0.33	0.33	0.33	0.33	0.33
0.29	0.33	0.33	0.33	0.33	0.33
0.50	0.45	0.44	0.44	0.38	0.39
0.71	0.70	0.54	0.56	0.48	0.47
1.03	0.85	0.67	0.56	0.49	0.48
1.24	0.96	0.72	0.59	0.50	0.49

Second, the knapsack program was tailor-made for this application. Thus, setup and data conversion times were eliminated. Thirdly, the conventional assignment process was achieved by modifying the knapsack routine to return when the first request to replace a variable on a given level was encountered. While this is an efficient procedure, other even more efficient procedures may be available.

(5)   Computer time requirements for any problem/method combination were in fact so small that available time would normally not be a significant constraint for the solution of problems of the size tested here.

4.   Analytic Effectiveness

The purpose of the analytic effectiveness evaluation was to determine the quality of solutions obtained using the different sequencing criteria. The test data generated in the computational efficiency phase was analyzed for the effect of different criteria and assignment methods on solution quality. The relative frequency at which the combinatorial approach or the sequential approach yielded the best results for a particular sequencing heuristic is displayed in Table VI-4. This table also displays the frequency at which individual urgency factors yielded solutions within 5% of the best solution found.

It is seen that the knapsack approach consistently improved the performance of the algorithm. This improvement was particularly apparent for factors exhibiting individual coefficient values within a relative narrow spread around their mean value. Factors with a wider spread of values (or with a minimum value equal to zero) exhibited smaller improvements. The "minimum slack" heuristic proved to be the traditional sequencing heuristic with the best performance. For this particular factor, it is interesting to note that while the combinatorial procedure was superior to the sequential procedure in 58% of the cases, the sequential procedure was superior to the

TABLE VI-4

ANALYTIC EFFICIENCY OF ALGORITHM WITH DIFFERENT URGENCY FACTORS[a]

Urgency factor	Best answer to problem		Solution quality[b]	
	Combinatorial (%)	Sequential (%)	Combinatorial (%)	Sequential (%)
Duration	75	25	18	12
Resource required	80	20	31	15′
Min slack	58	42	69	81
LFT	75	25	42	38
$e \dfrac{\text{slack}}{\text{max slack}}$	100	0	0	0
Log (slack)	55	45	11	22
Constant	72	28	18	18

[a] Table summarizes results obtained when 26 60–200 activity schedules were developed with and without the knapsack routine. $P = 0.4$.

[b] Percent of solutions within 5% of best solution found.

combinatorial procedure in finding solutions within 5% of the best known solution. No correlation between solution time and schedule duration could be developed.

The test data was also analyzed to determine if any of the urgency criteria exhibited superior performance for certain classes of problems such as those with unusually tight constraints or with loose network structures. No such dominance could be found. However, a study of the distribution of the range of solution values for different problems lead to other useful observations. First, the *range* of schedule durations obtained with the different factors for a particular problem was strongly dependent upon the information content in the project network. For networks with $R > 0.3$, the range of values was usually sufficiently narrow to be ignored. Second, the spread in schedule durations for networks of a particular restrictiveness was independent of constraint tightness for all but the most extreme tightness values.

E. A RESOURCE ALLOCATION/MANPOWER LEVELING SYSTEM

In this section we will review in detail the design of a commercially developed resource constrained scheduling package. You will quickly see that even though heuristic scheduling algorithms are conceptually simple, the implementation of an efficient algorithm to solve large problems is difficult and requires application of virtually all subjects encountered so far in this text. An overview of the system is shown in Figure VI-4.

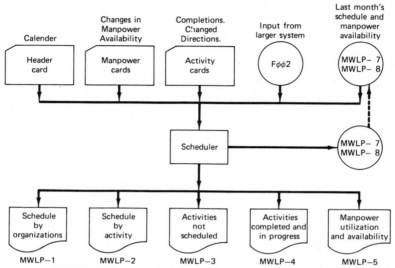

FIG. VI-4   Systems overview of manpower leveling program.

1.   Systems Overview

Under normal use, the program develops detailed daily schedules of manpower assignments to activities for all organizations within a government agency. The resulting schedules are provided, together with several different management reports, in informative formats. Manpower assignments are normally performed internally by the scheduler to ensure a high level of manpower utilization. However, facilities for user intervention and overrides are incorporated both to capitalize on the users' additional information and insight and to allow for special high priority jobs and unexpected changes.

As the program develops schedules for a fixed, reasonably short time horizon, it was possible to modify the basic heuristic scheduling algorithm presented in Fig. VI-2 to include a multiple pass feature. Using this feature, activities are partitioned into three sets of activities with different externally specified priorities. The first set containing "urgent" activities, the second set containing "normal" activities, and the third set containing "no rush" activities. All activities in the first set are scheduled before the second set of activities is scheduled, etc.

When properly used, this feature compensates for the common tendency of one-pass algorithms to schedule low priority–high slack activities as soon as excess resources are available. This tendency frequently results in the

TABLE VI-5
DATA RECORD FOR INDIVIDUAL ACTIVITIES

Field number	Contents	Field number	Contents
1	Activity duration	14	Pointer to next parallel act
2	Earliest feasible	15	Total float
3	Workdays this month	16	Free float
4	Computed urgency factor	17	Total man days required
5	Desired manpower level	18	Externally scheduled start
6	Not used		date
7	Status at end of month	19	CPM start date
8	Finish day	20	Project identifier
9	Actual start day	21	Activity sequence number
10	Pointer to next activity in	22	Organization code
	chain	23	I node name
11	Pointer to manpower	24	J node name
	organization	25	External priority
12	Pointer to I node	26	Accounting data
13	Pointer to J node		

prior utilization of resources that should rather be reserved to schedule more critical activities at a later time.

The scheduler must be provided with basic *calendar information, manpower availability data*, and *activity data* (including dates and manpower requirements). Facilities are provided for a separate data file (MWLP-7) for baseline manpower availability in different organizations. When this file is not used, manpower data must be provided in card format each month.

The prime source of input is a tape MWLP-8 generated by the scheduler at last month's scheduling session. This tape reflects the situation as of the first of this month under the assumption that the schedule developed last month was successively implemented. Changes in this data must be entered through cards.

An activities-on-links notation is used and activities are identified by their source node (INODE)-sink node (JNODE) pair. Data for each activity are contained in separate activity records (Table VI-5). These data are initially entered through cards (2 per activity). Later, if MWLP-8 is not used, updated data cards must be prepared each month for all activities including scheduled but-not-yet finished activities.

2. Activity Chains

The key to the program design is the use of linked activity records stored on random access storage devices. Only one such description is usually in core at any one instant. Activity records are linked together into several mutually exclusively chains of activities. The *candidate chain* is a dynamically changing chain identifying all activities eligible for scheduling at a given point in time. This includes (1) activities eligible for scheduling at earlier points in time but which have not yet been scheduled, and (2) activities released for scheduling at this time.

The order of appearance of activities in the chain reflects the relative urgency or criticality of particular activities. The most critical activity appears first. The least critical appears last.

In addition to the candidate chain, the program recognizes 31 different chains of activities, each identifying activities eligible for an early start on a particular date in the month.

Initially, these chains reflect the situation as it was described in the input data; however, as scheduling progresses, activities may be reassigned to new chains to reflect delays caused by limited resource availabilities.

Individual activities with common successors and predecessors are referred to as parallel activities. Unless such activities have a scheduled start time differing from their CPM start date, they are all assumed to be required o start at the same time. To facilitate this, separate chains are also used to denti fy different sets of parallel activities.

3.   The Algorithm

The algorithm follows the general one given in Fig. VI-2. However, several important observations must be made.

(1)   The algorithm develops a schedule for a fixed time span (usually one month). Many unscheduled activities may remain for scheduling at a later time.

(2)   The algorithm assumes that the CPM calculations have already been made.

(3)   Scheduling is performed in three passes. In the first pass, urgent activities are selected. In the second pass, normal activities are selected while in the last pass, nonurgent activities with large slack times are selected provided that resources are available.

4.   Detailed Program Design

The program is partitioned into four major modules. The EDIT module, the MERGE module, the SCHEDULING module, and the REPORT generator. Figure VI-5 illustrates the relationships between these modules and the various external and internal data files.

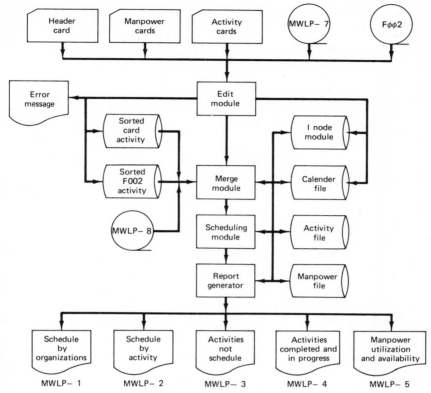

FIG. VI-5   Detailed systems overview.

a.   The EDIT Module

The major steps of the EDIT module are as shown in Fig. VI-6. A detailed discussion of individual program steps follows:

(1) *Set up calendar*   An internal calendar identifying both working days and the names of individual days in the month is developed from a built-in calendar (identifying the length and first day of the month for all years between 1974 and 1999).

(2) *Process the FØØ2 tape*   This step is executed only when MWLP is utilized as a subsystem of a larger management information system not discussed here.

(3) *Set up manpower file*   This section sets up an internal random access file used to maintain daily records on the availability and utilization of manpower from each organization. Data for this program section comes from cards or the MWLP-7 data tape.

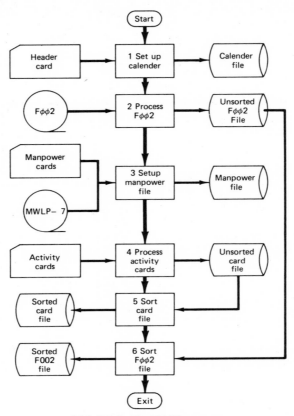

FIG. VI-6   The EDIT program.

(4)   *Process activity cards*   The purpose of this section is to edit and analyze activity information cards. The output of this section is an internal disc file containing activity records in a format suitable for future processing.

Activity cards are used either to introduce new activities into the system or to provide override information to data provided on the MWLP-8 file.

(5)   *Sort card file*   The purpose of this section is to order the activity card records in such a way that proper merging of data from the three different input media (cards, MWLP-8, and FØØ2) is ensured.

(6)   *Sort FØØ2 file*   The purpose and method of this section are similar to the ones in the previous section.

b.   The MERGE Module

In the MERGE module activity information from the various sources (tapes and/or card overrides) are merged into a single activity file. The activities in this file are then linked to appropriate records describing their source and sink nodes. While doing this, we also count how many predecessor activities a node has. Later we will use this information to ensure that the successor activities of a node are not started until all predecessors have been completed.

Each activity is also linked to a record describing the organization providing manpower for the task. This link will be utilized later to ensure that no activity is started unless sufficient manpower is available.

c. The SCHEDULE Module

The SCHEDULE module implements the scheduling algorithm discussed earlier and presented in Fig. VI-7.

d. The OUTPUT Module

The OUTPUT module generates all regular and optional reports and output files. These include graphic displays of activity schedules and manpower

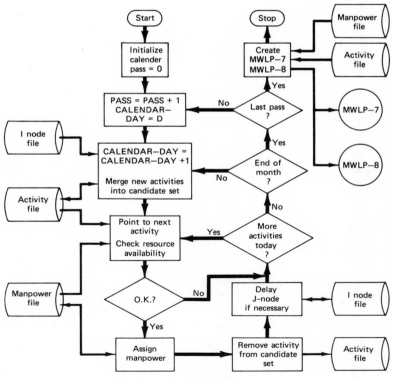

FIG. VI-7 The SCHEDULE module.

assignments as well as reports on manpower utilization and expected schedule progress during the month.

5. Conclusion

The design of a program capable of scheduling 40,000 or more activities from a large number of different networks has been presented. The program has been implemented on a Honeywell (GE) 465 computer and is currently undergoing field testing.

Through the use of five program overlays and a heavy use of linked lists stored on random access discs, it was possible to reduce the program core storage requirements to a minimal 16K 24 bit words. While this approach increases the amount of I/O required to execute the program, this increase was in most cases not significant. The slight increase that we did experience is easily traded off against the fact that the program is small enough to run in the background against larger and more resource consuming programs, thus utilizing excess resources that otherwise would not have been used.

PROBLEMS

1. The following project is given:

Activity:	A	B	C	D	E	F	G	H
Duration:	0	8	3	5	2	3	7	0
Predecessors:	—	A	A	C	C	B,D	E	F,G
Resource usage:	0	8	4	2	6	5	5	0

Develop schedules for this project using several different heuristic urgency factors under the following resource availabilities: (a) 16 units, (b) 10 units, (c) 8 units.

2. Solve the problem in Fig. VI-1 under the assumption that no sharing of resources is permitted. Is your solution optimal?

3. Solve the problem in Fig. VI-1 using the static heuristic algorithm with resource usage and slack times as urgency factors.

4. Write a front end program that reads in data for a resource constrained scheduling problem in a user friendly format and sets up the corresponding zero-one integer programming problem. Printout the constraint coefficient matrix.

5. Write and test a program that implements the heuristic scheduling algorithm in Fig. VI-2. (Allow each activity to use at least two different resources.)

6. Design appropriate printouts from a resource constrained scheduler

(such as the one discussed in Fig. VI-6) for the following people:
  (a) the company president,
  (b) the individual responsible for the overall performance of a specific project,
  (c) the individual responsible for the utilization of a particular resource,
  (d) the individual responsible for a particular activity.

7. How frequently should the reports defined in Problem 6 be generated?

8. How would you modify the integer programming approach to resource constrained scheduling to accommodate external constraints on earliest start times?

9. Modify the heuristic scheduling algorithm to force the start of a particular activity at the earliest possible moment.

10. Why are most users of heuristic scheduling algorithms in real life situations not overly concerned by the fact that their scheduling algorithm does not generate truly optimal (in a mathematical sense) schedules?

11. Design a project scheduling program utilizing a network data structure and input section as discussed in Chapter IV and a CPM subroutine as discussed in Chapter V. Allow for several different user selected urgency factors. To expedite the development process, modify the list processing routines given in Chapter II to form and maintain two linked lists: the first containing jobs in process (ranked on completion time), and the second containing jobs ready for scheduling (ranked on urgency).

BIBLIOGRAPHY

Baker, K. *Introduction to Sequencing and Scheduling.* Wiley, New York, 1974.

Davis, E. W., "Project Scheduling under Resource Constraints-Historical Review and Categorization of Procedures," *AIIE Trans.* (December 1973), 297–312.

Davis, E. W., and G. E. Heidorn, "An Algorithm for Optimal Project Scheduling under Multiple Resource Constraints," *Management Sci.* 17, No. 12 (August 1971), B803–816.

Davis, E. W., and J. H. Patterson, "A Comparison of Heuristic and Optimum Solutions Resource Constrained Project Scheduling," *Management Sci.* 21, No. 8 (April 1975), 994–955.

Mason, A. T., and C. L. Moodie, "A Branch and Bound Algorithm for Minimizing Cost in Project Scheduling," *Management Sci.* 18, No. 4, Part 1 (December 1971), B158–B178.

Moodie, C. L., and D. D. Mandeville, "Project Resource Balancing by Assembly Line Balancing Techniques," *Ind. Eng.* 17, No. 7 (July 1966),

Patterson, J. H., and W. D. Huber, "A Horizon-Varying, Zero-One Approach to Project Scheduling," *Management Sci.* 20, No. 6 (February 1974), 990–998.

Pritsker, A. A. B., L. J. Watters, and P. M. Wolfe, "Multi-Project Scheduling with Limited Resource: A Zero-One Programming Approach," *Management Sci.* 16, No. 1 (September 1969) pp. 93–108.

Thesen, A., "Heuristic Scheduling under Resource and Precedence Restrictions," *Management Sci.* **23**, No. 4, (December 1976), 412, 422.

Thesen, A., "A Manpower Levelling/Project Planning Program," *Comput. Ind. Eng.* **1**, No. 4 (1977).

Thesen, A., "Measures of the Restrictiveness of Project Networks," *Networks* **4**, No. 3 (1977).

Wiest, T. D., "A Heuristic Model for Scheduling Large Projects with Limited Resources," *Management Sci.* **13**, No. 6 (February 1976), B359–B377.

Wiest, J., "Project Network Models: Past and Future," Paper presented at the *Fall Joint National ORSA/TIMS Meeting, November 1975.*

CHAPTER VII

LINEAR PROGRAMMING METHODS

Linear programming (LP) problems form a class of problems that occur with great frequency in a wide variety of different problem settings. Since these problems also frequently have great economic significance, it is comforting to know that most LP problems at least in principle can be solved in a straightforward manner on a digital computer using readily available algorithms.

However, substantial practical problems arise when such solutions are attempted. These relate both to problems in organizing the large amounts of data usually affiliated with LP problems and to problems relating to the potentially excessive computer resources required to solve large LP problems. These problems are discussed in this chapter.

A. THE LINEAR PROGRAMMING PROBLEM

1. A Simple Problem

A linear programming problem is a constrained optimization problem illustrated by the following example problem:

Maximize $Z = 3x_1 - 2x_2 - x_3$

subject to $\quad 2x_1 + 2x_2 - x_3 \leqslant 2$

$$x_1 + 2x_2 - x_3 = 1$$

$$-4x_1 + x_2 + x_3 \geqslant 2$$

$$x_1, x_2, x_3 \geqslant 0.$$

Here all variables are restricted to be nonnegative, and equality as well as inequality constraints are allowed. Since LP algorithms have difficulties dealing with inequalities, *slack variables* are added to the constraints to absorb unused "resources" and thus to force equalities to appear. When slack variables are introduced, the problem previously discussed becomes

Maximize $\quad Z = 3x_1 - 2x_2 - x_3$

subject to $\quad 2x_1 \qquad + 2x_2 - x_3 + x_4 \qquad = 2$

$$x_1 \qquad + 2x_2 - x_3 \qquad = 1$$

$$-4x_1 \qquad + x_2 + x_3 \qquad - x_5 = 2$$

$$x_i \geqslant 0, \qquad i = 1, ..., 5.$$

Here x_4 is interpreted as the amount of the first "resource" not being utilized, and x_5 is interpreted as the amount of usage of the third resource in excess of two units.

It is convenient to use matrix notation when LP problems are discussed. Using such notation the general LP problem is stated as

Maximize $\quad Z = CX$

subject to $\quad AX = b$

$$x_i \geqslant 0, \qquad i = 1, ..., n,$$

where C is a 1 by n vector of coefficients in the objective function, X is a n by l vector of decision variables, A is a m by n matrix of constant coefficients, b is the vector of resource availabilities, n is the number of decision variables (including slacks), and m is the number of constraints. Using this notation, the above problem is expressed as

$$\text{Maximize} \quad Z = \begin{bmatrix} 3 & -2 & -1 & 0 & 0 \end{bmatrix} \begin{bmatrix} x_1 \\ x_2 \\ x_3 \\ x_4 \\ x_5 \end{bmatrix}$$

subject to

$$\begin{bmatrix} 2 & 2 & -1 & 1 & 0 \\ 1 & 2 & -1 & 0 & 0 \\ -4 & 1 & 1 & 0 & -1 \end{bmatrix} \begin{bmatrix} x_1 \\ x_2 \\ x_3 \\ x_4 \\ x_5 \end{bmatrix} = \begin{bmatrix} 2 \\ 1 \\ 1 \end{bmatrix}$$

$$x_1, x_2, x_3, x_4, x_5 \geq 0$$

2. A Larger Problem[†]

To illustrate a typical use of LP, we present an application of LP to the development of a long-range land use plan for an army base. This example also presents a practical application of many of the network concepts presented in Chapter IV.

a. Problem Statement

Assume that specified amounts of various urban land uses are to be distributed within a community partitioned into several internally homogeneous geographical sectors or zones. Furthermore, assume that these zones are interconnected by existing networks of sewers, waterlines, electrical wires, and the like. The capacities of all current links in these networks are known, as are the costs of additional capacity in any link in any network. Economic activities locating in each zone will (a) incur public construction expenses in that zone (for schools, streets, etc.), (b) fill available vacant land, and (c) generate new demands for utility services in quantities proportional to the extent of their development.

New utility demands in a zone, in turn, will create additional utility flows in the chain of utility network links from this zone to the zone supplying this utility. When this flow is combined with the flows to other sectors, the capacities of one or more existing utility conduits may be exceeded. In this eventuality, additional public expenditures to expand capacitated utility links must be undertaken.

It follows that some patterns of land use development may result in lower public costs than others. In the following sections we present a model that distributes land uses such that the sum total land development cost and utility network expansion cost is minimized.

---

† This example is taken from Bagby, G., and A. Thesen, "A Network Flow Model for Allocation of Land Uses to Sectors," *Management Sci.* **22**, No. 11 (July 1976), by permission of the publisher.

b. A Hypothetical Example

One thousand units of new residential development and one thousand units of new industrial growth are expected in a community during the time period under consideration. Regardless of where it is located, one unit of industrial floorspace is assumed to require two units of electricity and five units of water and to occupy nine units of land. Similarly, one unit of residential floorspace demands three units of electricity, four units of water, and utilizes seven units of land.

The region can be divided into five internally homogeneous zones such that construction and utility distribution costs are constant within zones but differ between zones. To simplify the solution procedure, the first zone is an overflow zone with infinite capacity. Zones 2–5 have available 3000, 200, 10,000, and 7000 acres respectively for development. A very large penalty (M) is assessed against land uses choosing to locate in zone 1 (the overflow zone) while land use development in all other areas is assumed costless.

The layout of the zones and their interconnecting utility networks is shown in Fig. VII-1. Numeric data for this problem are presented in this figure and in Table VII-1.

The dashed and dotted links between the zones denote electrical and water networks respectively. Utilities may flow in the existing network at no cost. When the capacity of a utility link is exceeded, new links must be installed at a cost proportional to the expected flow in the link. Incremental costs represent the expense of providing new utility links. Capacity represents a bound on existing utility line capacity. The unit capacity expansion cost for a given utility link is assumed proportional to the length of the links. Thus, the expansion cost for different links in the same network differ.

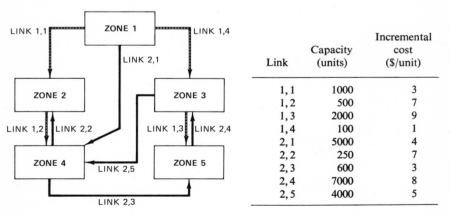

Link	Capacity (units)	Incremental cost ($/unit)
1, 1	1000	3
1, 2	500	7
1, 3	2000	9
1, 4	100	1
2, 1	5000	4
2, 2	250	7
2, 3	600	3
2, 4	7000	8
2, 5	4000	5

FIG. VII-1 Utility flows in a hypothetical problem.

TABLE VII-1

DATA AND ALLOCATIONS FOR EXAMPLE PROBLEM

Zone	Available land	Construction cost		Allocation	
		Residential	Industrial	Residential	Industrial
1	0	99999	99999	0	0
2	3000	0	0	161.9	0
3	200	0	0	28.6	0
4	10000	0	0	142.9	1000
5	7000	0	0	666.7	0
Dual variable				53	49
Land usage rate				7	9
Utility usage rate, utility 1 (electricity)				3	2
Utility usage rate, utility 2 (water)				4	5

Network	Link	To	From	Available capacity	Cost of new per unit capacity	Flow	Dual variable	New link flow
		Zones				Solution existing link		
1	1	2	1	1000	3	1000	3	1914.3
(electricity)	2	4	2	500	7	500	7	1928.6
	3	5	3	2000	9	2000	7.3	0
	4	3	1	100	1	100	1	1985.7
2	1	4	1	5000	4	5000	4	4000
(water)	2	2	4	250	7	250	7	397.6
	3	5	4	600	3	600	3	2181
	4	3	5	7000	8	114.3	0	0
	5	4	3	4000	5	0	0	0

The problem is to find the distribution of new factories and residences over the five regions that minimizes total cost of land development and new utility links.

c. Model Formulation

Let X_{ij} signify the amount (measured in units of floorspace) of land use i (1 for residential, 2 for industrial) locating in zone j. Let Y_{uk} measure the flow of utility u (1 for electric, 2 for water) through an expansion of the kth link, and let Z_{uk} symbolize the flow of utility u through the existing link k. Then, using these parameters and conventional network arc-incidence notation, the example is represented by the following linear program.

Minimize $Z = MX_{11} + MX_{21} + 3Y_{11} + 7Y_{12} + 9Y_{13} + 1Y_{14}$

$$+ 4Y_{21} + 7Y_{22} + 3Y_{23} + 8Y_{24} + 5Y_{25} \qquad (1)$$

subject to
$$X_{11} + X_{12} + X_{13} + X_{14} + X_{15} = 1000 \qquad (2)$$

$$X_{21} + X_{22} + X_{23} + X_{24} + X_{25} = 1000 \qquad (3)$$

$$3X_{11} + 2X_{21} - Y_{11} - Y_{14} - Z_{11} - Z_{14} \geqslant 0 \qquad (4)$$

$$3X_{12} + 2X_{22} + Y_{11} - Y_{12} + Z_{11} - Z_{12} = 0 \qquad (5)$$

$$3X_{13} + 2X_{23} - Y_{13} + Y_{14} - Z_{13} + Z_{14} = 0 \qquad (6)$$

$$3X_{14} + 2X_{24} + Y_{12} + Z_{12} = 0 \qquad (7)$$

$$3X_{15} + 2X_{25} + Y_{13} + Z_{13} = 0 \qquad (8)$$

$$4X_{11} + 5X_{21} - Y_{21} - Z_{21} \geqslant 0 \qquad (9)$$

$$4X_{12} + 5X_{22} + Y_{22} + Z_{22} = 0 \qquad (10)$$

$$4X_{13} + 5X_{23} + Y_{24} - Y_{25} + Z_{24} - Z_{25} = 0 \qquad (11)$$

$$4X_{14} + 5X_{24} + Y_{21} - Y_{22} - Y_{23}$$

$$+ Y_{25} + Z_{21} - Z_{22} - Z_{23} + Z_{25} = 0 \qquad (12)$$

$$4X_{15} + 5X_{25} + Y_{23} - Y_{24} + Z_{23} - Z_{24} = 0 \qquad (13)$$

$$7X_{11} + 9X_{21} \geqslant 0 \qquad (14)$$

$$7X_{12} + 9X_{22} \leqslant 3000 \qquad (15)$$

$$7X_{13} + 9X_{23} \leqslant 200 \qquad (16)$$

$$7X_{14} + 9X_{24} \leqslant 10,000 \qquad (17)$$

$$7X_{15} + 9X_{25} \leqslant 7000 \qquad (18)$$

$$Z_{11} \leqslant 1000 \qquad (19)$$

$$Z_{12} \leqslant 500 \qquad (20)$$

$$Z_{13} \leqslant 2000 \qquad (21)$$

$$Z_{14} \leqslant 100 \qquad (22)$$

$$Z_{21} \leqslant 5000 \qquad (23)$$

$$Z_{22} \leqslant 250 \qquad (24)$$

$$Z_{23} \leqslant 600 \qquad (25)$$

$$Z_{24} \leqslant 7000 \qquad (26)$$

$$Z_{25} \leqslant 4000. \qquad (27)$$

Here the redundant constraints (4), (9), and (14) are included for completeness.

The objective function calculates the cost consequences of any particular assignment. Needless to say, investment costs of flows through existing utility links having excess capacity are zero.

Constraints (2) and (3) assert that all land use growth must be allocated, while the next ten constraints [(4)–(13)] ensure that standard flow conservation conditions are met (i.e., flow out of a zone equals flow into the zone less flow required by land uses located within the zone). Constraints (4) and (9) allow a positive outflow from zone 1. This guarantees sufficient availability of the two utilities. Constraints (14)–(18) prevent the land allocated to factories and houses in a zone from exceeding the total vacant land available, and the remaining nine constraints provide upper bounds on utility flows through existing links.

Table VII-1 portrays the initial data and the resulting solution for this example. Zonal shadow prices indicate the total increase in utility system cost resulting from an additional acre of residences or factory floorspace. As expected, the shadow price on additional capacity in existing links never exceeds the price for new parallel links. (In one case the shadow price was less than this value. In this case the shadow price reflects the cost of flow through alternative paths.) It is seen that one more unit of residential floorspace would add $53 to the municipal budget when all resultant shifts in utility flows have been accounted for.

d. The General Model

In general, the paths of utility flows are modeled as directed branches in a network where the nodes represent activity zones. Separate networks are used for each utility. For simplicity it is assumed that electric and water flows are from the source to the activity node while the sewerage flows are in the opposite direction. Furthermore, it is assumed that all conduits are dimensioned such that a utility flows at identical speeds in all links.

The total utility flow emanating from a source is equal to the total amount of utility services demanded by activities residing in each zone. Utility flows in the existing network are assumed costless. However, links in the existing network have a fixed capacity determined from the size and number of conduits in the link. When existing capacity has been exhausted, additional capacity in a link is made available at a fixed charge per unit capacity required. This charge is computed as a unit cost multiplied by the length of the link. The constant velocity assumption renders it possible to compute conduit size from capacity requirement.

The problem of distributing K activities to minimize total network expansion costs can thus be formulated as follows:

$$\text{Minimize} \quad F = \sum_{i=1}^{n(a)} \sum_{j=1}^{n(z)} c_{ij} X_{ij} + \sum_{k=1}^{n(u)} \sum_{l=1}^{n(z)} d_k f_{kl} Y_{kl}$$

subject to

(allocate everything) $\quad \sum_{j=1}^{n(z)} X_{ij} = A_i, \qquad i = 1, 2, ..., n(a),$

(flow conservation) $\quad \sum_{i=1}^{n(a)} \alpha_{ki} X_{ij} + \sum_{l=1}^{n(k)} b_{jk}(Y_{kl} + Z_{kl}) = 0,$

$$k = 1, 2, ..., n(u),$$

$$j = 1, 2, ..., n(z) \quad \text{except terminal zones.}$$

(utility availability) $\quad \sum_{l=1}^{n(k)} b_{J_k kl}(Y_{kl} + Z_{kl}) \leqslant C_k,$

$$\text{where} \quad k = 1, 2, ..., n(z),$$

c_{ij} construction cost (dollars/ft^2 floorspace),
d_k cost/ft per unit of new capacity for links in utility network k,
f_{kl} length of link,
J_k index of terminal zone for kth utility network,
$n(a)$ number of activities,
$n(k)$ number of links in a utility network,
$n(u)$ number of utility networks,
$n(z)$ number of zones,
X_{ij} level of new activity development i in zone j (ft^2 floorspace),
Y_{kl} utility flow in the lth new link in utility network k,
Y_{kl}^u upper bound of flow in new link,
Z_{kl} additional utility flow in the existing link,
$Z_{kl}^{(u)}$ available unused capacity in the existing link.

The structure of this model can be visualized from Fig. VII-2, where the boldface numeral **1** denotes a summation vector composed of ones, I signifies identity matrices of appropriate dimension, 0 defines sundry null vectors and matrices, Greek letters represent the scalars mentioned in the equations, and B represents the utility network's branch-node incidence matrices. This figure also illustrates the fact that the existing network and the expansion network need not have identical layouts.

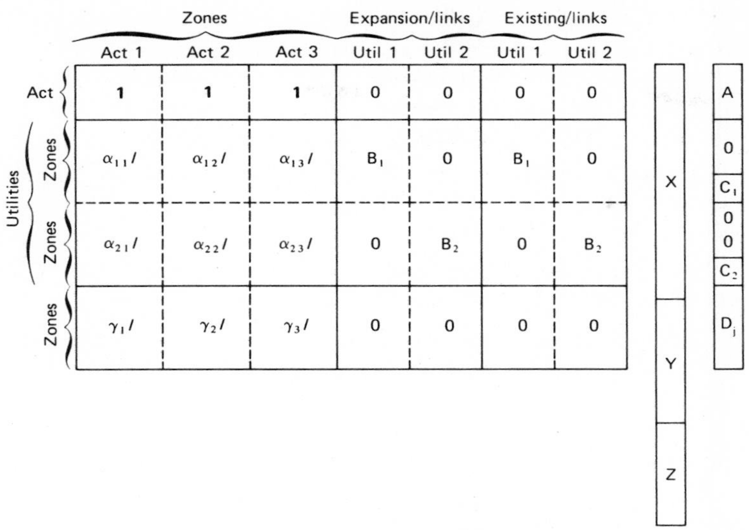

FIG. VII-2 Structure of general problem.

e. Solving the Problem

The model just discussed was used to develop a long-range land use plan for an army base. Three different utilities, three different types of land uses, and 25 different land use zones were identified. This resulted in an LP with 105 rows, 272 structural variables, and 881 nonzero entries. After the necessary slack variables were added, the constraint matrix had 105 rows, 372 columns, and 981 nonzero entries. The corresponding matrix density was $981/372 * 105 = 0.0251$ or about 2.5%. This level of sparsity is typical for constraint matrices of this size. After the problem was formulated, a proprietary LP program (the CDC OPHELIE) was used to solve the problem in less than six central processing unit (CPU) seconds. (The actual solution is of no concern and is omitted here.)

B. MATHEMATICAL PROGRAMMING SYSTEMS

1. Special Considerations

A typical commercial use of LP is found in the meatpacking industry where it is used every week to determine the optimum hot dog recipe given the current beef (and chicken?) availability and prices. This is a rather small problem (a few hundred rows at most) that is routinely solved by any commercially available algorithm. However, a few considerations not usually stressed in the classroom are presented:

(a)   Extensive post optimality analysis is desired.

(b)   The basic structure of the problem does not change from week to week.

(c)   Some feasible or near feasible solution is usually known.

(d)   Even this "small" problem may have almost 100,000 individual co-efficients in the constraint matrix. Thus, efficient data handling facilities are required.

(e)   The constraint matrix is likely to be quite sparse (with no more than 10% nonzero elements).

It is obvious that while some of these considerations (such as the matrix sparsity) may have algorithmic impact, most relate to the manner in which data is handled and the manner in which the initial problem is formulated. Thus, most commercial LP packages (frequently referred to as mathematical programming systems) have extensive data handling and/or matrix generation facilities. In fact, many commercial LP packages may be thought of as extensive data base management systems with an accidental simplex algorithm thrown in.

A different class of commercial LP problems is illustrated by the use in the oil industry of LP in production planning systems to determine the daily production mix for oil refineries. Such problems are unusually large (some exceed 10,000 rows and 50,000 columns) and are correspondingly difficult to solve in a reasonably short time. However, the use of LP in this context is of sufficient economic significance to justify the acquisition of a computer fully dedicated to this task.

2.   Mathematical Programming Software

All major computer manufacturers provide extremely sophisticated mathematical programming systems for solution of problems of this kind. These systems which have evolved over many years usually include mixed integer programming as well as LP facilities. Many also include matrix (i.e., tableau) and/or report generators. The current industry standard appears not unsurprisingly to be the IBM Mathematical Programming System Extended/370 (MPSX/370). However, the Control Data Corporation APEX-III system with the accompanying PDS/MAGEN matrix generator system is also highly respected. The UNIVAC corporation also provides a competent system, the FMPS math programming system. Several software houses also provide mathematical programming systems. These compete with the computer manufacturers' systems both in price and in performance. A par-

TABLE VII-2
Key Mathematical Programming Systems

System name	APEX-III	MPSIII	MPSX/370	FMPS-LP
Vendor	Control Data Company 8100 34th Avenue S. Minneapolis, Minnesota 55440	Mgmt. Science Syst. 7700 Leesburg Pike Falls Church, Virginia 22043	IBM World Trade 821 United Nation Plaza New York, New York 10017	SPERRY UNIVAC P.O. Box 3942 St. Paul, Minnesota 55165
Computer	CDC 6000 CYBER 70 series CYBER 170, 760 CYBER 76	IBM/360 IBM/370	IBM/370	UNIVAC 1110 UNIVAC 1108
Minimum core	65K 60 bit words	128K 32 bit words	120K 32 bit words(OS) 250K 32 bit words(DOS)	26K 36 bit words
Algorithms	Revised simplex MIP	Revised simplex MIP, GUB	Revised simplex Devex	Revised simplex GUB
Input format	MPS	MPS	MPS	MPS, LP1108, LP90, etc.
Matrix/report generator (separately priced product)	PDS/MaGen	Dataform	MGRW	GAMMA 3.4
Control language	MPS also FORTRAN	PCL	ECL also PL/1	FMPS (FORTRAN like)
Max rows	8191	16K standard 64K with GUB	16383	8192
Max columns	32767	512K standard unlimited with GUB	Unlimited	Unlimited
Typical monthly cost (lo–hi)	500–1350	100–2500	367–787	NA
Date of information	October 1976	October 1976	October 1976	November 1976

ticularly successful and sophisticated system of this kind is the MPSIII system from Management Science Systems, Inc. This system is fully compatible with MPSX/370, and, in fact, portions of MPSIII may be used in conjunction with (i.e., as an extension of) MPSX/370. A comparison of key attributes of four representative mathematical programming systems is given in Table VII-2.

MPS and its competitors provide elaborate control languages for the formulation of solution strategies for mathematical programming problems. A discussion of these languages is beyond the scope of this text (the reader is referred to the users' guides cited in the bibliography for more information). However, we provide in Table VII-3 a shortened overview of the commands available in the MPS control language. Individual instructions in this language bring in quite elaborate sections of code designed to execute the step as efficiently as possible. The detailed operations carried out in these steps are discussed later in this chapter.

TABLE VII-3
SELECTED MPS COMMANDS

INPUT AND STARTUP

CONVERT	Reads input data. Generates problem file
REVISE	Modifies existing problem file
SAVERHS	Adds another right-hand-side to problem
SETUP	Reads problem file. Allocates storage. Builds working files.
MOVE	Selects specific right-hand-side, objective function, bounds or ranges to be used for problem

OPTIMIZATION

CRASH	Finds initial starting basis
DUAL	Finds optimal solution using the dual simplex algorithm
INVERT	Recomputes the basis inverse
PRIMAL	Finds optimal solution using a primal algorithm

POST OPTIMAL ANALYSIS

PARACOL	Performs parametric analysis on specific column
PARAOBS	Performs parametric analysis on objective function
PARARHS	Performs parametric analysis on the right-hand-side
PARARIM	Performs parametric analysis on the rime of the problem
PARAROW	Performs parametric analysis on a specified row
RANGE	Determines variable and rhs for which solution is optimal

OUTPUT

PICTURE	Creates pictorial representation of portion of matrix
SOLUTION	Prints complete solution in standard format
STATUS	Prints current status of problem
TRANCOL	Shows cost of utilizing one unit of non-basic variables

3. The MPS Input Format

Since all LP packages are designed to solve the same problem using essentially the same algorithm (the revised simplex method), it is not unsurprising that a standard format for input of LP data has emerged. Nor is it surprising that the standard format is the one first used by IBM in its MPS system.

As illustrated in Fig. VII-3, the MPS format is a rather rigid format containing four mandatory and two optional data blocks each preceded by a properly encoded identification card. An illustration of the use of this format is provided in Fig. VII-4 where the problem introduced in Section A.1 is described.

The first input card is a NAME card assigning an 8 character name to the problem for identification purposes. This name is then reprinted later at appropriate places in the output. This card is followed by the ROWS data block. Here each problem row is assigned a unique 8 character name and the nature of each row is identified by one of the codes E, G, L, or N (for =, ⩾, ⩽, or unconstrained rows, respectively). A problem may have more than one objective function (code N) specified. The row name of the function to be used in a particular solution is then specified later in the MPS program itself.

The COLUMNS section is designed to identify all nonzero data values in

Section	Columns						Comments
	00 00 00000111 11	11111222 22	222223333333 333	44444444 44	555555555566		
	12 34 56789012 34	56789012 34	567890123456 789	01234567 89	012345678901		
1	NAME	problem name					mandatory head card
2	ROWS	blank	blank	blank	blank		mandatory section
	type row name						types are L,G,E, or N one card per row
3	COLUMNS						mandatory section
	variable name	row name	value	row name	value		one or two non zero coefficients per card
4	RHS						mandatory section
	set name	row name	value	row name	value		several sets allowed
5	BOUNDS						optional section
	type set name	column name	value				several sets allowed
6	ENDATA						last card

FIG. VII-3 MPS input format.

```
NAME              PROBL.A1
ROWS
  N OBJ.FUNC
  L ROW ONE
  E ROW TWO
  G ROW THRE
COLUMNS
      X(1)        ROW ONE      2.0
      X(1)        ROW TWO      1.0
      X(1)        ROW THRE    −4.0
      X(2)        ROW ONE      2.0
      X(2)        ROW TWO      2.0
      X(2)        ROW THRE     1.0
      X(3)        ROW ONE     −1.0
      X(3)        ROW TWO      1.0
      X(3)        ROW THRE     1.0
      X(1)        OBJ.FUNC     3.0
      X(2)        OBJ.FUNC    −2.0
      X(3)        OBJ.FUNC    −1.0
  RHS             ROW ONE      2.0
                  ROW TWO      1.0
                  ROW THRE     2.0
ENDATA
```

FIG. VII-4   Illustration of use of MPS input format.

the tableaux matrix. To identify the location of specific data elements in this matrix, it is necessary to assign names to each column in the tableaux matrix in addition to the already assigned row name. These names are introduced as needed in the COLUMNS section. We note that by selecting meaningful names for rows and columns (i.e., constraints and variables) it may be possible to have an almost self-documented LP model.

The RHS section contains the right-hand side values for the constraint matrix. A special feature of most math programming systems is the fact that many different right-hand side vectors may be specified for a given problem. The particular vector to be used is then selected in the program specifications when the problem is to be solved.

The optional BOUNDS section is used to specify upper or lower bounds on different variables. Several different sets of bounds may be specified, with the specific set to be used for a specific solution being specified at solution time.

The optional RANGES section is used when one or more rows are constrained to fall between a lower and upper bound. The *range* of the constraint (i.e., the difference between the upper and lower bound) is specified in this section. This information is combined with the information provided in the ROWS section to construct the bound value not provided there. For example, if constraint i was defined as a less-than-or-equal-to constraint in the rows section, then the RANGES section would be used to introduce a greater-than-or-equal-to constraint involving the same row but with a bound of $C_i - r_i$, where r_i is the range value specified in the RANGES section.

The MPS input data section is terminated by an ENDATA card.

C. THE SIMPLEX METHOD

The key reason for the wide use of LP models of real life situations is the availability of the simplex method for efficient solution of LP problems. The fundamental steps of this method (Figure VII-5) have not changed since they were first formulated at the Rand Corporation in the early fifties (Dantzig, Orden, and Wolfe, 1954). The basic premise of this method is the fact that the optimal solution is one with exactly as many nonzero variables as there

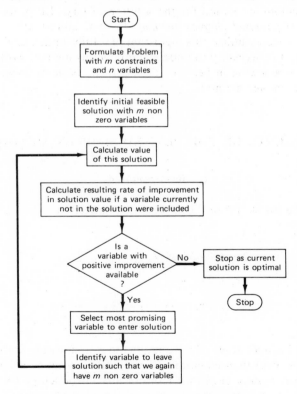

FIG. VII-5 Overview of simplex method.

are constraints. Briefly, the method describes a procedure whereby a sequence of improved solutions is generated. Each solution is developed from the previous solution by replacing a variable in the solution by a variable currently not in the solution. When no further improvements can be made in the present solution, then it is guaranteed that the present solution is optimal.

Many different varieties of the simplex method are available. The *tableau* method used in most standard texts (Wagner, 1969) is well suited for hand calculations; however, the method requires too many operations and too much core storage to be well-suited for computer implementation. The *dual simplex* method possesses the feature of working in the infeasible rather than the feasible domain. Such a feature renders this method an efficient algorithm for the solution of problems where near-optimal but infeasible solutions are known. Such situations arise when a sequence of related problems, possibly with an increasing number of constraints, is to be solved. The dual simplex method is readily implemented on a computer and many dual simplex algorithms (such as DUPLEX at the University of Wisconsin) are available.

The most common method for the solution of large LP problems on the computer is the *revised simplex method*. In fact, almost all commercially available LP systems utilize this algorithm. To fully understand and utilize these systems, it is necessary to understand how this method works. For this reason we are reviewing in Sections D and E the basic premises and steps of the revised simplex method.

D. ELEMENTS OF THE REVISED SIMPLEX METHOD

1. Basic Solutions

Consider the simple LP problem presented in Section A.1:

Maximize $\quad Z = 3x_1 - 2x_2 - x_3$

$$
\begin{aligned}
\text{subject to} \quad 2x_1 + 2x_2 - x_3 + x_4 \qquad &= 2 \\
x_1 + 2x_2 - x_3 \qquad\quad &= 1 \qquad\qquad (28) \\
-4x_1 + x_2 + x_3 \quad - x_5 &= 2 \\
x_i \geqslant 0, \qquad i = 1, \dots, 5.
\end{aligned}
$$

This problem includes a set of m equations in n unknowns. Since there are more variables (five) than equations (three), infinitely many solutions exist. However, it can readily be shown (consult any introductory LP text), that the *optimal* solution is one where only m of the n variables take on nonzero values. Solutions of this kind are referred to as *basic solutions*, and the vector of nonzero variables is referred to as the *basis*. The number of different basic solutions available for a given problem is finite. In fact, the number of different basic solutions is computed as $n!/m!(n-m)!$ (or for the preceding example, $5!/((5-3)! * 3!) = 10$ different solutions, many of which are infeasible).

One approach to finding the optimal solution to an LP problem would be to explicitly enumerate all basic solutions. This indeed is a quite practical approach to the above problem. However, consider a somewhat larger (but still small) problem with 50 variables and 20 constraints. In this case, exhaustive enumeration will involve $50!/(20! * 30!) \doteq 4.7 * 10^{13}$ solutions. Evaluating all these solutions is clearly not desirable and probably not feasible. Thus, it is nice to know that neither is it necessary since the simplex method and its descendants provide efficient algorithms that evaluate only an insignificant fraction of these alternatives before the optimal solution is found.

2. The Basis Matrix

When the identity of the variables in a given basic solution is known, then the proper values of these variables can readily be determined by solving the corresponding m equations in m unknowns formed by the initial constraint set. For example, a basic solution in x_1, x_2, and x_3 for the above problem is found by solving the set of equations

$$2x_1 + 2x_2 - x_3 = 2,$$
$$x_1 + 2x_2 - x_3 = 1, \tag{29}$$
$$-4x_1 + x_2 + x_3 = 2,$$

or, using matrix notation,

$$\begin{bmatrix} 2 & 2 & -1 \\ 1 & 2 & -1 \\ -4 & 1 & 1 \end{bmatrix} \begin{bmatrix} x_1 \\ x_2 \\ x_3 \end{bmatrix} = \begin{bmatrix} 2 \\ 1 \\ 2 \end{bmatrix}$$

$$\begin{bmatrix} x_1 \\ x_2 \\ x_3 \end{bmatrix} = \begin{bmatrix} 2 & 2 & -1 \\ 1 & 2 & -1 \\ -4 & 1 & 1 \end{bmatrix}^{-1} \begin{bmatrix} 2 \\ 1 \\ 2 \end{bmatrix} \tag{30}$$

$$\begin{bmatrix} x_1 \\ x_2 \\ x_3 \end{bmatrix} = \begin{bmatrix} 1 & -1 & 0 \\ 1 & -\frac{2}{3} & \frac{1}{3} \\ 3 & -\frac{10}{3} & \frac{2}{3} \end{bmatrix} \begin{bmatrix} 2 \\ 1 \\ 2 \end{bmatrix} = \begin{bmatrix} 1 \\ 2 \\ 4 \end{bmatrix} .$$

The matrix of constraint coefficients for the variable in the basis is referred to as the *basis matrix*, and in general the matrix computations in (30) are expressed as

$$X' = B^{-1}b,$$

where B is the basis matrix, b the resource availability vector for the original problem, and X' the vector of variables in the basis, with the variables appearing in the same order as their columns do in the basis matrix. The inverse of B will exist for all well defined problems. The inverse will not exist for problems where some constraints are linear functions of each other.

An alternative approach to the solution of the set of equations in Eq. (29) would be to perform *row manipulations* on the initial set of equations such that the answer could be immediately read when x_4 and x_5 were set equal to zero. This is achieved by adding and subtracting rows from each other (and thus changing their form but not their overall information content) until the following set of equations emerges:

$$
\begin{aligned}
x_1 \quad\quad\quad + \; x_4 \quad\quad &= 1 \\
x_2 \quad + \; x_4 - \tfrac{1}{3}x_5 &= 2 \\
x_3 + 3x_4 - \tfrac{2}{3}x_5 &= 4.
\end{aligned}
\tag{31}
$$

Solving this set of equations for the case when x_4 and x_5 are set equal to zero is, of course, trivial.

The coefficient matrix corresponding to a set of constraint equations manipulated such that the coefficients of the variables in the present basis forms an identity matrix will be referred to as the *present tableau matrix (A')*.

3.   The Importance of B^{-1}

The importance of the basis matrix B (or rather its inverse B^{-1}) stems from the fact that all coefficients in the present tableau matrix A' can be derived from B^{-1} and the initial tableau matrix A. This means that core space need not be reserved for A'. Thus larger problems may be solved.

We have already seen that X' can be computed as $B^{-1} * b$. Since the row transformations used to convert b into X' are the same row transformations that were applied to A, it follows that any column A'_j in A' can be constructed from the corresponding column in the original tableau matrix as

$$A'_j = B^{-1}A_j.$$

For example, A'_4 is readily computed for the case where the basis contains x_1, x_2, and x_3 as

$$
A'_4 =
\begin{bmatrix}
1 & 1 & 0 \\
1 & -\tfrac{2}{3} & \tfrac{1}{3} \\
3 & -\tfrac{10}{3} & \tfrac{2}{3}
\end{bmatrix}
\begin{bmatrix}
1 \\
0 \\
0
\end{bmatrix}
=
\begin{bmatrix}
1 \\
1 \\
3
\end{bmatrix},
$$

where B^{-1} was obtained from Eq. (30). This answer is readily verified by consulting Eq. (31).

E. THE REVISED SIMPLEX METHOD

We are now able to discuss the revised simplex method and show why this method is particularly well suited for computer implementation. Individual steps will be discussed first. This discussion is followed by a summary of the algorithm. Computational considerations in implementing this algorithm are discussed in the following section.

1. Obtaining the Initial Feasible Solution

We need an initial solution with m nonzero variables from which we can start the iterations. Such a solution is usually achieved by the addition of *artificial variables* to the constraint set such that an initial solution is immediately found when all but m variables are set equal to zero. For our example problem Eq. (28), this is achieved by the addition of two variables x_6 and x_7 resulting in the following constraint set:

$$
\begin{aligned}
2x_1 + 2x_2 - x_3 + x_4 &&&&= 2 \\
x_1 + 2x_2 - x_3 &&+ x_6 && = 1 \\
-4x_1 + x_2 + x_3 && - x_5 && + x_7 = 2.
\end{aligned}
$$

A solution containing x_4, x_6, and x_7 is now immediately available. The fact that x_6 and x_7 carry no physical meaning is, of course, troublesome, and the first goal in any LP code is to rid the solution of all such variables. If this is not possible, then no feasible solution to the problem is available.

Most manual LP algorithms achieve this by assigning these variables an infinitely high cost (the big M method) such that the optimal solution will never contain such variables if another solution is available. Computer algorithms use a slightly different approach. First, a procedure called *crashing* is used. Here rows are manipulated in a search for an initial solution with as few artificial variables as possible. Then the problem is solved with an artificial objective function (Z_2) constructed such that its maximum value is attained when all artificial variables are removed from the solution.

To develop this function we first introduce a new artificial variable x_{n+1} equal to the negative sum of all the other artificial variables. Since all variables are restricted to be nonnegative, it follows that x_{n+1} can only be zero if *all* artificial variables are equal to zero and x_{n+1} will be negative if one or more artificial variables are positive. Thus, the maximum value of x_{n+1} is zero and this value is reached only if all artificial variables are set equal to zero.

The relationship between x_{n+1} and the other variables is expressed as

$$x_{n+1} = \sum x_i = \sum a_{jk} x_k - \sum b_j,$$

where the limits are chosen for

all $i \ni x_i$ is artificial,
all $j \ni j$th constraint has an artificial variable,
all $k \ni x_k$ is not artificial.

To comply with our standards for writing constraints, this can be rewritten as

$$\sum a_{jk} x_k - x_{n+1} = \sum b_j, \tag{32}$$

where i, j, k are defined as above.

For our example problem, this constraint is written as

$$-3x_1 + 3x_2 \quad -x_5 \quad -x_8 = 3.$$

We are now able to eliminate all artificial variables from the solution by maximizing $Z_2 = x_{n+1}$ (or $Z_2 = x_8$ for the example problem).

No feasible solution exists if the optimal solution has a value less than zero. A feasible solution is found if $Z_2 = 0$. In this case, we immediately continue to solve the original problem by optimizing the original objective function Z_1.

2. Selecting the Incoming Variable

The identity of the next variable to be introduced into a given solution is determined by computing the rate of change in the objective function that would be experienced if each variable currently not in the solution were to enter it. The variable causing the largest positive improvement per unit introduced is usually selected to enter (although there is no guarantee that this variable will cause the largest *total* improvement).

This rate of change is determined by computing a quantity $c_j - Z_j$, where c_j is the coefficient in the objective function for the candidate variable x_j and Z_j is the aggregate reduction in the objective function due to changes in other variable levels caused by the entry of x_j. As an illustration of how variables currently in the basis must change their values when a new variable enters, consider the entry of x_4 into the basis of Eq. (30). We know that regardless of the value assigned to x_4 the following must always hold:

$$x_1 \qquad + \; x_4 = 1$$
$$x_2 \quad + \; x_4 = 2$$
$$x_3 + 3x_4 = 4.$$

If x_4 is introduced at a level of one, then the reduction in the other variables are $\Delta x_1 = 1$, $\Delta x_2 = 1$, and $\Delta x_3 = 3$; and the corresponding reduction in the objective function is

$$Z_4 = c_1 \Delta x_1 + c_2 \Delta x_2 + c_3 \Delta x_3$$
$$= 3(1) + (-2)(1) + (-1)(3) = -2,$$

and $c_4 - Z_4 = 0 - (-2) = 2$. Thus, the value of the objective function will increase by two units for each unit of x_4 that is introduced into the basis. Introduction of x_4 will therefore cause an improvement of the solution value. (But we do not know by how much since we do not yet know how much of x_4 we can introduce.)

From these calculations, we see that Δx_i is obtained in general as $\Delta_k x_i' = a_{ij}'$, where x_i' is the variable currently in the ith position in the basis, $\Delta_k x_i'$ the change in value in x_i' caused by the introduction of x_k, and a_{ij}' the coefficient value in the present tableau matrix. Therefore, $c_j - Z_j$ can be computed as

$$c_j - Z_j = c_j - \sum_{i=1}^{m} c_i' a_{ij}', \tag{33}$$

where c_i' is the coefficient in the objective function for the variable currently in the ith position in the basis. Since A_j' is readily obtained from the original tableau matrix as $A_j' = B^{-1} A_j$, it is possible to compute $c_j - Z_j$ for any column of interest without actually having A' available in core, and this is indeed the approach used in the revised simplex method. In fact, since the coefficients of A are always needed for a whole column at one time, storage of A on an offline storage device is fairly efficient since the cost of seeking out and reading in this information can be amortized over all entries in the column.

3. Identifying the Departing Variable

The choice of the variable to enter the solution explicitly identifies both the variable to leave the solution and the values of all variables in the new solution. While this may not be intuitively obvious, it follows directly from the requirement that the solution is to have no more than m nonnegative variables. Let us follow the transformation from the ith to the $(i+1)$th basis. We first append the entering variable x_j to the ith basis at zero level. Then we gradually increase its value. In order to satisfy the constraints, the other variables in the basis must also change their values. Some may increase in value while some may decrease in value. For example, if we wish to introduce x_4 into the basis in Eq. (30) at some specified value θ then the following set of equations must always hold:

$$x_1 \qquad\qquad\qquad = 1 - \theta$$
$$x_2 \qquad\qquad = 2 - \theta$$
$$x_3 \quad = 4 - 3\theta$$
$$x_4 = \theta.$$

As we increase the value of θ from zero, we have 4 nonzero variables until θ reaches the value of one. At this point x_1 is equal to zero. Further increase in θ (and thus x_4) is not feasible because the corresponding solution will have at least one negative variable. Thus, if x_4 is to enter the solution, x_1 *must* leave if a basic feasible solution is to be retained. This observation which when generalized is referred to as the θ-*rule* is stated more formally in the following: compute $\theta_k = b'_k / a'_{ki}$ for each constraint. If at least one θ_k is positive, replace all negative θ's by innfiity, and find the position in the basis matrix of the departing variable j such that θ_j is the smallest θ. Let the entering variable x_i occupy this position in the new basis. If no θ_k's have positive values, then x_i may enter at an infinitely high value without driving any other variables from the solution. The value of the resulting solution is *unbounded*. This situation only appears for ill or poorly defined problems.

As in the case of $c_j - Z_j$, it is possible to compute the θ_k's without actually having A' available. This is again achieved by first computing A'_i as $B^{-1} A_i$. This is the approach used in the revised simplex method.

4.   Finding the New Solution

The most straightforward approach to finding the value of a new solution is to construct its basis matrix from A and solve (by inversion) the resulting m equations in m unknowns. For example, the value of the basis variables resulting from a replacement of x_1 by x_4 in Eq. (30) can be found as

$$
\begin{bmatrix} x_4 \\ x_2 \\ x_3 \end{bmatrix} =
\begin{bmatrix} 1 & 2 & -1 \\ 0 & 2 & -1 \\ 0 & 1 & 1 \end{bmatrix}^{-1}
\begin{bmatrix} 2 \\ 1 \\ 2 \end{bmatrix}
$$

$$
= \begin{bmatrix} 1 & -1 & 0 \\ 1 & \tfrac{1}{3} & \tfrac{1}{3} \\ 0 & -\tfrac{1}{3} & \tfrac{2}{3} \end{bmatrix}
\begin{bmatrix} 2 \\ 1 \\ 2 \end{bmatrix} =
\begin{bmatrix} 1 \\ 1 \\ 1 \end{bmatrix}. \tag{34}
$$

Alternatively, we can develop the new solution by performing row manipulations on the set of equations in Eq. (31), restated here as

$$x_1 \qquad\quad + x_4 \qquad\qquad = 1$$
$$x_2 \quad + x_4 - \tfrac{1}{3}x_5 = 2$$
$$x_3 + 3x_4 - \tfrac{2}{3}x_5 = 4.$$

By manipulating these rows such that x_4 is eliminated from all but the first equation, we shall again have a situation where the solution of the equations for the specified nonzero variables is trivial. This situation is achieved by subtracting the first equation in Eq. (31) from the second and by subtracting three times the first equation from the third equation yielding

$$x_1 \qquad\qquad + x_4 \qquad\qquad = 1$$
$$-x_1 + x_2 \qquad\qquad - \tfrac{1}{3}x_5 = 1$$
$$-3x_1 \qquad + x_3 \qquad - \tfrac{2}{3}x_5 = 1.$$

The same results are achieved by premultiplying the present tableau matrix A and the solution vector X by an elementary row transformation matrix E:

$$
\begin{bmatrix} 1 & 0 & 0 \\ -1 & 1 & 0 \\ -3 & 0 & 1 \end{bmatrix}
\begin{bmatrix} 1 & 0 & 0 & 1 & 0 & | & 1 \\ 0 & 1 & 0 & 1 & -\tfrac{1}{3} & | & 2 \\ 0 & 0 & 1 & 3 & -\tfrac{2}{3} & | & 4 \end{bmatrix}
$$

$$
= \begin{bmatrix} 1 & 0 & 0 & 0 & 0 & | & 1 \\ -1 & 1 & 0 & 0 & -\tfrac{1}{3} & | & 1 \\ -3 & 0 & 1 & 0 & -\tfrac{2}{3} & | & 1 \end{bmatrix}.
$$

This transformation matrix differs from an identity matrix only in the column corresponding to the column in the basis matrix for the entering variable. E can always be constructed by inspection from the present tableau matrix as

$$E = [e_{ij}] \qquad \text{where}$$

$$e_{ij} = 0 \qquad \text{if} \quad i \neq j \quad \text{and} \quad j \neq k,$$

$$e_{ii} = \begin{cases} 1 & \text{if} \quad i \neq k, \\ 1/a'_{kl} & \text{if} \quad i = k, \end{cases}$$

$$e_{ik} = -a'_{il}/a'_{kl} \qquad \text{if} \quad i \neq k,$$

(where k is the column in the basis matrix for entering (and leaving) variables, and l the index of entering variables), or, if the present tableau matrix is not available, E can be constructed from the initial tableau matrix by first developing A'_l as $B^{-1}A_l$.

Using this transformation matrix, a new solution may be developed from an old one as

$$X'_{new} = EX'_{old}.$$

This, of course, requires substantially less effort than what is required to develop the new B^{-1} by constructing and inverting B.

In fact, E may also be used to develop the new B^{-1} from the old B^{-1}. Since $X'_{old} = B_{old}^{-1} b$ and since $X'_{new} = B_{new}^{-1} b = EX'_{old}$, it follows that

$$B_{new}^{-1} = EB_{old}^{-1}.$$

This feature is one of the key reasons for the efficiency of the revised simplex matrix. For, as we have seen, when B_{new}^{-1} is known, all elements of interest in A'_{new} may be constructed from A without actually developing the new current tableau matrix.

5. The Algorithm

We are now able to state the revised simplex method for solution of maximization type LP problems (this algorithm follows the general steps of Figure VII-5):

(a) Formulate the problem using the accepted format.

(b) Add slack and artificial variables as required.

(c) Form an initial basic solution.

(d) If artificial variables are used, then

    (1) introduce x_{n+1} and the corresponding constraint as defined in Eq. (32),

    (2) redefine the objective function to be Max $Z_2 = x_{n+1}$.

(e) For each variable currently not in the solution, compute $A'_j = B^{-1}A_j$, then use Eq. (33) to compute the rate of change $(c_j - Z_j)$ in the objective function resulting from the introduction of x_j into the solution.

(f) If no change is positive, then

    (1) if artificial variables are still in the solution, stop as no solution is feasible;

    (2) if the artificial objective function Z_2 is being optimized, then restore the original objective function and go to step (e) as all artificial variables have been removed;

    (3) if the original objective function is being optimized, stop as the optimal solution has been found.

(g) Otherwise, select the variable with the largest $c_j - Z_j$ to enter the solution.

(h) Use the θ-rule to identify the departing variable. Stop if no variable is found since the present solution is unbounded.

(i) Develop the inverse of the new basis matrix from the inverse of the old basis matrix.

(j) Develop the value of the new solution.

(k) Go to (e) to see if the present solution may be improved.

F. COMPUTATIONAL CONSIDERATIONS

The implementation and execution of programs carrying out the revised simplex method for relatively small problems is a fairly straightforward matter. However, substantial complications arise when algorithms designed to handle larger problems are developed. The most serious of these problems relates to excessive computer time and storage requirements. However, the potential for lost numerical accuracy due to the large number of iterations is also a concern. These problems are strongly related and the solution of one problem will usually also solve the other ones. In this section we will discuss several ways in which these problems may be solved.

1. Dealing with Sparse Tableau Matrices

Packing and unpacking of sparse matrices is often made difficult or impossible by the fact that the sparsity of the matrix changes over the course of the solution process. For example, no convenient way of storing A' in a packed format is available if the standard tableau method for solving LP problems is used.

This problem does not emerge when the revised simplex method is used. The tableau matrix now is stored in its original form A, and A does, of course, not change over time.

A particularly efficient method for storing A in a packed format is available since our only use for A is to produce columns of the current tableau matrix A'_j through a simple matrix multiplication ($A'_j = B^{-1}A_j$). We observe that the elements of A are always accessed in a columnwise fashion and that the elements within a column are accessed in a strict sequential order. This suggests that a linked list similar to the one used in Chapter IV for networks is an efficient data structure. To illustrate such a scheme, the matrix

$$A = \begin{bmatrix} 2 & & -1 & 1 & & & & \\ & 2 & -1 & & & 1 & & \\ -1 & 1 & & & -1 & & 1 \end{bmatrix}$$

is readily stored in three lists as

AFIRST	1	3	5	7	8	9	10	11		
ADATA	2	-1	2	1	-1	-1	1	-1	1	1
AROW	1	3	2	3	1	2	1	3	2	3

The interpretation of these lists should be self evident. While this organization did not result in any reduction of storage requirements for this matrix, it is easy to verify that substantial savings are available for larger matrices. For example, our 105 row problem has 981 nonzero elements. Thus, $2 \cdot 981 + 106 = 2068$ locations are required to store the packed A matrix, while $981 \cdot 105 = 103,005$ locations are required to store the unpacked matrix.

An added bonus when this storage scheme is used is the fact that the effort in computing A'_j as $B^{-1}A_j$ is (slightly) less than it would be if an unpacked A_j were used. This is because all operations involving zero valued elements are now implicitly eliminated. When the unpacked format is used, explicit operations either eliminating or carrying out operations involving zero valued elements are required.

This packed format is also fairly efficient when disc storage is used. This is because whole columns (sometimes blocks of columns) can be read in one operation. Thus search and read time can be amortized over all elements in the column rather than over a single element as normally is the case when random access storage is used.

2. Storing and Updating B^{-1}

For a one thousand row problem B^{-1} will have one million elements. Most of these elements will initially be zero and a packed storage format appears attractive. However, as iterations progress, more and more elements take on nonzero values. Thus a packed format such as the one used to store A cannot be used. (This declining sparsity also suggests that the effort in computing $A'_j = B^{-1}A_j$ increases with the number of operations as an increasing number of multiplications must be performed to compute the value of a single element.)

To circumvent these problems, B^{-1} is not stored in its complete form. Instead, it is stored as a sequence of elementary transformation matrices, with each transformation matrix describing the changes since the last solution. Traditionally, these matrices were the elementary row transformation matrices discussed in Section D.4:

$$B^{-1} = E_i E_{i-1} E_{i-2} \cdots E_2 E_1.$$

This is referred to as the *product form* of the inverse. More recently an alternative representation involving the decomposition of B into an upper triangular and a lower triangular matrix L is used:

$$B = LU,$$
$$B^{-1} = U_1^{-1} U_2^{-1} \cdots U_{i-1}^{-1} U_i^{-1} L_i^{-1} L_{i-1}^{-1} \cdots L_2 L_1.$$

This is referred to as the *elimination form* of the inverse. Here the U_i's (L_i's) are similar to the E_i's except that all elements below (above) the diagonals are zero. The main advantage of the LU vectors over the E vectors lies in the fact that the rate of growth in nonzero elements is substantially less than the rate of growth for the E vectors. The procedure for decomposition of L and U and for the development of U_i and L_i are beyond the scope of this text. The interested reader is referred to Forrest and Tomlin (1972).

The main advantage of storing B^{-1} in either its product form or its elimination form is the fact that both of these forms lend themselves extremely well to storage in the packed format already used to store A since individual vectors do not change as the inverse changes.

As the number of iterations increase, the number of transformation vectors will increase, as will the number of nonzero elements in each new vector. (The numerical accuracy of data elements is likely to exhibit a corresponding decrease in quality.) Eventually, the size of the file of transformation vectors may even exceed the size of the unpacked B^{-1}. To eliminate these compounding resource and accuracy problems, the basis matrix is usually reinverted at regular intervals from the initial tableau matrix. This inversion will reduce the number of transformation matrices and restore the numerical accuracy of the corresponding data elements.

3. Selecting Incoming Variables

The simplex algorithm specifies that the incoming variable x_i is selected as the variable with the largest positive $c_j - Z_j$. However, any variable with a positive $c_j - Z_j$ will yield an improved solution, and there is no guarantee that the variable with maximum $c_j - Z_j$ will yield maximum improvement. The absence of such a guarantee is fortunately of no consequence for large scale LP algorithms since it would not be practical to conduct a sequential search of tens of thousands of $c_j - Z_j$'s to find the largest one.

In fact, since the calculation of $c_j - Z_j$ involves the operations of first bringing A_j in from the disc and then multiplying it by B^{-1}, it is not even desirable to compute $c_j - Z_j$ for more than a small subset of the candidate variables.

To minimize this effort, many algorithms employ a two stage selection process: $c_j - Z_j$'s are computed until 100 (or fewer) promising variables are identified. One of these is selected to enter, and the $c_j - Z_j$'s are recomputed but now only for the variables in the identified subset of promising variables. Iterations continue in this manner until no further improvement can be obtained from this subset. At this time $c_j - Z_j$ are again computed for the general candidate variables until another promising subset is found or until the optimality of the present solution is proven.

4. Generalized Upper Bounding

Generalized upper bounding (GUB) is a powerful procedure used to reduce the size and complexity of many LP problems. To explain and illustrate the use of GUB in a major mathematical programming system, we reproduce in this section the discussion of GUB in Management Science System's MPSIII General Description booklet.

Generalized Upper Bounding (GUB) is a powerful special purpose optimizer, which extends the LP solution capabilities of MPS III far beyond those of the Basic System.

GUB is a special purpose optimizer in that it focuses on certain broad classes of LP models. It solves all models in these classes with great speed and efficiency by taking advantage of the special structure (described in the following) that all such models share. GUB is particularly effective in solving *large* LP models having this structure because it reduces both the computer time *and* the core storage required to achieve a solution. Thus, GUB provides two major benefits:

Solution Economy   Reduced dollar cost per answer
New Applications   Many very large models, otherwise intractable, are well within the state of the art for GUB and can be solved reliably and economically.

The GUB implementation in MPS III is incorporated in the optional VAR FORM optimizer, and has been in field use since 1969. MPS III's GUB routinely solves appropriately structured LP models containing more than 10,000 constraints and 100,000 variables.

GUB APPLICATION AREAS

LP models with the GUB structure arise in a number of well-known applications, including:

transportation (pure, bounded, and capacitated networks)
multi-product blending
raw material and/or production resource allocation (forest management,

machine loading, plant scheduling)
operations planning (combined production/inventory/distribution planning)
resource assignment (i.e., freight cars, personnel)
combinations of the above (as in large scale models of economic sectors)

Thus, although GUB is a special purpose optimizer, it actually is effective for a large proportion of all LP models.

Also, MSS has found that almost all very large LP models originate in the application areas listed above. As a result, most large LP models have the GUB structure, and can take advantage of GUB's solution power.

GUB MODEL STRUCTURE

GUB models contain two sets of rows (constraints):

A set of ordinary LP rows, which may be of any size or structure

A set of GUB rows, which have a very special structure

The special structure of the GUB rows conforms to these rules:

All of the elements in *each* GUB row are either $+1$ or -1.
No two GUB rows have any columns in common.
The right-hand-side values of the GUB rows are non-negative.

In MPS III GUB, variables that interact with GUB rows may be upper bounded and the GUB rows themselves may be ranged.

Virtually all LP models contain some GUB rows and can therefore be solved faster with GUB. However, GUB's full solution power applies only when a substantial portion (say $> 40\%$) of the rows are GUB rows. The application areas listed above always lead to models having such proportions.

The set of variables that interact with a GUB row is called a GUB set or a group. Following are examples of various GUB row structures, showing the GUB set or group coefficients:

1	1	1	1	.	.	.	.	.	.	1	$= g_p$	Product demand, raw material
1	1	1	1	1	.	.	.	.	1	1	$\leqslant g_p$	availability, plant capacity
1	1	1	1	1	.	.	.	-1	-1	-1	$= 0$	Material balance
1	1	1	1	1	1	.	.	.	.	1	$= 1$	Convexity (for λ-Method separable programming)

THE LOGIC OF GUB

An important characteristic of GUB rows is that they contain very little information about the problem. The unit elements in a GUB row constitute a *logical* statement that:

Each GUB variable is upper bounded at g_p

The sum of all variables may not exceed g_p

but they convey no *technological* information. In models which contain a high proportion of GUB rows, most of the matrix coefficients actually contribute little or nothing to the essential problem definition.

Moreover, the contribution of all GUB rows to the pricing of variables during each iteration can only be:

πp for all variables in GUB row p

0 for all other variables in the model

Therefore, any time spent on pricing computations in the GUB rows of a model is wasted.

To avoid this waste of space and time, the GUB procedure eliminates GUB row constraints in much the same way that bounded variables eliminate individual bound constraints. Specifically the GUB procedure permits GUB rows to be physically *deleted* from the explicit model representation processed by MPS III. Thus, a model involving, say, 100 LP rows and 1000 GUB rows, will be input and handled by GUB as a 100-row model rather than an 1100-row model, with all that this implies in terms of reduced basis size and increased solution speed. This reduction in effective problem size is what gives GUB its great solution power.

GUB SOLUTION SPEED

GUB's solution speed advantage over conventional solution procedures is a direct function of the proportion of GUB rows in the model: the greater the proportion of GUB rows, the greater is GUB's speed advantage. Also, the economic benefits of GUB's solution speed advantage increase directly with increasing problem size.

When no GUB rows exist in a model, or none are recognized as such, MPS III GUB automatically solves the model as a standard LP solution procedure would. Such cases do not lead to any speed degradation with respect to standard LP procedures.

PROBLEMS

1. Write an input processor for an existing LP subroutine accepting input data in the standard MPS format.

2. Write a special purpose matrix generator that accepts CPM activity data in a convenient format and generates data for the corresponding LP problem in MPS format.

3. Test the LP program available at your installation to see if the order of variables or constraints has a measurable effect on execution time.

4. Test the efficiency of the LP program available at your installation to see how solution speed is affected by tableau matrix density.

5. Develop an algorithm for the generation of random LP problems.

6. Develop a scheme whereby hash coding is used to store the elements in a sparse matrix.

7. Determine the range of matrix densities where hash coding is more efficient (less space, same speed) than the conventional method for storing a 100 by 100 matrix.

8. Write a program that reads suitable data for the problem described in Section A.2 and generates the corresponding LP problem utilizing the standard MPS format.

9. Write a program that multiplies two matrices (both stored in a packed format) giving the result in a packed format.

BIBLIOGRAPHY

Bagby, G., and **A. Thesen,** "A Network Flow Model for Allocation of Land Uses to Sectors," *Management Sci.* **22**, No. 11 (July 1976), 1221, 1228.

Bonner and Moore Software Systems, "*Univac 1100 Series—Exec. 8, Functional Mathematical Programming System—Users Reference Manual,*" Houston, Texas, August, 1973.

Control Data Corporation, "APEX III Reference Manual, "Publication No. 76070000. Minneapolis, Minnesota, 1974.

Control Data Corporation, PSD/MAGEN User Information Manual, Publication No. 8400900. Minneapolis, Minnesota, 1974.

Dantzig, G. B., A. Orden, and **P. Wolfe,** *Notes on Linear Programming.* The Rand Corp., April 1954.

Geoffrion, A. M., "Elements of Large-Scale Mathematical Programming Parts I and II," *Management Sci.* **16**, No. 11 (July 1970), 651–691.

Forrest, J. J. H., and **J. A. Tomlin,** "Updating Triangular Factors of the Basis to Maintain Sparsity in the Product Form Simplex Method," *Math. Programming* **2**, No. 3 (1972), 263–278.

Forrest, J. J. H., J. P. H. Mirst, and **J. A. Tomlin,** "Practical Solutions of Large Mixed Integer Programming Problems with UMPIRE," *Management Sci.* **20**, 736–773 (1974).

International Business Machines, "IBM Mathematical Programming System Extended/370 (MPX/370) Primer," Compagnie IBM France, Paris-la-Defence, 1974.

Kalan, J. E., "Aspects of Large-Scale Incore Linear Programming," *Proc. 1974 Ann Conf. ACM, August 3–5, 1974,* pp. 304–313.

Management, Science Systems, Inc., "MPSIII General Description," Rockville, Maryland, 1976.

Miller, M. H., *On Round-off Errors in Linear Programming.* Springer Verlag, New York, 1970.

Orchard-Hays, W., *Advanced Linear Programming Computing Techniques.* McGraw-Hill, New York, 1968.

Scientific Control Systems, Ltd., *UMPIRE Users Guide*, London, June, 1970.

Tomlin, J. A., "Maintaining a Sparse Inverse in the Simplex Method," *IBM Develop.* **16**, No. 4 (July 1972), 415–423.

Tomlin, J. A., "A Survey of Computational Methods for Solving Large Scale Systems," Report 72-75, OR Department, Univ. Stanford, California, October, 1972.

White, W. W., "A Status Report on Computing Algorithms for Mathematical Programming," *ACM Computing Surveys*, **5** (1973), 135–166.

Wagner, H., *Principles of Operations Research*. Prentice-Hall, Englewood Cliffs, New Jersey, 1969.

CHAPTER VIII

BRANCH AND BOUND METHODOLOGY

A. THE BRANCH AND BOUND CONCEPT

The branch and bound method is a solution strategy that has emerged over the last decade as one of the major practical tools for the solution of real life optimization problems. The attractiveness of this method stems from its ability to implicitly eliminate large groups of potential solutions to a problem without explicitly evaluating them. However, like dynamic programming, branch and bound is a strategy, not an algorithm, and the strategy must be merged with the structure of the specific problem at hand to form an implementable solution algorithm.

There are at least four major reasons for the growing acceptance of branch and bound algorithms:

(1) The method is conceptually simple and easy to understand.

(2) The method is easily adaptable to a wide range of different problem situations.

(3) The method is well-suited for computer implementation.

(4) Alternative methods are usually not available.

The strategy is based on the premise that the problem to be solved has the following attributes:

(1) *Combinatorial nature* A combinatorial problem has at the minimum

171

the following properties:

> (a) A finite set of objects is given.
> (b) Each object can take on a certain range of attributes.
> (c) A *solution* to a problem is developed by fixing the attribute values for all objects.
> (d) Only certain combinations of attribute values are allowed.

(2) *Branchability*   This implies that

> (a) it must be possible to construct a finite and countable set containing all the different solutions to the problem (this follows from 1);
> (b) it must be possible to recursively partition a nonempty set of solutions into a nonoverlapping subset.

(3) *Rationality*   A rational problem is one where

> (a) each solution has a unique *value* calculated from the values of its attributes;
> (b) the "best" solution is the one with the highest (or lowest) value.

(4) *Boundability*   An *estimate* of the value of the best solution contained in any set of solutions can be obtained such that

> (a) the actual value of the best solution in the set is inferior or equal to the estimate (thus the estimate is an upper *bound*);
> (b) minimal effort is expended in obtaining this estimate;
> (c) the estimate is reasonably close to the actual value.

The branch and bound concept exploits these properties to (a) implicitly and explicitly construct a tree describing all solutions to the problem, and (b) conduct a guided search in this tree for the best solution.

B. AN ILLUSTRATION

An overview of a simple branch and bound strategy is given in Fig. VIII-1. To illustrate its use in combinatorial optimization, we will consider the following zero-one integer programming problem:

$$\text{Maximize} \quad Z = x_1 + x_2 - x_3$$
$$\text{subject to} \quad x_1 + 2x_2 + 3x_3 \leqslant 4$$
$$x_1 + x_2 + 2x_2 \geqslant 2$$
$$x_i = 0 \text{ or } 1, \quad i = 1, 2, 3.$$

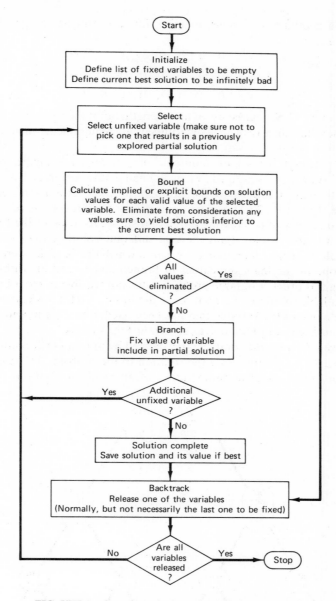

FIG. VIII-1   Overview of a branch and bound strategy.

From a combinatorial point of view, this problem has 2^3 *possible* solutions, namely:

$$x_1: \quad 0 \quad 0 \quad 0 \quad 0 \quad 1 \quad 1 \quad 1 \quad 1$$
$$x_2: \quad 0 \quad 0 \quad 1 \quad 1 \quad 0 \quad 0 \quad 1 \quad 1$$
$$x_3: \quad 0 \quad 1 \quad 0 \quad 1 \quad 0 \quad 1 \quad 0 \quad 1$$

This certainly is a countable list of finite length. Since the value and feasibility of each solution also is readily determined, all requirements of a combinatorial nature are readily satisfied.

If we partition the set of solutions into successively smaller, mutually exclusive subsets of solutions, we will finally have developed a tree containing different solutions to the problem at each terminal node. This is shown in Fig. VIII-2. This partitioning was performed by selecting *one* variable in a set and by creating a different subset for each of the two values that the variable could attain. Several different solution trees could have been developed depending upon the order in which the variables were selected. In fact, one of the main difficulties in branch and bound algorithms is determining this order. For large problems, it is not feasible to record the entire set of available solutions in a node as we did in Fig. VIII-2. Instead we usually write the name of the variable that has been fixed at that point and the value it has been fixed at in the node as shown in Fig. VIII-3.

If we were to trace the complete tree defined by our set partitioning strategy (Chapter III), we would locate the solution to the problem. However, this is paramount to a complete enumeration of all problem solutions. To avoid

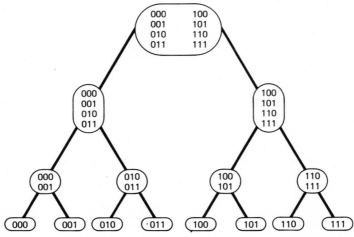

FIG. VIII-2 Tree structure describing successive partitions of sets of solutions to sample problem by complete tabulation of all sets.

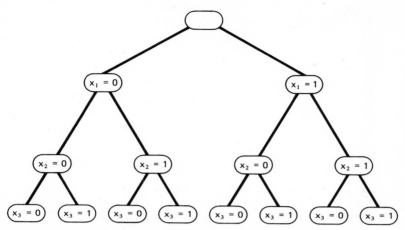

FIG. VIII-3 Tree structure describing successive partitions of sets of solutions to sample problem by specifying where and how variable values are fixed in different stages.

this, we determine on each level a bound on the best solution attainable for each node emerging from this level. Many of these bounds will be inferior to the best solution already obtained and the corresponding nodes can safely be ignored. The remaining nodes can then be explored one at a time until it is established that the best solution has been found or that the bound was not very tight such that the actual solution was substantially inferior to the bound (and in fact inferior to the current best solution).

The success of a branch and bound algorithm hinges to a great extent upon the manner in which the bounds are calculated. Since the bound is to be calculated many times, we want a bound that is easy to calculate. However, we also want a bound that is reasonably close to the actual value of the best solution. The bounding problem is simplified by the fact that since we are after a bound rather than an exact solution, we may relax several of the troublesome constraints in the initial problem. In our integer programming problem this means that we may calculate the bound by relaxing the integer constraint on the variables and solving the resulting linear programming (LP) problem (Chapter VII). Using the strategy in Fig. VIII-1, we first decide to fix x_1 to its two possible values of 0 and 1 and determine the bounds of solutions with $x_1 = 1$ or $x_1 = 0$ by solving the linear program:

$$\text{Maximize} \quad Z(0) = 0 + x_2 - x_2 \qquad \text{Maximize} \quad Z(1) = 1 + x_2 - x_3$$
$$\text{subject to} \quad 0 + 2x_2 + 3x_3 \leqslant 4 \qquad \text{subject to} \quad 1 + 2x_2 + 3x_3 \leqslant 4$$
$$0 + x_2 + 2x_3 \geqslant 2 \qquad\qquad 1 + x_2 + 2x_3 \geqslant 2$$
$$0 \leqslant x_i \leqslant 1 \qquad\qquad\qquad 0 \leqslant x_i \leqslant 1.$$

We find that $Z(0) = 0.5$ for $x_1 = 0$, $x_2 = 1$, and $x_3 = 0.5$; and $Z(1) = 2$ for $x_1 = 1$, $x_2 = 1$, and $x_3 = 0$. Since $Z(1)$ is more promising than $Z(0)$, we decide to explore this alternative first. If the value of the actual solution turns out to be less than the bound we obtained for solutions with $x_1 = 1$, then we will explore solutions with $x_1 = 0$; otherwise we will not have to do this.

We now select a value for x_2. Again we fix the value both ways and determine the bounds of the best attainable solutions by solving the following two LP's:

$$\text{Maximize} \quad Z(1,0) = 1 + 0 - x_3 \qquad \text{Maximize} \quad Z(1,1) = 1 + 1 - x_3$$
$$\text{subject to} \quad 1 + 0 - 3x_3 \leqslant 4 \qquad \text{subject to} \quad 1 + 2x_2 + 3x_3 \leqslant 4$$
$$1 + 0 + 2x_3 \geqslant 2 \qquad \qquad 1 + x_2 + 2x_3 \geqslant 2$$
$$0 \leqslant x_i \leqslant 1 \qquad \qquad \qquad 0 \leqslant x_i \leqslant 1.$$

Here $Z(1,0) = 0$ for $1,0,1$; and $Z(1,1) = 2$ for $1,1,0$; since the second solution is equal to the highest bound encountered, we know that we will never be able to find a solution of higher value. Since the solution also is an *integer*, we know that this is a feasible solution to the initial problem. Thus, we have found the optimal solution by explicitly considering four *partial* solutions $[(x_1 = 0), (x_1 = 1), (x_1 = 1, x_2 = 0), (x_1 = 1, x_2 = 1)]$ and by implicitly considering the 12 other remaining partial solutions.

Normally, we would not have been so lucky as to find the optimal solution in the first branch enumerated. If, at the end of the first branch we had not developed a feasible solution better than or equal to any of our remaining bounds, we would have had to backtrack in the tree (just as for any other tree search algorithm) until we found a node with a better bound. On that level, we then continue the search along the more promising path, etc.

C. DESIGN CONSIDERATIONS

From Fig. VIII-1 it is apparent that a branch and bound algorithm designer is faced with a sequence of four difficult design choices:

(1) Selection of the next variable:

> use next in sequence?
> use one with best bound?
> use one with best estimated solution?

(2) Selection of proper variable value:

> use next value?

use value with best bound?
use value with best estimated solution?
(3) Calculation of bounds and estimates:
   from scratch?
   from previous estimate?
(4) Backtracking:
   to the next variable on previous level?
   to the most promising variable on previous level?
   to the most promising variable anywhere?

The most important concern in selecting a variable for inclusion in a partial solution is to make sure that the resulting partial solution is one that has not previously been explored (otherwise an infinite loop would result). This is achieved by implicitly or explicitly forming lists of all variables eligible for inclusion in particular partial solutions. As variables are included in the solution, they are removed from the eligibility list. Separate lists are maintained for each different level in the solution tree. One list per level is usually sufficient since the branch and bound algorithm usually will maintain only one partial solution at any time.

Initially the eligibility list for the first level will be full while all other lists will be empty. The other lists will fill up as we explore partial solutions further down in the tree. Lists corresponding to partial solutions further down in the tree than the node currently being explored (i.e., with more fixed variables) will be empty.

The generation and management of such a set of lists has the potential of becoming a complex task. However, as we will show in Section D, it is indeed possible to design algorithms where the list generation and maintenance task are trivial. This is achieved by selecting variables in increasing order of their subscripts and releasing variables in decreasing order of their subscripts. In this case, the current variable on a level explicitly defines the remaining unexplored variables on the level. This results in extremely short programs requiring minimal core storage. However, the selection rule ignores the issue of solution quality thus resulting in a large number of alternatives being needlessly explored. This approach may be acceptable when you are unable to distinguish with any precision between the qualities of different potential solutions. (In this case you may have to explore all these alternatives anyway.) The approach may also have some merit when the bounding rules are unusually strong such that a search of unpromising alternatives is truncated fast.

A more complex list management procedure is required if you have a bounding rule that is precise enough to warrant the selection of a variable other than the next variable. In this case, items may be removed from the middle of the list. This calls for flags or pointers to maintain an up-to-date list. In this case care must also be taken to avoid the possibility of generating the same partial solution through different paths.

Selection of a variable value may be achieved by picking the one with the most promising bound. However, since the bounding algorithm must be designed to be consistently biased, it may in some cases be fruitful to apply a separate prediction mechanism that instead estimates the most likely solution value. This procedure may increase the rate at which the algorithm converges toward the optimum solutions.

D. A RECURSIVE BRANCH AND BOUND METHOD FOR ZERO-ONE PROGRAMMING

Thesen (1975) provides a simple illustration of design and implementation of branch and bound algorithms in his approach to the knapsack problem. This method differs from other methods in that its principal focus is on the development of computationally efficient branching and bounding rules.

1. The Problem

There are N objects. Each object has a fixed utility v_i. The combined utility of a set of objects is equal to the sum of the utilities of the individual object. No penalty is invoked if an object is not chosen. Each object i requires a fixed amount w_{ji} of K different resources. Only a limited amount W_j of each resource is available. If no more than $L(L \leqslant N)$ of these objects may be chosen, find the combination of objects with the highest combined utility. (The upper bound on the number of projects is not always explicity stated.) The integer programming formulation of this problem reads as follows:

$$\text{Maximize} \quad Z = \sum_{i=1}^{N} v_i x_i \tag{1}$$

$$\text{subject to} \quad \sum_{i=1}^{N} w_{ji} x_i \leqslant W_j, \qquad j = 1, ..., K \tag{2}$$

$$\sum_{i=1}^{N} x_i \leqslant L, \tag{3}$$

$$x_i = 0 \text{ or } 1, \qquad i = 1, ..., N. \tag{4}$$

It is further assumed that the variables are ordered such that $v_i \geqslant v_{i+1}$ and that all $w_i \geqslant 0$.

2. Branching

A tree structure called the combinatorial tree can be used to define all combinations of objects that may be formed from a set of objects. The importance of this tree stems from the ease with which it may be generated.

Definition A combinatorial tree of size L, N is a tree with L levels where the pointers from a node labeled i on the lth level point to nodes with the following labels:

Condition:	$l < L, i < N$	$l = L, i < N$	$i = N$
FON	$i+1$	Empty	Empty
NOS	$i+1$	$i+1$	Empty

where i, l, N, and L are positive integers, $1 \leqslant l \leqslant L$ and $1 \leqslant i \leqslant N$.

An example of a combinatorial tree (CT) with $L = 3$ and $N = 4$ is given in Fig. VIII-4 where the double arrow signifies the NOS pointer and the single arrow signifies the FON pointer. The relevance of the CT is due to the one to one correspondence between nodes and combinations. An obvious implication of this observation is the fact that a CT has $\sum_1^L \binom{N}{i}$ nodes. Indeed, the CT in Fig. VIII-5 has 14 nodes since 14 unique nonempty combinations of three or fewer objects can be drawn from a set of four objects.

It is clear that a CT of size L, N represents all feasible and many infeasible solutions to the problem defined in Eqs. (1)–(4) and that although the capacity constraints (2) may be violated, the zero-one constraints (4) never are.

3. Bounding

Each potential solution is represented by a (possibly incomplete) branch in the CT. By exploiting both the order in which variables appear along a branch and the upper limit on the number of nodes along a branch, an upper bound on the value of a solution may be obtained.

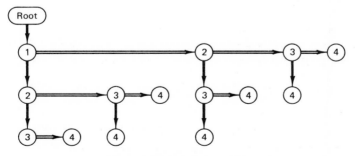

FIG. VIII-4   Combinatorial tree of size 3, 4.

Let l be the number of variables in the current solution $(1 \leqslant l \leqslant L)$, $R(i)$ the index of the ith variable in the current solution $(1 \leqslant i \leqslant l,\ R(i) < R(i+1))$, $Z(l) = \sum_{i=1}^{l} V_{R(i)}$ (value of current solution), and $B(l,n)$ the upper bound on the value of the current solution. This bound may be expressed as

$$B(l,n) = Z(l-1) + \sum_{i=n}^{\min(N, n+L-l)} v_i, \tag{5}$$

where $\min(N, n+L-l)$ is the index of the last variable that might be included. It is easy to verify that Eq. (5) is an upper bound since $v_i > v_{i+1}$. This bound may be determined recursively from previous bounds through the following relationships:

$$B(1,1) = \sum_{i=1}^{L} v_i, \tag{6}$$

$$B(l, n+1) = B(l,n) - v_n + v_{n+L-l+1}, \tag{7}$$

$$B(l+1, n+1) = B(l,n). \tag{8}$$

4. The Algorithm

The following enumerative algorithm utilizes the concepts discussed in the previous section to solve the problem defined in Eqs. (1–4). An overview of the enumerative nature of the algorithm is given in Fig. VIII-5.

Step 1 INITIALIZATION OF VARIABLES

Define r_k as the current usage of the kth resource. Define Z^* as the value of the best solution yet found. Set $l, n = 0$; $v_i = 0$ for $i = N+1$ through $N+L$; $r_k = 0$ for $k = 1$ through K. Set $B(1,1) = \sum_{i}^{L} v_i$, Z and $Z^* = 0$. Compute a bound on $\sum x_i$ as $\min(g_j)$, where g_j is the maximum number of nonzero variables possible in the jth constraint. Set L equal to this bound unless a stricter bound is given. Proceed to Step 2.

Step 2 ADD NEW VARIABLE ON NEW LEVEL

(a) If $l = L$ or $n = N$, this step is not possible; in this case, proceed to Step 4, otherwise continue to Step 2(b).

(b) Set $l = l+1$; $n = n+1$; $Z = Z+v_n$; $r_k = r_k + w_{n,k}$ for $k = 1$ through K; $R(l) = n$. Calculate bound on lateral step on this level from equation

$$B(l, n+1) = B(l,n) - v_n + v_{n+L-l+1}. \tag{7}$$

Proceed to Step 3.

Step 3 TEST FEASIBILITY AND OPTIMALITY OF SOLUTION

(a) If for at least one resource k, $r_k > W_k$, then the step was infeasible; in this case, proceed to Step 4, otherwise proceed to Step 3(b).

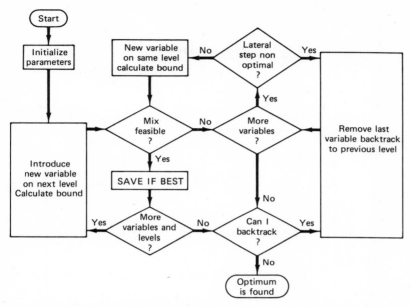

FIG. VIII-5 Overview of algorithm for solution of knapsack problem.

(b) If $Z > Z^*$ then the current solution is best so far; in this case, save the current solution by setting $Z^* = Z$, $l^* = l$, and $R^*(i) = R(i)$ for $i = 1$ through l^*. In either case, attempt inclusion of other variables by proceeding to Step 2.

Step 4 REPLACE VARIABLE ON CURRENT LEVEL
(a) If $n = N$ step is not possible, in this case, proceed to Step 5, otherwise go to Step 4(b).
(b) If $B(l, n+1) < Z^*$ step will not yield an improved solution, in this case, proceed instead to Step 5.
(c) Account for resource consumption by setting the following for all k: $r_k = r_k - w_{n,k} + w_{n+1,k}$. Also set $Z = Z - v_n + v_{n+1}$, $n = n + 1$ and $R(l) = n$. Calculate bound on lateral step as

$$B(l, n+1) = B(l, n) - v_n + v_{n+L-l+1}.$$

Proceed to Step 3.

Step 5 BACKTRACK TO PREVIOUS LEVEL
(a) If $l = 1$ search is completed, proceed to Step 6.
(b) Remove the variable on the lth level by setting $Z = Z - v_n$, $r_k = r_k - W_{n,k}$ all k, $l = l - 1$, and retrieve the index of the variable on this level as $n = R(l)$. Return to Step 4.

TABLE VIII-1
Steps in Calculation for Numerical Example

Seq	Comment	Stage	l	n	R	Z	r	Z^*	R^*	Bounds
1	Initialize	1	0	0	0	0	0,0,0	0	0	$B(1,1) = v_1 + v_2 + v_3 = 21$
2	Step down	2	1	1	1	10	2,2,1			$B(1,2) = B(1,1) - v_1 + v_4 = 14$
3	Feasible and best	3						10	1	
4	Step down	2	2	2	1,2	17	8,5,1			$B(2,3) = B(1,2) + v_1 - v_2 = 17$
5	Not feasible	3								
6	Sidestep attractive	4		3	1,3	14	3,6,3			$B(2,4) = B(2,3) - v_3 + v_5 = 14$
7	Feasible and best	3						14	1,3	
8	Step down	2	3	4	1,3,4	17	3,7,6			$B(3,5) = B(2,4) + v_3 - v_5 = 15$
9	Not feasible	3								
10	Sidestep attractive	4		5	1,3,5	15	3,7,5			$B(3,6) = B(3,5) - v_5 + v_6 = 15$
11	Feasible and best	3						15	1,3,5	
12	Cannot step down	2								
13	Cannot sidestep	4								
14	Backtrack	5	2	3	1,3	14	3,6,3			
15	Sidestep unattractive	4								
16	Backtrack	5	1	1	1	10	2,2,1			
17	Sidestep unattractive	4								
18	Backtrack	5	0							
19	Optimum found	6								

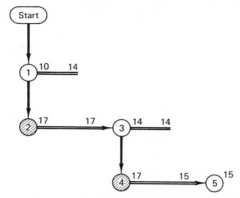

FIG. VIII-6   Tree traced in search for optimal solution.

Step 6   FINISH

Optimal solution is contained in the first l^* elements of the vector R^*. Its value is Z^*.

5.   Numerical Example

As an illustration the following problem is solved:

Maximize $Z = 10x_1 + 7x_2 + 4x_3 + 3x_4 + 1x_5$

subject to

$$2x_1 + 6x_2 + \ x_3 \qquad\qquad\qquad \leqslant 7$$
$$2x_1 + 3x_2 + 4x_3 + \ x_4 + x_5 \leqslant 8$$
$$x_1 \qquad\quad + 2x_3 + 3x_4 + x_5 \leqslant 5$$
$$x_1 + \ x_2 + \ x_3 + \ x_4 + x_5 \leqslant 3, \quad x_i = 0 \text{ or } 1.$$

Table VIII-1 presents the detailed calculations for this example while the tree traced is illustrated in Fig. VIII-6. Shaded nodes represent infeasible solutions, values along the double arrows represent bounds, and numbers adjacent to a node represent the value of the corresponding solution.

E.   BRANCH AND BOUND WITH CONTINUOUS VARIABLES

We have discussed branch and bound algorithms only in the context of discrete optimization problems. However, the method can also be applied to solve many different pseudocombinatorial problems with continuous type variables. To illustrate a branch and bound approach to one such problem, we will show how the simplex method for solution of linear programming problems can be developed through the branch and bound approach.

1.   The Problem

The problem has the same mathematical formulation as the zero-one integer programming problem discussed previously except that the binary all-or-nothing-at-all concept is modified to allow any nonnegative fraction of an object:

$$\text{Maximize} \quad Z = \sum_{j=1}^{N} v_j x_j \tag{9}$$

$$\text{subject to} \quad \sum_{j=1}^{N} w_{ij} x_j \leqslant W_i, \qquad i = 1, ..., K. \tag{10}$$

Research has shown that except in the case of a few illconstructed problems, the optimal solution to this problem will have exactly K nonzero variables. We shall have occasion to use this finding.

In our proposed approach, we will have some difficulties in handling the inequalities utilized in this formulation. However, additional variables serving no other purpose than to absorb (at no cost) unused resources can be introduced such that all constraints always hold as equalities. Thus the problem becomes

$$\text{Maximize} \quad Z = \sum_{j=1}^{N} v_j x_j \tag{11}$$

$$\text{subject to} \quad \sum_{j=1}^{N+K} w_{ij} x_j = W_i \qquad i = 1, ..., K. \tag{12}$$

One *slack variable* is assumed to absorb the excess for each constraint.

The following illustrates a problem of this kind:

$$\text{Maximize} \quad Z = 10x_1 + 7x_2 + 4x_3 + 3x_4 + x_5$$

$$\begin{aligned}
\text{subject to} \quad & 2x_1 + 6x_2 + x_3 && + x_6 && = 7 \\
& 2x_1 + 3x_2 + 4x_3 + x_4 + x_5 && + x_7 && = 8 \\
& x_1 \qquad + 2x_3 + 3x_4 + x_5 && + \quad + x_8 && = 5 \\
& && x_i \geqslant 0, \\
& && i = 1, ..., 8.
\end{aligned}$$

This problem consists of eight variables and three equations. However, we already know that of these eight variables only three will be nonzero for the optimal solution. Also, once the identity of the optimal nonzero variables is determined, their value can be uniquely computed by regarding the constraints as three equations in three unknowns.

2. Branching

An N variable problem with K (equality) constraint has a total of

$$\binom{N}{K} = \frac{N!}{(N-K)!\,K!}$$

different possible solutions (i.e., combinations of nonzero variables) that must be investigated for optimailty. For the simple example problem, this means that we have

$$\binom{8}{3} = \frac{8!}{5!\,3!} = 56$$

possible solutions which must be explored.

To develop a solution tree describing these solutions, some new terminology relating to the state of particular variables is required:

(1)   A variable is *included* if it is in a solution at a nonzero level.

(2)   A variable is *excluded* if it is in a solution at a zero level.

(3)   A variable is *free* if its inclusion or exclusion has not yet been decided.

(4)   A variable is *fixed* if the actual value of an included variable is determined.

(5)   The solution is *partial* if some free variables still exist.

(6)   The solution is *complete* if all variables are either fixed or excluded.

Using this terminology, a solution tree is drawn to represent all partial and complete solutions as chains of included variables in a combinatorial tree. An incomplete solution tree for the sample problem is presented in Fig. VIII-7. The optimal solution can now be found by searching this tree for the one complete path with the largest value.

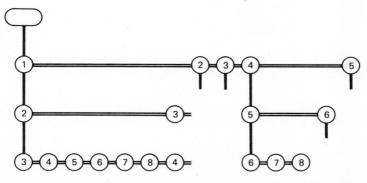

FIG. VIII-7   Incomplete solution tree for continuous variable example.

3.   Bounding

In the present approach, all nodes on a given level are first evaluated. The resulting bounds will determine the *order* in which variables at a given level are considered for inclusion. This order will be determined as a function of the relative quality of the anticipated solutions.

However, calculation of bounds in this context is somewhat difficult. Instead we will therefore use a pseudobound, the change in solution value that would occur if one unit of the new variable were to be included. To determine this, we first compute how much the value of the variable in the present solution must change to accommodate one unit of the candidate variable j. This is easily accomplished when we recall that we assumed all constraints to always hold as equalities. Then we compute the corresponding change in the objective function Z_j. Finally we compute the *total* change in the objective function $c_j - Z_j$. Since we are maximizing, any candidate variable with a negative $c_j - Z_j$ can be ignored, and large positive values are indications of a potential for vastly improved solutions. (The details of these calculations were presented in the discussion of the simplex method in Chapter VII.)

4.   Backtracking

All tree searching algorithms include backtracking features that allow the search to step back and continue on a higher level when the search in a given subtree has been completed. This backtracking traditionally implied that the search would step back along the very path followed to reach a node. However, a few algorithms allow branching (or jumping) in the backtrack step such that a different path is followed when backtracking.

Such branching is advantageous because we can then release the *least attractive* rather than the *most recently included* variable in the present solution. This usually improves the convergence rate. However, the resulting computer program is usually substantially more complex than that of the traditional backtrack programs. Furthermore, for some problem situations, it is difficult or impossible to formulate backtrack branching steps so as to guarantee that the optimal solution can be reached in a finite number of steps. Neither of these difficulties arises here.

To illustrate the concept of branching in the backtracking step, we will allow such branching in the present formulation. For our example, if the solution 2, 3, 5 were reached through a normal search, backtracking would bring us back to 2, 3. With branching, we could instead reach 2, 5 or 3, 5. While this backtracking appears as jumping in Fig. VIII-7, this tree could easily be redrawn as an acyclic network where these steps would be represented as bonafide branches. (The drawing of this network is left as an exercise.)

5. The Algorithm

The presentation of the algorithm follows:

Step 1 INITIALIZE

Define an initial solution to include the slack variables $X_{N+1}, \ldots, X_{N+K}$. Fix the level of these variables such that all constraints hold with equality. Exclude all other variables.

Step 2 BOUND

Calculate contribution to present solution by including one unit of each excluded variable while altering values of presently fixed variables to retain feasibility. Otherwise identify the variable with the largest positive solution. If there is no positive contribution, go to Step 5.

Step 3 BACKTRACK

Identify the fixed variable whose removal would accommodate the largest number of new units of the new variable. Remove this variable from the solution.

Step 4 BRANCH

Modify present solution by including the excluded variable identified in the bound stage. Fix the level of all included variables such that feasibility is retained. Go to Step 2.

Step 5 STOP

The present solution is optimal.

This algorithm differs from most branch and bound algorithms in that it exhibits zero overshoot since the optimal solution is immediately recognized as such when branching is allowed in the backtrack stage.

We must always take care that the algorithm does not get stuck in an infinite loop. A large number of authors have studied the occurrence of this problem in the simplex algorithm, and it appears that looping will not occur for correctly formulated problems. However, it may occur for improperly formulated problems where linear dependencies between the constraints are present.

F. AN EVALUATION

1. Methodology

The algorithm presented in Section D was coded in FORTRAN and implemented and tested on a Harris-Datacraft 6024/3 mini computer with 32K 16 bit words. Since the algorithm is highly recursive and requires insignificant amounts of intermediate storage, the resulting code is short and requires a minimum of core storage (10K words). Several hundred test problems were solved using this code and two reference codes, the first based on the basic Balas algorithm (Geoffrion, 1967) and the second on an extension of this algorithm (Zionts, 1972). Attempts to implement Geoffrion's improved algorithm, RIP30C, (Geoffrion, 1967; Geoffrion and Nelson, 1968) on the Harris-Datacraft were unsuccessful due to hardware restrictions.

A series of tests using randomly generated problems with controlled attributes was performed to determine both how various problem attributes affected the efficiency of the present algorithm and how this code performed relative to the reference codes. Then, published test problems were used to provide reference data facilitating the order of magnitude comparisons with evaluations performed elsewhere.

2.   Generation of Test Problems

In order to develop a random problem generator for this class of problems, we perform a preliminary study to determine those attributes of the problem at hand that had the most significant impact on solution time.

The following parameters are identified:

(1)   problem size (K and N),
(2)   constraint density ($D = \Pr\{w_{ij} > 0\}$),
(3)   constraint tightness ($T = \sum(\sum w_{ij}/W_i)$),
(4)   difference between adjacent v_j's.

Capital budgeting problems of the Lori–Savage type typically have a density close to unity and a tightness of between one and two, while set covering problems on the other hand may have densities as low as 0.02–0.11 and a corresponding tightness of 2–15 depending on problem size.

Before we can proceed, we need to make additional assumptions:

(1)   Each w_{ij} is independent of any other w_{ij} .
(2)   The range of all w_{ij}'s is in the same range $[a \leqslant w_{ij} \leqslant b]$.
(3)   All W_i's have the same value ($W_i = 1$).
(4)   The difference between adjacent v_i's is either constant or drawn from an exponential distribution with mean $e + f \times i$.

These assumptions imply that we will generate a problem where all constraints are approximately of equal tightness. However, it would be relatively easy to generate constraints of differing tightness by assigning some distribution to the W_i's.

To generate constraints of the specified tightness T, it is necessary to determine the values of a and b that correspond to the problem attribute parameter T (tightness) and D (density). Unfortunately, only one relationship is available:

$$T = \frac{a+b}{2} * N * D \quad \text{or} \quad \frac{a+b}{2} = T(ND).$$

To explicitly determine the value of a and b we therefore also need to specify the range $R = b - a$ of the w_{ij}'s such that

$$b = T/(ND) + R/2, \qquad a = T/(ND) - R/2.$$

If we define $q_i = -v_i + v_{i-1}$, then three different patterns of relationships between adjacent v_i's can be identified:

(a) $q_i = q_j + \varepsilon, \qquad 2 \le i \le j \le N,$
(b) $q_i > q_j + \varepsilon,$
(c) $q_i < q_j + \varepsilon.$

In the first case, the v_i's are linearly decreasing with i. In the second case, the v_i's are decreasing at a decreasing rate, while in the third case the v_i's are decreasing at an increasing rate. The following recursive expression may be used to generate either one of these relationships:

$$v_N = K, \qquad v_{N-1} = K - A,$$
$$v_i = (1+a)v_{i+1} - av_{i+2}, \qquad i = N - 2, ..., 1.$$

A wide range of different values can be chosen for the constant K without affecting the performance of the algorithm. We find 100 to be a good choice.

The choice of the initial increment A has substantial effect on the performance of an algorithm. Small values usually render a problem hard to solve with large values having the opposite effect. Similar considerations apply to the rate of increase factor a.

We have now identified eight factors that can be used to control the attributes of randomly generated knapsack problems:

N	number of variables,
M	number of constants,
v_n	value of last cost factor in the objective factor,
$v_{n-1} - v_n$	initial change in cost factors,
B	subsequent rate of change in cost factors,
T	constraint tightness,
R	range of values on constraint matrix,
D	constraint density.

The design of an algorithm that generates random problems controlled by these parameters is a reasonably straightforward procedure. The actual development of the algorithm is left as a problem assignment.

3. Results

Randomly generated problems with controlled attributes were solved to determine the effect of these attributes on solution time. To keep cost down, the size of these problems was, whenever possible, kept to 5×15. Spot checks indicate that the trends developed for these problems do extrapolate to problems of larger size.

Constraint tightness Performance of the present algorithm and the two reference algorithms showed a strong dependence upon constraint tightness. This is shown in Fig. VIII-8 where the relationship between solution time and constraint tightness for the case with evenly spaced v_j's is plotted. It is seen that solution time for all three algorithms increased as the tightness was increased from 0.5 to approximately 1.5–1.6. Further increases caused a corresponding reduction in solution time. For relatively unconstrained problems the Balas–Geoffrion code was 20 to 30% faster than the Zionts' code. On the other hand, for most constrained problems ($t > 1.6$) the Zionts' code was 20 to 30% more efficient than the other code. This behavior is explained by the fact that Zionts' extension of the Balas algorithm involves an exploitation of bounds on variables induced by tight constraints. For relatively unconstrained problems, the additional work required by this approach is not offset by the benefits gained. The present code showed the same sensitivity to constraint tightness with problems in the tightness range of 1–2.5 again being the hardest to solve. However, as a rule of thumb, this code required approximately one-tenth of the solution time required by the two reference codes for problems of this size.

Objective function The three codes also exhibited a strong sensitivity to the relative values of the terms in the objective functions. For example, the

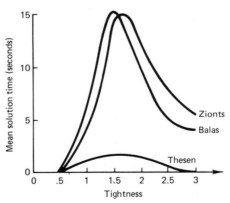

FIG. VIII-8   Effect of constraint tightness: $n = 15$, $m = 5$, $d_n/d_1 = 1$.

average solution time for 10 randomly generated 5-constraint 15-variable problems with $t = 2$ and equal v_j's was 18.36, 24.03, and 2.13 seconds, respectively, for the Balas, Zionts, and Thesen codes. These times dropped exponentially as the ratio between the largest and the smallest of coefficients in the objective function d_n/d_1 was increased. For $d_n/d_1 = 5$, the times were 6.63, 5.53, and 0.12 seconds. Similar trends were found for other problem sizes and tightnesses. The relative effect of the objective function on solution time appeared to be independent of problem tightness and similar for all three codes.

Problem size   Random problems of successively larger size were generated and solved to determine the effect of problem size on solution time. Figure VIII-9 shows the solution time for the present code and the two reference codes for random problems with a tightness of 1.0 and $d_n/d_1 = 1$. It is seen that the magnitude and rate of increase in solution times is substantially less for the present code than for the two reference codes. However, it is still increasing as the problem time increases. The rate of increase in solution time was found to be dependent upon constraint tightness. While on the average 1 minute was required to solve a 30-variable problem with $t = 2$, a 50-variable problem could be solved in the same time if the tightness was reduced to 1.

Bounds   Tests were made to determine the effect on the solution speed of the bound on the number of nonzero variables. Figure VIII-10 shows this effect on Peterson's problem number 5. It is seen that a tight bound (or accurate estimate) on the number of nonzero variables in the optimal solution will play an important role in reducing the computer time required to solve a problem. This property will be partciularly useful when large problems with relatively few nonzero variables are to be solved.

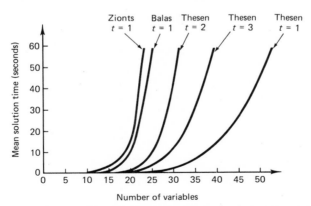

FIG. VIII-9   Effect of problem size on time, $m = 5$, $d_n/d_1 = 1$.

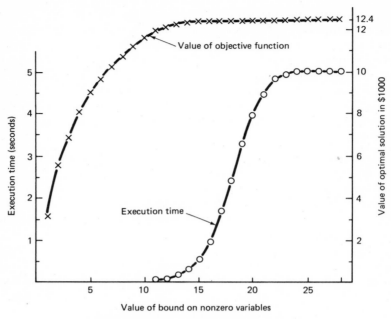

FIG. VIII-10   Effect of bound on nonzero variables.

Most branch and bound type algorithms exhibit improved performance when a tight bound on the value of the optimal solution is known. Such a bound cannot be exploited directly in the present algorithm. This bound may, however, be used to calculate a bound on the number of nonzero variables, thus indirectly resulting in improved performance.

PROBLEMS

1.   Draw the complete solution tree for the following problem:

Maximize $Z = 3x_1 + 4x_2 - x_3 + x_4$

subject to $x_1 + x_2 + x_3 + x_4 \leqslant 2$

$$x_i = 0 \text{ or } 1, \quad i = 1, \ldots, 5.$$

2.   How could you incorporate the constraint in the procedure in Problem 1 into the BOUND step of the algorithm in Fig. IV-1?

3.   Solve the following problem using the procedure described in Section B and your conclusion in Problem 2:

Maximize $Z = 2x_1 + 3x_2 + 4x_3 - 5x_4 + x_5$

subject to

$$x_1 + x_2 - x_3 + 2x_4 - x_5 \geqslant 2$$
$$x_1 - x_2 + x_3 + x_4 + x_5 \leqslant 3$$
$$2x_1 + x_2 - x_3 + x_4 - x_5 \leqslant 5$$
$$x_1 + x_2 + x_3 + x_4 + x_5 \leqslant 3$$
$$x_i = 0 \text{ or } 1, \quad i = 1, \ldots, 5.$$

4. Demonstrate an analogy between the binary search algorithm and a branch and bound algorithm.

5. Is a branch and bound algorithm still a tree search procedure if jumping is allowed in the backtracking stage?

6. In the general flowchart in Fig. IV-1 we required that a bound on the solution be calculated for all feasible values for a selected variable. Did we have to do this when we studied the simplex algorithm?

7. Write a program for the solution of the knapsack program with 1 constraint and up to 30 variables.

8. Write a random knapsack problem generator.

9. Evaluate the computational efficiency of the algorithm written in Problem 7. In particular show how the mean solution time increases with problem size and decreases with constraint tightness.

BIBLIOGRAPHY

Balas, E., "An Additive Algorithm for Solving Linear Programs with Zero-One Variables," *Operations Res.* **13** (July–August 1965), 517–549.

Geoffrion, A. M., "Integer Programming by Implicit Enumeration and Balas' Method," *SIAM Rev.* **9** (April 1967), 178–190.

Geoffrion, A. M., "An Improved Implicit Enumeration Approach for Integer Programming," *Operations Res.* **17** (May–June 1969), 437,454.

Geoffrion, A. M., and **A. B. Nelson,** "Users Instructions for Integer Programming Code RIP30C"*RM-5627-PR* The Rand Corporation, Santa Monica, California, 1968.

Greenberg, H., and **R. L. Hegerich,**"A Branch Search Algorithm for the Knapsack Problem," *Management Sci.* **16** (1972), 327–332.

Kolesar, P. J., "A Branch and Bound Algorithm for the Knapsack Problem," *Management Sci.* **9** (May 1967), 497–520.

Murphree, E. L., and **S. Fenves,** "A Technique for Generating Interpretive Translators for Problem Oriented Languages," *Nordisk Tidskr. Informationsbehandling (BIT)* (October 1970), 310–323.

Petersen, Clifford C., "Computational Experience with Varients of the Balas Algorithm Applied to the Selection of R&D Projects," *Management Sci.* **13** (May 1967), 736–750.

Thesen, A., "A Recursive Branch and Bound Algorithm for the Multi-dimensional Knapsack Problem," *Naval Res. Logist. Quart.* **22**, No. 2 (June 1975), 341–353.

Zionts, Stanley, "Generalized Implicit Enumeration Bounds on Variables for Solving Linear Program with Zero-One Variables," *Naval Res. Logist. Quart.* **19** (1972), 165–181.

CHAPTER IX

RANDOM NUMBER GENERATORS

A. THE MULTIPLICATIVE CONGRUENTIAL RANDOM NUMBER GENERATOR

Sequences of random numbers are required for such computer applications as automated design of experiments, monte carlo studies, and discrete event simulation. Such numbers are readily available in tabular form in the literature. However, such tables are not efficiently handled in a computer. To save I/O time and storage space, we would prefer to generate the numbers one by one in the computer as we need them. Unfortunately, it is not feasible to generate truly random sequences of numbers in the computer. However, we are able to generate sequences that, although we know they are not random, do pass all statistical tests that a truly random sequence should pass. Such sequences are referred to as pseudorandom sequences.

There is a large number of different pseudorandom number generators available today. Of them, the multiplicative congruential method for generation of uniformly distributed random numbers is one of the most effective. In fact, the random number generators provided with most FORTRAN compilers and with the GASP, GPSS, SIMULA, and SIMSCRIPT simulation languages are all of this kind. This is good news since even though the name is complex, the multiplicative congruential method is one of the simplest of all pseudorandom number generating schemes.

Numbers are generated recursively from the following congruence relationship:

$$u_{i+1} \equiv a \cdot u_i \,(\text{mod}\, m).$$

Translated into English, this means that the $(i+1)$th random number is obtained as the remainder of a constant a times the last number u_i divided by another constant m.

To illustrate this method, we will investigate the sequence generated by a generator with $a = 6$, $m = 23$, and $u_0 = 13$:

$u_1 \equiv 6 \cdot 13 \,(\text{mod}\, 23) \equiv 78 \,(\text{mod}\, 23) \equiv 3 \cdot 23 + 9 \,(\text{mod}\, 23), \qquad u_1 = 9$

$u_2 \equiv 6 \cdot 9 \,(\text{mod}\, 23) \equiv 54 \,(\text{mod}\, 23) \equiv 2 \cdot 23 + 8 \,(\text{mod}\, 23), \qquad u_2 = 8.$

The full sequence generated by this generator is

$$S_1 = 6, \quad 13, \quad 9, \quad 8, \quad 2, \quad 12, \quad 3, \quad 18, \quad 16, \quad 4, \quad 1, \quad 6, \dots$$

This *cycle* will be generated repeatedly regardless of the value of u_0 as long as u_0 is a member of the cycle. If we choose a u_0 that is not a member of S_1 (for example, 5), the following cycle is generated:

$$S_2 = 5, \quad 7, \quad 19, \quad 22, \quad 17, \quad 10, \quad 14, \quad 15, \quad 21, \quad 11, \quad 20, \quad 5, \dots$$

We have now seen that even though the generator has a potential of generating a sequence of up to 22 different numbers, the actual length of the cycle was substantially less. The resulting length of a sequence depends upon the values chosen for the modulus m and the multiplier a. For example, if the multiplier were changed from 6 to 7, a single 22 number sequence would be developed regardless of the value of u_0:

$$S_3 = 1, \quad 7, \quad 3, \quad 21, \quad 9, \quad 17, \quad 4, \quad 5, \quad 12, \quad 15, \quad 13, \quad 22, \quad 16,$$
$$20, \quad 2, \quad 14, \quad 6, \quad 19, \quad 18, \quad 11, \quad 8, \quad 10, \quad 1, \dots$$

It is desirable to generate sequences with cycles as long as possible. This ensures a coverage of as many points as possible in the interval over which numbers are generated.

To generate long cycles it is desirable to use as large a value of m as possible. (The resulting random numbers can later be scaled to fit a more practical range.)

Research has shown that the longest cycles are developed if m is chosen as the largest prime number available in the computer. This choice also eliminates certain potentially strong correlations between consecutive pairs of numbers that would be present if the largest available integer were chosen.

Considerable theoretical and empirical research has been conducted to determine the value of good multipliers a for given values of m. Details of this work are given by Knuth (1969). The importance of research to determine good combinations of multiplier and modulus stems from the differences in design of different computers. A generator that works well on the 36 bit Univac 1110 does not work well on the 32 bit IBM 370 since the higher modulus feasible on the 1110 is not realizable on the 370. We summarize in Table IX-1 the combinations of a and m that have been shown to give good results for several different computers. A random number implementing these recommendations for the Harris-Datacraft 6024/3 minicomputer is given in Fig. IX-1.

B. TESTING UNIFORM RANDOM NUMBER GENERATORS

A pseudorandom uniform number generator must satisfy two key criteria:

(1)   The numbers must appear to be drawn from uniform distribution on the interval [0–1].

(2)   The order of numbers in the sequence must appear to be completely random.

A battery of different statistical procedures are available to test the hypothesis that the above criteria are satisfied. We recommend that several different tests be applied to any random number generators of unknown quality. In this section we review four such procedures. The first two procedures test assumptions regarding the distribution of the numbers regard-

TABLE IX-1

Constants for Multiplicative Generators for Different Computers

Typical computer	Word size	a	m	m^{-1}
Harris-Datacraft	24	3125	$2^{23}-15$	$1.192095 \cdot 10^{-7}$
IBM 370	32	65539 or 16807	$2^{31}-1$	$4.656613 \cdot 10^{-10}$
UNIVAC 1110	36	3125	$2^{35}-31$	$2.910383 \cdot 10^{-11}$

```
FUNCTION UNIF(A,B)
DATA ISEED/235621/
X=ISEED
X=X*3125,
IF(X.LT.0.)X=-X
X=AMOD(X,8388593,)
ISEED=X
X=X/8388593,
UNIF=A+(B-A)*X
RETURN
END
```

FIG. IX-1   Uniform random number generator for the Harris-Datacraft 6024/3 computer.

less of their sequence. The last two procedures test the hypothesis that the numbers appear in a random sequence.

In addition to the test discussed here, Knuth (1969) recommends that a *spectral* test be applied to explore the presence of autocorrelation in the generated sequence. This test is unfortunately so complex that its application and interpretation are beyond the scope of this text.

1. Tests for Distribution

a. The Kolmogorov–Smirnov Test

The Kolmogorov–Smirnov test is a relatively simple procedure designed to test the hypothesis that a given set of observations was drawn from a particular distribution. The test statistic D used in this test is a measure of the observed maximum difference between the theoretical distribution and an empirical distribution function constructed from the observed data. It can be shown that D is a random variable. The likelihood that D exceeds a given value if the hypothesis is correct can be computed for samples of different sizes.

The following is an application of the Kolmogorov–Smirnov test to evaluate the assumption that a pseudorandom number generator generates numbers uniformly distributed between 0 and 1:

(1) *Formulate hypothesis* H_0: Numbers are drawn from uniform distribution on the interval [0–1].

(2) *Draw sample of size n* Knuth (1969) suggests $n = 1000$. Call ith sample value x_i.

(3) *Determine the empirical cumulative distribution function* $Fn(x)$ *such that* $Fn(x) = $ (count of $x_i \leqslant x$)/n. This is easily achieved by:

    (a) sorting the values such that $x_i \leqslant x_{i+1}$,

    (b) computing the corresponding cumulative value as

$$Fn(0) = 0,$$
$$Fn(x_i) = i/n, \qquad i = f, \dots, n.$$

(4) *Calculate the Kolmogorov–Smirnov statistic*

$$D = \max[Fn(x) - x], \qquad 0 \leqslant x \leqslant 1.$$

(5) *Consult a table of acceptable limits for the Kolmogorov–Smirnov test* to determine the acceptability of the resulting value of D. (For a sample size of 50 and a 10% risk level, this value is 0.172.)

To illustrate the use of the Kolmogorov–Smirnov test, we will apply the test to the first 50 two-digit random numbers in the table given by Gordon (p. 94, 1969).

(1) *Formulate hypothesis* H_0: Numbers are drawn from uniform distribution.

(2) *Draw sample of size* 50.

0.10	0.32	0.76	0.13	0.34
0.37	0.04	0.64	0.74	0.24
0.08	0.68	0.19	0.09	0.23
0.99	0.02	0.09	0.70	0.38
0.12	0.99	0.80	0.36	0.64
0.66	0.74	0.34	0.76	0.36
0.31	0.10	0.45	0.82	0.35
0.85	0.77	0.02	0.65	0.68
0.63	0.32	0.05	0.74	0.90
0.73	0.42	0.03	0.64	0.35

(3) *Determine empirical distribution function*

(a) *Step* 1: Sort the data.

1	0.02	11	0.12	21	0.35	31	0.64	41	0.74
2	0.02	12	0.13	22	0.36	32	0.65	43	0.77
3	0.03	13	0.19	23	0.36	33	0.66	43	0.80
4	0.04	14	0.23	24	0.37	34	0.68	44	0.82
5	0.05	15	0.24	25	0.38	35	0.68	45	0.85
6	0.08	16	0.31	26	0.42	36	0.70	46	0.90
7	0.09	17	0.32	27	0.45	37	0.70	47	0.94
8	0.09	18	0.34	28	0.63	38	0.73	48	0.97
9	0.10	19	0.34	29	0.64	39	0.74	49	0.99
10	0.10	20	0.35	30	0.64	40	0.74	50	0.99

(b) *Step* 2: Construct $Fn(x)$.

$Fn(0.00) = 0.00$	$Fn(0.12) = 0.22$	$Fn(0.36) = 0.43$	$Fn(0.65) = 0.64$	$Fn(0.85) = 0.90$
$Fn(0.02) = 0.04$	$Fn(0.13) = 0.24$	$Fn(0.37) = 0.48$	$Fn(0.66) = 0.66$	$Fn(0.90) = 0.92$
$Fn(0.03) = 0.06$	$Fn(0.19) = 0.26$	$Fn(0.38) = 0.50$	$Fn(0.68) = 0.70$	$Fn(0.94) = 0.96$
$Fn(0.04) = 0.08$	$Fn(0.23) = 0.28$	$Fn(0.42) = 0.52$	$Fn(0.70) = 0.74$	$Fn(0.97) = 0.98$
$Fn(0.05) = 0.10$	$Fn(0.24) = 0.30$	$Fn(0.45) = 0.54$	$Fn(0.73) = 0.76$	$Fn(0.99) = 1.00$
$Fn(0.08) = 0.12$	$Fn(0.31) = 0.32$	$Fn(0.63) = 0.56$	$Fn(0.74) = 0.82$	
$Fn(0.09) = 0.16$	$Fn(0.32) = 0.34$	$Fn(0.64) = 0.62$	$Fn(0.77) = 0.84$	
$Fn(0.10) = 0.20$	$Fn(0.34) = 0.38$		$Fn(0.80) = 0.86$	
	$Fn(0.35) = 0.42$		$Fn(0.82) = 0.88$	

(4) *Calculate the Kolmogorov–Smirnov Statistic* Maximum value of $x - Fn(x)$ occurs for $f(0.38)$ with $D = 0.12$.

(5) *The critical value is* 0.172 *for a* 90% *level of significance* Thus the Kolmogorov–Smirnov test has not identified any reason for rejecting the null hypothesis.

b. The Chi-square Test

The chi-square test is another well-known test used for testing of hypotheses regarding the universe from which independent samples are drawn. This test differs from the Kolmogorov–Smirnov test in that the chi-square is designed for discrete rather than continuous distribution. This does not pose any problem, however, because the continuous distribution can be broken up into appropriate intervals. The test is based on the premise that deviations between actual and expected frequences of occurrence of observations are independently distributed and follow the normal distribution. The test statistic χ^2 is based on aggregated squares of these deviations. To apply the chi–square procedure to test a uniform number generator, follow this procedure:

(1)   *Formulate hypothesis H_0* : Numbers are drawn from the Uniform distribution on the interval [0–1].

(2)   *Break the distribution into k intervals* such that the probability of an observation being drawn from the ith interval is $p(i)$.

(3)   *Make a preliminary decision on the sample size.*

(4)   *Adjust the sizes* (they need not be identical) *of the k intervals* such that the expected number of observations in an interval $np(i)$ exceeds four.

(5)   *Modify the sample size* if (4) could not be carried out.

(6)   *Obtain sample.*

(7)   *Determine the* actual *frequency f(i) of observations in each interval.*

(8)   *Form the test statistic*:

$$\chi_{n-1}^2 = \sum_{i=1}^{k} \frac{(f(i)-np(i))^2}{np(i)}.$$

(9)   *Under the assumption that the null hypothesis* (1) *is true*, this test statistic will follow the chi-square distribution with $k-1$ degrees of freedom.

(10)   *Reject the null hypothesis if x^2 has a value that only infrequently.(say less than 5% of the time) is generated by the x^2 distribution with $k-1$ degrees of freedom.* For a risk level of 5% and 9 degrees of freedom, the largest acceptable value for the test statistic is 16.9.

To illustrate the use of the χ^2 test on the distribution of the data generated by a uniform random number generator, we shall again evaluate the data from Gordon's table:

(1)   *Formulate hypothesis H_0*: The data is drawn from a universe of uniformly distributed numbers on the interval [0–1].

(2)   *Form ten intervals of equal size* such that

$$p(i) = 0.1, \qquad i = 1, ..., 10.$$

(3)   *Collect 50 sample values.*

(4)   *The expected number of observations in each interval* $np(i)$ *is* 5   Thus, no modification will be required.

(5)   *Not necessary.*

(6)   *Use the sample obtained for the Kolmogorov–Smirnov test.*

(7)   *Determine the actual frequency of observation in each interval*   By inspection the following counts are established:

$$f(1) = 8, \qquad f(2) = 5, \qquad f(3) = 2, \qquad f(4) = 10, \qquad f(5) = 2,$$
$$f(6) = 0, \qquad f(7) = 8, \qquad f(8) = 7, \qquad f(9) = 3, \qquad f(10) = 5.$$

(8)   *Form the test statistic:*

$$\chi_9^2 = \frac{\begin{array}{c}(8-5)^2 + (5-5)^2 + (2-5)^2 + (5-10)^2 + (2-5)^2 \\ + (0-5)^2 + (8-5)^2 + (7-5)^2 + (3-5)^2 + (5-5)^2\end{array}}{5}$$

$$= \frac{9}{5} + \frac{0}{5} + \frac{9}{5} + \frac{25}{5} + \frac{9}{5} + \frac{0}{5} + \frac{9}{5} + \frac{4}{5} + \frac{4}{5} + \frac{0}{5}$$

$$= 12.0.$$

(9)   5% *of all* x^2 *values exceed* 16.9 *for 9 degrees of freedom.*

(10)   *Since* χ^2 *lies below this value,* there is no reason (as far as this test is concerned) to reject the null hypothesis.

2.   Tests for Random Sequence

Determination that a generator provides numbers from a given distribution is not enough. You must also ascertain that their sequence is random.

In this section we will review several tests designed for this purpose. One important test, the spectral test, is omitted due to its complexity.

a.   The Run Test

A *run* is defined as a string of numbers appearing in monotonically increasing *or* decreasing order. For example, the string $03, 23, 57, 92$ contains one run. The string $03, 23, 19, 07, 92$ contains three runs: $(03, 23)$, $(19, 07)$, (92). To accurately count the number of runs in a sequence, it is helpful to replace a number in the string by a plus sign $(+)$ if it is larger than the previous number and by a minus sign $(-)$ if it is less than this number. Do not use any symbol at all for the first number. The number of runs is then counted as one plus the number of sign changes. Using this replacement, the string $03, 23, 19, 07, 92$ becomes $+--+$. The presence of three runs is now easily verified.

The *run test* is based on the premise that the number of runs in a randomly ordered sequence of numbers is in itself a random variable. For a sequence with more than 20 entries it can be shown that this count is approximately normally distributed with a known mean and variance. Thus, too many or too few runs may indicate that the number of runs has been drawn from a distribution other than the one expected in a randomly ordered sequence.

The run test can be operationalized as follows:

(1) *Form the null hypothesis H_0* The order of appearance of numbers in a sequence of numbers is random.

(2) *Select a sample sequence of length n ($n > 20$).*

(3) *Define a run of entries as a subsequence* for which either $a_{i-1} > a_i \leqslant a_{i+1} \leqslant \cdots \leqslant a_{i+m} > a_{i+m+1}$ or $a_{i-1} < a_i \geqslant a_{i+1} \geqslant \cdots \geqslant a_{i+m} < a_{i+m+1}$.

(4) *Define the test statistic r* as the number of runs (up *and* down) in the sample.

(5) *If $N > 20$ and H_0 is true*, then r is approximately normally distributed with the parameters

$$E(r) = \tfrac{1}{3}(2n-1), \qquad \text{Var}(r) = \tfrac{1}{90}(16n-29).$$

(6) *Accept H_0 if* for an acceptable risk level α,

$$\alpha \leqslant Z\left(\frac{r - E(r)}{\sqrt{\text{Var}(r)}}\right) \leqslant 1 - \alpha.$$

To illustrate this procedure, we will again evaluate the aforementioned random number table:

(1) H_0: The numbers appear in a random order.

(2) Employ the 50 item sample used for the Kolmogorov–Smirnov test.

(3) The following runs are counted:

10	37	08	99	12	66	31	85	63	73
+	−	+	−	+	−	+	−	+	−
32	04	68	02	99	74	10	77	32	42
−	+	−	+	−	−	+	−	+	+
76	64	19	09	80	34	45	02	05	03
−	−	−	+	−	+	−	+	−	+
13	74	09	70	36	76	82	64	74	64
+	−	+	−	+	+	−	+	−	−
34	24	23	38	64	36	35	68	90	35
−	−	+	+	−	−	+	+	−	

(4) $r = 36$.

(5) $E(r) = \tfrac{1}{3}(2n-1) = \tfrac{1}{3}(2 \cdot 50 - 1) = \tfrac{101}{3} = 33.67$

$$\text{Var}(r) = \tfrac{1}{90}(16n - 29) = \tfrac{1}{90}(16 \cdot 50 - 29) = \tfrac{771}{90} = 8.57$$

$$\frac{r - E(r)}{\sqrt{\text{Var}(r)}} = \frac{36 - 33.67}{\sqrt{8.57}} = 0.80$$

and from a table for the normal distribution $Z(0.8) = 0.7881$

(6) H_0 is accepted at the 10% risk level since

$$0.5 \leqslant 0.7881 \leqslant 0.95.$$

b.   The Gap Test

A "gap" is a measure of the interval between two numbers in a specific range in a sequence of random numbers. If the numbers are randomly ordered and ten intervals of equal size are used, then it can easily be deduced that the gap is a random variable x following the distribution

$$\Pr\{x \,|\, k\} = \Pr\{k \text{ followed by exactly } x \text{ numbers not in the same interval as } k\}$$

$$= 0.1\,(0.9)^x, \qquad x = 0, 1, 2, \dots.$$

This theoretical distribution can now be compared to an observed empirical distribution, and a chi-square or a Kolmogorov–Smirnov test can be applied to test the hypothesis that data in the empirical distribution were drawn from the theoretical distribution.

To illustrate this test, we will apply the test to the data used for the run

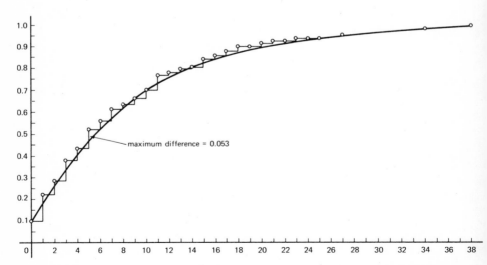

FIG. IX-2   Empirical and theoretical distributions for gap data for example problem.

TABLE IX-2
GAP DATA FOR EXAMPLE PROBLEM

Length	Digits 0	1	2	3	4	5	6	7	8	9	Summary of gaps Observed	Expected	Cumulative distribution Theoretical	Empirical	Difference
0		1	2	1		2	1		2		9	9.0	0.100	0.100	0
1	2		3	4	1		1				11	8.1	0.190	0.220	0.03
2	3		1		2						6	7.3	0.271	0.289	0.018
3	1		2		1	1	3				8	6.6	0.344	0.378	0.034
4	1	1	1		1		1	1			6	5.9	0.410	0.444	0.035
5	1		1	2	1	1		1			7	5.3	0.469	0.522	0.053
6	1		1	1		1					4	4.8	0.522	0.567	0.045
7		1		2		1		1			5	4′3	0.570	0.622	0.052
8			1				1				2	3.9	0.613	0.644	0.031
9		1			1						2	3.5	0.651	0.667	0.016
10			1	1			1				3	3.1	0.686	0.700	0.014
11		1	2	1	1		1				6	2.8	0.718	0.767	0.049
12	1										1	2.5	0.746	0.778	0.032
13			1								1	2.3	0.771	0.789	0.018
14						1					1	2.1	0.794	0.800	0.006
15	1	1	1				1				4	1.9	0.815	0.844	0.029
16					1						1	1.7	0.833	0.856	0.023
17		1					1				2	1.5	0.850	0.878	0.028
18	1	1									2	1.4	0.865	0.900	0.035
19											0	1.2	0.878	0.900	0.022
20							1				1	1.1	0.891	0.911	0.020
21					1						1	1.0	0.902	0.922	0.020
22						1					1	0.9	0.911	0.933	0.022
23						1					1	0.8	0.920	0.944	0.022
24											0	0.7	0.928	0.944	0.016
25											0	0.6	0.935	0.944	0.009
26				1							1	0.6	0.942	0.956	0.014
27											0	0.6	0.948	0.956	0.008
28											0	0.5	0.953	0.956	0.003
29	1										1	0.5	0.958	0.967	0.009
30											0	0.4	0.962	0.967	0.005
31						1					1	0.4	0.966	0.978	0.012
32											0	0.3	0.969	0.978	0.009
33											0	0.3	0.972	0.978	0.006
34											0	0.3	0.975	0.978	0.003
35											0	0.3	0.977	0.978	0.001
36			1								1	0.3	0.980	0.989	0.009
37											0	0.2	0.982	0.987	0.005
38			1								1	0.2	0.984	1.000	0.016

test. However, we will now concatenate the numbers into a string of single digits:

```
1 0 3 7 0 8 9 9 1 2 6 6 3 1 8 5 6 3 7 3 3 2 0 4 6
8 0 2 9 9 7 4 1 0 7 7 3 2 4 2 7 6 6 4 1 9 0 9 8 0
3 4 4 5 0 2 0 5 0 3 1 3 7 4 0 9 7 0 3 6 7 6 8 2 6
4 7 4 6 4 3 4 3 4 2 3 3 8 6 4 3 6 3 5 6 8 9 0 3 5
```

Ninety different gaps are identified by considering each digit to occupy a different interval. The empirical and theoretical frequency distributions in Table IX-2 are obtained. These two distributions are plotted in Fig. IX-2. The maximum difference between the theoretical and empirical distribution is found to be 0.053. Since the critical value for a Kolmogorov–Smirnov test on the 90% significance level is 0.13, H_0 is accepted as true.

C. EXPONENTIALLY DISTRIBUTED VARIATES

1. The Distribution Function

The exponential distribution is frequently used to describe interarrival times in queueing simulations. Its suitability for this purpose stems from its key postulate that the probability that an event takes place in a given short interval is proportional to the length of the interval and is independent of events prior to the interval. This is often a valid assumption for queueing type situations.

The exponential distribution is defined as

$$f(x) = \lambda e^{-\lambda x}, \qquad 0 \leqslant x < \infty,$$

$$F(x) = \int_0^x f(t)\, dt = \int_0^x \lambda e^{-\lambda t}\, dt = [1 - e^{-\lambda t}]_0^x = 1 - e^{-\lambda x}.$$

The mean of the function is

$$E(x) = \int_0^\infty t f(t)\, dt = \int_0^\infty t \lambda e^{-\lambda t}\, dt = \frac{1}{\lambda}.$$

The variance is

$$\mathrm{Var}(x) = \int_0^\infty (t - E(x))^2 f(t)\, dt = \int_0^\infty \left(t - \frac{1}{\lambda}\right)^2 \lambda e^{-\lambda t}\, dt = \frac{1}{\lambda^2}.$$

Relevant parameters for this and other distributions are summarized in Table IX-3.

TABLE IX-3
Summary of Random Variables, Distribution Functions, and Generators

Distribution	Random variable	Range	Mean	Var	Functions	Generator
Uniform	U	$0 \leqslant U \leqslant 1$	$\dfrac{1}{2}$	$\dfrac{1}{12}$	$f(x) = 1 \quad F(x) = x$	$U_{i+1} = AU_i \bmod(B)$
Uniform	$R(a,b)$	$a \leqslant R \leqslant b$ $-\infty < a < b < \infty$	$\dfrac{a+b}{2}$	$\dfrac{(a+b)^2}{12}$	$f(x) = \dfrac{1}{a+b} \quad F(x) = \dfrac{x}{a+b}$	$R = a + U(b-a)$
Exponential	$E(\lambda)$	$0 \leqq E$ $0 < \lambda < \infty$	$\dfrac{1}{\lambda}$	$\dfrac{1}{\lambda^2}$	$f(x) = \lambda e^{-\lambda x}$ $F(x) = 1 - e^{-\lambda x}$	$E = -\dfrac{1}{\lambda}\log U$
Erlang	$Z(\lambda, k)$	$0 < Z$ $0 < \lambda < \infty$ $k = 1, 2, \ldots$	$\dfrac{k}{\lambda}$	$\dfrac{k}{\lambda^2}$	$f(x) = \dfrac{\lambda^k x^{k-1} e^{-\lambda x}}{(k-1)!}$	$Z = \sum\limits_{i=1}^{k} E_i = \dfrac{\log \prod_{i=1}^{k} U_i}{\lambda}$
Normal	$N(\mu, \sigma)$	$-\infty < N < \infty$ $0 < \sigma < \infty$	μ	σ^2	$f(x) = \dfrac{1}{\sigma\sqrt{2\pi}}\exp\left(-\dfrac{1}{2}\left[\dfrac{x-\mu}{\sigma}\right]^2\right)$	$N = \left(\sum\limits_{i=1}^{12} U_i - 6\right)\sigma + \mu$
Chi-square	$\chi(n)$	$0 < \chi < \infty$ $n = 1, 2, \ldots$	n	$2n$	$f(x) = \dfrac{x^{n/2-1}e^{-n/2}}{[n/2-1]!\,2^{n/2}}$	$\chi = \sum\limits_{i=1}^{n} N_i^2$ For even n's use $\chi = Z(n/2, 1/2)$
Poisson	$P(\lambda)$	$P = 0, 1, \ldots$ $0 < \lambda < \infty$	λ	λ	$\Pr(P = k) = \dfrac{e^{-\lambda}\lambda^k}{k!}$	$\prod\limits_{i=1}^{P} U_i \geqslant e^{-\lambda} > \prod\limits_{i=1}^{P+1} U_i$

2. Generation of Random Deviates $E(\lambda)$

For any random deviate x drawn from any distribution function F, there corresponds a unique, uniformly distributed random variable p such that $F(\chi) = p$. (In fact p is the probability that a random deviate drawn from F is less than x.) Thus, the distribution function F specifies the value of p for a given x. In certain cases the reverse mapping is possible and the value of x for a given p can be computed as $x = F^{-1}(p)$. This is referred to as the principle of *inverse transformation*.

The exponential distribution offers an example of application of this principle to the generation of random deviates:

$$r = F(t) = 1 - e^{-\lambda t}, \qquad 1 - r = e^{-\lambda t},$$

$$\log(1-r) = -\lambda t, \qquad t = -(1/\lambda)\log(1-r).$$

Random deviates from an exponential distribution E with mean equal to $1/\lambda$ can now be generated by drawing a random number U between 0 and 1 and using the transformation

$$E = -\frac{1}{\lambda}\log U.$$

U is used in place of $1 - U$ to reduce the amount of effort required to determine E. Clearly both U and $1 - U$ are uniformly·distributed random deviates between 0 and 1.

D. ERLANG DISTRIBUTED VARIATES

1. The Distribution Function

The Erlang distribution has been proven to be useful in describing the arrival process in complex queueing systems. Thus, a close kinship between the Erlang and exponential distribution is to be expected. In fact, the Erlang random variable Z is the sum of k independent exponentially distributed random variables E, *each* with a mean of $1/\lambda$. Thus, in the special case of $k = 1$, the Erlang and exponential distributions are identical.

The Erlang distribution is defined as

$$f(x,k) = \frac{\lambda^k x^{(k-1)} e^{-\lambda x}}{(k-1)!}, \qquad k = 1, 2, \ldots,$$

$$F(x,k) = 1 - e^{-\lambda x} \sum_{m=1}^{k} \frac{(\lambda x)^{m-1}}{(m-1)!}.$$

When k is allowed to be noninteger, the Erlang distribution is generalized into the Gamma distribution.

The mean and variance of these distributions are

$$E(x) = k/\lambda \quad \text{and} \quad \text{Var}(x) = k/\lambda^2.$$

These parameters can easily be derived from the Erlang density function. However, they follow immediately from the fact that an Erlang random variable is defined as the sum of k independent exponential random variables.

2. Generation of Random Deviates $Z(K, \lambda)$

Erlang distributed random deviates may be generated by summing up exponentially distributed deviates:

$$Z = \sum_{i=1}^{k} E_i = \sum_{i=1}^{k} -\frac{1}{\lambda} \log U_i = -\frac{1}{\lambda} [\log U_1 + \log U_2 + \cdots + \log U_k].$$

The calculation of these logarithms is a fairly time consuming endeavor. Thus, we use one of the fundamental laws of logarithms to reduce the number of logarithms that need to be computed:

$$Z = -\frac{1}{\lambda} \log(U_1 U_2 \cdots U_k) = -\frac{1}{\lambda} \log \prod_{i=1}^{k} U_i.$$

An efficient FORTRAN function for calculation of Erlang distributed random deviates is given in Fig. IX-3.

```
      FUNCTION ERLANG(TMEAN ,K)
      REAL LAMBDA
C
C THIS FUNCTION GENERATES AN ERLANG DISTRIBUTED RANDOM  DEVIATE
      LAMBDA=K/TMEAN
C
      ERLANG=0.
      IF(LAMBDA.GT.0.)GOTO 1000
      WRITE(6,100)LAMBDA
  100 FORMAT('  ERLANG(AMEAN,K) AMEAN =',F8.2,' IS NEGATIVE!)
      RETURN
 1000 ERLANG=TMEAN
      IF(K.GT.0.AND.K.LE.100)GOTO 1010
      WRITE(6,101) K
  101 FORMAT('  ERLANG(AMEAN,K) K =',I8,' IS NOT BETWEEN 1 AND 100')
      RETURN
 1010 PROD = 1.
      DO 1020 I = 1,K
        PROD = PROD * UNIF(0.,1.)
 1020 CONTINUE
      IF(PROD.LE.0)GOTO 1030
      ERLANG=-ALOG(PROD)/LAMBDA
      RETURN
 1030 ERLANG=1./LAMBDA
      RETURN
      END
```

FIG. IX-3 FORTRAN function for generation of Erlang distributed random deviates.

E. NORMALLY DISTRIBUTED VARIATES

1. The Distribution Function

A large number of natural processes may be described by random deviates drawn from a normal distribution with a given mean μ and variance σ^2. Furthermore, the law of large numbers states that when independent random variates of any distribution are sufficiently aggregated, they too follow the normal distribution. In mathematical terms this law is stated as:

$$\Pr\left\{\lim_{n\to\infty}\left[\frac{\sum_{i=n}^{n}r_i-n\mu}{\sqrt{n}\,\sigma}<b\right]\right\}=\Phi\left(\frac{b-\mu}{\sigma}\right)$$

The normal distribution is defined as

$$f(x)=\frac{1}{\sigma\sqrt{2\pi}}\exp\left(-\frac{1}{2}\frac{(y-\mu)^2}{\sigma^2}\right),\qquad E(x)=\mu,\qquad \mathrm{Var}(x)=\sigma^2$$

This function may be *normalized* to a function with $\mu=0$ and $\sigma=1$ by the substitutions

$$x=\frac{y-\mu}{\sigma}$$

$$\phi(x)=f\left(\frac{y-\mu}{\sigma}\right)=\frac{1}{\sqrt{2\pi}}\exp\left(-\frac{x}{2}\right)^2,\qquad \Phi(x)=P(Y<y)=F\left(\frac{y-\mu}{\sigma}\right)$$

Both $\phi(x)$ and $\Phi(x)$ are readily available in standard tables.

2. Generation of Random Deviates $N(v,\sigma)$

It follows from the law of large numbers that $x=\lim_{n\to\infty}\sum_{i=1}^{n}r_i$ is normally distributed regardless of the distribution of r_i. If r_i is drawn from the uniform distribution, it can be shown that x is approximately normally distributed for any $n\geq 10$. The mean of the uniform distribution is $\frac{1}{2}$ and the variance of the distribution is $\frac{1}{12}$. Thus an approximately normally distributed variable with $v=0$ and $\sigma=1$ can be generated as

$$N=\frac{\sum_{i=1}^{n}U_i-n/2}{\sqrt{n}\cdot(1/\sqrt{12})}$$

This expression can be substantially simplified if n is chosen to be 12.

$$N=\frac{\sum_{i=1}^{12}U_i-6}{\sqrt{12}\,(1/\sqrt{12})}=\sum_{i=1}^{12}U_i-6.$$

```
      FUNCTION ANORM(AMEAN,STDV)
C
C THIS FUNCTION GENERATES A NORMALLY DISTRIBUTED RANDOM
C DEVIATE WITH THE SPECIFIED MEAN AND VARIANCE
C
      ANORM=AMEAN
      IF(STDV.GT.0.)GOTO 1000
      WRITE(6,100)STDV
  100 FORMAT(' ANORM(AMEAN,STDV) STDV ='F8.2,' IS ZERO OR NEGATIVE')
      RETURN
 1000 SUM = -6.0
      DO 1010 I = 1,12
        SUM = SUM + UNIF(0.,1.)
 1010 CONTINUE
      ANORM=SUM*STDV+AMEAN
      RETURN
      END
```

FIG. IX-4 FORTRAN function for generation of normally distributed random deviates.

To generate normally distributed random deviates with an arbitrary (but known) mean and variance the expression is modified as

$$N = \left(\sum_{i=1}^{12} U_i - 6 \right) \sigma + \mu.$$

A FORTRAN function utilizing this expression to generate normally distributed deviates with a mean μ and variance σ is given in Fig. IX-4.

F. CHI-SQUARE DISTRIBUTED VARIATES

1. The Distributed Function

The chi-square distribution is a skewed distribution which frequently fits empirically collected data reasonably well. Thus, there is often a need to generate chi-square distributed random deviates in simulation models of different kinds.

A chi-square random variable with n degree of freedom is the sum of n independent, squared, normal random deviates with $v = 0$ and $\sigma = 1$:

$$\chi = \sum_{i=1}^{n} N_i^2 .$$

The chi-square density function is

$$f(x) = \frac{1}{2^{n/2}(n/2-1)!} x^{n/2-1} e^{-x/2}, \qquad 0 \leqslant x < \infty, \quad n = 1, 2, \ldots,$$

and

$$E(x) = n, \qquad \text{Var}(x) = 2n.$$

2. Generation of Random Deviates $x(n)$

By substituting $k = n/2$ and by introducing the constant $\lambda = \frac{1}{2}$, we get

$$f(x) = \frac{1}{(k-1)!}\left(\frac{1}{2}\right)^k x^{k-1} e^{-x/2} = \frac{1}{(k-1)!} \lambda^k x^{k-1} e^{-x/2}.$$

This, of course, is the density function for the Erlang distribution. Thus, for even values of n (such that $n/2$ is an integer), a chi-square random deviate with n degrees of freedom is identical to an Erlang deviate with $k = n/2$ and $\lambda = \frac{1}{2}$.

For deviates with an odd number of degrees of freedom, an alternate approach is necessary. In this case, we utilize the original chi-square process differently and generate the deviate as $\sum_{i=1}^{n} N_i^2$. In Fig. IX-5 we present a FORTRAN function for the generation of random deviates from the chi-square distribution with N degrees of freedom.

```
      FUNCTION CHISQ(N)
C
C THIS FUNCTION GENERATES CHI-SQUARE DISTRIBUTED RANDOM
C DEVIATES WITH N DEGREES OF FREEDOM
C
      CHISQ=0.
      IF(N.GT.0.AND.N.LE.100)GOTO 1000
      WRITE(6,100) N
  100 FORMAT(' CHISQ(N) N =',I8,' IS NOT BETWEEN 1 AND 100')
      RETURN
C---------------------------------------------------------------
 1000 K=N/2
      IF(N.GT.K*2)GOTO 1020
C
C DEGREES OF FREEDOM IS EVEN. GENERATE DEVIATE FROM ERLANG
C DISTRIBUTION WITH K = N/2 AND LAMBDA = 1/2
C
      PROD = 1.
      DO 1010 I = 1,K
        PROD = PROD * UNIF(0.,1.)
 1010 CONTINUE
      CHISQ=PROD*2.
      RETURN
C---------------------------------------------------------------
 1020 CONTINUE
C
C ODD NUMBER OF DEGREES OF FREEDOM. GENERATE DEVIATE AS SUM
C OF N SQUARED NORMAL DEVIATES WITH MEAN = 0. AND VAR = 1.
C
      CHISQ = 0.
      DO 1040 I = 1,N
        ANORM = -6.
        DO 1030 J = 1,12
          ANORM = ANORM + UNIF(0.,1.)
 1030   CONTINUE
        CHISQ = CHISQ + ANORM * ANORM
 1040 CONTINUE
      RETURN
      END
```

FIG. IX-5 FORTRAN function for generation of chi-square distributed random deviates.

G. POISSON DISTRIBUTED VARIATES

1. The Distribution Function

The Poisson distribution describes the *number of events* (P) that take place in an interval of unit length on the assumption that the interval between individual events follows the exponential distribution with a mean of $1/\lambda$. The Poisson distribution is defined as

$$\Pr(P = k) = \frac{e^{-\lambda}\lambda^k}{k!}$$

The corresponding mean and variance are

$$E(P) = \lambda \quad \text{and} \quad \text{Var}(P) = \lambda.$$

2. Generation of Random Deviates $P(\lambda)$

Poisson deviates are obtained by counting how many randomly generated events with exponentially distributed interarrival times with a mean of $1/\lambda$ fit in an interval of unit length

$$\sum_{i=1}^{P} E_i \leqslant 1 < \sum_{i=1}^{P+1} E_i.$$

To improve the efficiency of this procedure, we modify the above relationship slightly:

$$\sum_{i=1}^{P} -\frac{1}{\lambda}\log(U_i) \leqslant 1 < \sum_{i=1}^{P+1} -\frac{1}{\lambda}\log(U_i),$$

$$-\frac{1}{\lambda}\log\prod_{i=1}^{P} U_i \leqslant 1 < -\frac{1}{\lambda}\log\prod_{i=1}^{P+1} U_i,$$

$$\prod_{i=1}^{P} U_i \geqslant e^{-\lambda} > \prod_{i=1}^{P+1} U_i.$$

We now see that Poisson deviates can be obtained by forming the products of consecutive uniformly distributed random variables until the value of the product falls below $e^{-\lambda}$. The deviate is one less than the number of terms in this product. In Fig. IX-6 we show a FORTRAN function that implements this procedure.

```
      FUNCTION IPOISN(AMEAN)
C
C THIS FUNCTION GENERATES POISSON DISTRIBUTED RANDOM DEVIATES
C WITH MEAN LAMBDA
C
      IF(AMEAN.GT.0.AND.AMEAN.LE.100)GOTO 1000
      WRITE(6,100)AMEAN
  100 FORMAT(' IPOISN(AMEAN) AMEAD ='F8.2,' IS NOT BETWEEN 0 AND 100')
      RETURN
C
 1000 CONST = EXP(-AMEAN)
      PROD = 1.
 1010 PROD = PROD * UNIF(0.,1.)
      IF(PROD.LT.CONST)RETURN
      IPOISN=IPOISN+1
      IF(IPOISN.GT.999)RETURN
      GOTO 1010
      END
```

FIG. IX-6   FORTRAN function for generation of Poisson distributed random deviates.

PROBLEMS

1. Write a program that performs a Kolmogorov–Smirnov test on the distribution of numbers generated by a uniform random number generator such as the one in Fig. IX-1. Use a significance level of 10%.

2. Repeat Problem 1 for the chi-square test.

3. Repeat Problem 1 for the run test.

4. Repeat Problem 1 for the gap test.

5. Modify the random number generator in Fig. VIII-2 to generate 10 independent streams of numbers.

6. Write a FORTRAN function able to provide exponentially distributed random deviates with mean $1/\lambda$ from any of 10 independent streams of deviates.

7. The normal distribution is a good approximation for the Erlang distribution for large values of k. Determine a realistic maximum value for which the function in Fig. IX-3 is practical or feasible. Modify this function to generate normal deviates with appropriate parameters for larger values of k.

8. Determine a reasonable upper limit of N for the chi-square random deviate generator in Fig. IX-5. Modify the function to reject requests for deviates with higher degrees of freedom.

9. Repeat Problem 8 for the Poisson generator in Fig. IX-6.

10. What is the cycle length of a multiplicative congruential generator with $\mu_0 = 1$, $a = 10$, and $m = 23$?

11. What happens when the generator in Problem 10 is modified such that $m = 25$?

12. Test the assumption that the last four columns of digits in a telephone directory may be used as a source of uniformly distributed random digits.

BIBLIOGRAPHY

Fishman, G. S., *Concepts and Methods in Discrete Event Simulation*. Wiley, New York, 1976.

Gordon, G., *System Simulation*. Prentice-Hall, Englewood Cliffs, New Jersey, 1969.

Greenberger, M., "Methods of Randomness," *Comm. ACM* **8**, No. 3 (March 1965), 177–179.

Hutchinson, D. W., "A New Uniform Pseudo Random Number Generator," *Comm. ACM* **9**, No. 6 (June 1966), 432–433.

Lewis, P. A. W., A. S. Goodman, and J. M. Miller, "A Pseudo Random Number Generator for the System 360," *IBM Systems J.* **8**, (1969) 136–149.

Knuth, D. E., *The Art of Computer Programming*. Vol. 2, Seminumerical Algorithm. Addison-Wesley, Reading, Massachusetts, 1969.

Rand Corporation, *A Million Random Digits with 1,000,000 Normal Deviates*, Free Press, 1955.

Schmidt, J. W., and R. E. Taylor, *Simulation and Analysis of Industrial Systems*, Richard D. Irwin, Inc., Homewood Illinois, 1970.

CHAPTER X

DISCRETE EVENT SIMULATION PROGRAMMING

A. INTRODUCTION

Discrete event simulation models are used to study performance characteristics of simple waiting line systems (such as bank tellers and barbershops) as well as of more complex queueing systems (such as steelmills and aircraft flight patterns). All discrete event simulation models describe how "customers" or "entities" flow through a system over time. A basic premise which applies to such models is that all changes in the state of a system are instantaneous changes at specific points in time. Such changes are discrete (as opposed to continuous), and the occasion of such a change can be termed an event—thus, the term "discrete event simulation" is explained.

The two main advantages of adopting a discrete event philosophy when a complex system is to be modeled, studied, and analyzed are (1) that all discrete event models can be synthesized from a set of basic building blocks or components and (2) that computer languages are available to allow the analyst to put together simulation models based on these building blocks.

Several different special purpose computer simulation languages such as GPSS or SIMSCRIPT are available. Such languages are particularly useful to describe certain classes of simulation problems. However, they lack the versatility of general purpose languages such as FORTRAN.

In this text, we are primarily concerned with discrete event simulation models. However, there are several other model classes, the most important of these is the class of continuous time or dynamic simulation models. Models in this class differ from discrete event models in that changes are assumed to take place continuously over time. Dynamic simulation models are well-suited for analysis of situations involving feedback and control.

B. ELEMENTS OF A DISCRETE EVENT SIMULATION MODEL

1. Two Modeling Philosophies

Two fundamentally different approaches to discrete event simulation modeling are available. We shall illustrate these by modeling a simple two chair barbershop situation (Fig. X-1) both ways.

First, as shown in Fig. X-2, the situation can be described in a diagram by showing the potential flows of the customer through the system. Termed a *process flow* diagram, each block in this diagram describes an activity related to the customer as he passes through the shop. These activities may involve instantaneous events (such as occupy chair); however, certain activities take time (such as the haircut) or imply a wait (such as the queue).

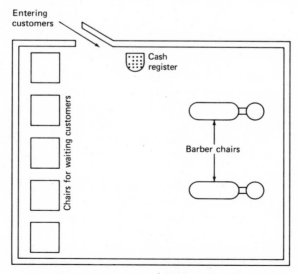

FIG. X-1 Simple two chair barbershop situation.

FIG. X-2 Process flow model for barbershop.

In addition, the diagram may allow for a conditional branching or the splitting of a customer into several different entities. While the process flow diagram describes how a single customer may flow through the system, the rate of arrival of customers may be such that many different customers actually occupy the system at one time. The most prominent simulation language based on the process flow modeling approach is the GPSS family of simulation languages.

An alternative to the process approach is the *event scheduling* approach as illustrated in Fig. X-3. This approach is centered around two key items: (a) individual descriptions of events that change the state of the system at various points in time and (b) a dynamically changing "list of future events" that keeps track of when these events are to take place. SIMSCRIPT, GASP, and WIDES (Chapter 1) are typical event scheduling oriented simulation languages.

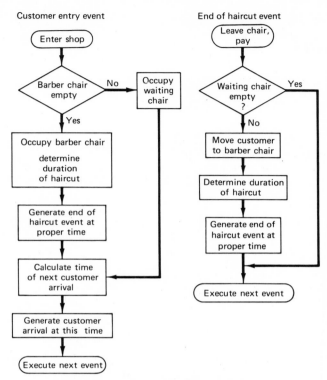

FIG. X-3 Event based model of barbershop.

2. Entity Attributes

It is assumed that the state of a system at any given instant is described by the states of the entities in the system at that time (e.g., how many customers are waiting for a haircut, how many are currently receiving haircuts, etc.). Individual entities are described by their *attributes*. The barbershop customers may, for example, be described by the attributes

(1) sex,
(2) age,
(3) length of hair,
(4) money in pocket,
(5) time of arrival (i.e., time entity was created).

While attributes 1, 2, and 5 (hopefully) do not change during the visit to the barbershop, attributes 3 and 4 clearly will. It is possible to develop simulation models where the entities are not described by any attributes at all, but the concept of attributes is an important one and most simulation languages allow an entity to be described by several different attributes. These attributes will be affiliated with the particular entity as it moves through the simulated system.

3. Queues

Discrete event simulation models usually take the form of an interacting network of queues and service centers. In the barbershop example, customers waiting for a haircut form a queue as do customers waiting to pay for their haircut. While the content and configuration of queues depend upon the particular problem being studied, each queue is subject to a specific "discipline":

(1)   Entries in the queue are ranked on the value of one of their attributes.
(2)   The queue is ordered in either increasing or decreasing value of this attribute.

The barbershop customers waiting for a haircut would, for example, be most likely to be ranked on attribute 5 (time of entry), with lowest value first (first come, first served).

Computer based discrete event simulation models must include subroutines that (1) can automatically insert a new entry in a queue in its proper place, (2) can remove the first entry in the queue (when it is to be served), and (3) do collect data on the utilization of the queue.

4. Events

The state of an entity is described by the value of its attributes. These values are changed by specific events. One of the main tasks in modeling a system for a discrete event simulation study is to identify all the different events that may take place and to describe the different inputs to and outputs from such events. For example, the events in the barbershop may be as follows:

(1)   Customer enters.
(2)   Customer sits down in chair.
(3)   Barber finishes haircut.
(4)   Customer leaves.

An event may be modeled either as a *recurrent* event or as a *triggered* event. A recurrent event is one that, among other things, generates a similar event to take place some time in the future. A triggered event is one that is caused by some action taking place inside the simulated system (such as barber finishing haircut). In addition, some models require exogenous events (these are manually scheduled events assumed to have originated in the environment).

When the event scheduling approach is used, the identification and description of all events is left to the user—while the simulation language processor takes care of the scheduling of these events at proper times.

When the process flow approach is used, the model does not always explicitly describe events. However, the language processor identifies all implied events, and events are scheduled just as for the event scheduling approach. In this case, the event subroutines are intrinsic elements of the language processor rather than of the user written program.

5. Random Number Generators

Discrete event simulation models duplicate the pattern of the naturally occurring variations in the intervals between events in real life by random numbers. These are drawn from probability distributions with appropriately specified parameters. Likewise, naturally occurring random variations in attribute values in real life are duplicated by drawing random numbers from probability distribution functions with appropriately specified parameters.

Thus, generation of random variables is a necessary function of any computer based discrete event simulation model. The development of random number generators suitable for discrete event simulation models were discussed in Chapter IX.

C. THE ADVANTAGE OF COMPUTER SIMULATION LANGUAGES

A language is a set of symbols with affiliated semantical and syntactic rules. A computer simulation language is a language designed so that it can be used to describe commonly occurring problem situations and so that descriptions in the language are readily translated (via a compiler or a program generator) into an executable computer simulation program. Thus, a computer simulation language serves two purposes: (a) it is a modeling language (focusing on the problem situation), and (b) it is a higher level programming language (focusing on the computer). The hierarchy of operations performed in the development of a computer simulation program using a simulation language is shown in Fig. X-4.

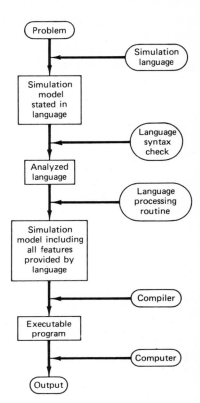

FIG. X-4   Hierarchy of simulation model processing.

1.   Modeling

As a modeling language, a simulation language assists the modeler by providing a modeling framework (such as the one discussed in Section B) and thus by providing "building blocks" corresponding to typical elements and operations in the problem situation. Modeling is substantially simplified when the modeling philosophy of a particular language is adopted. This is because the specific kinds of things that the model is to contain are now specified and the otherwise infinitely many design choices are correspondingly reduced.

All discrete event simulation languages provide a modeling framework essentially similar to the one presented in Section B (but note the two alternative timeflow mechanisms (discrete event and process flow)). However, some languages are substantially richer in modeling elements and operations than others. To illustrate a particularly powerful modeling language we will in the next chapter review aspects of modeling using the GPSS language. Since the choice of language frequently is a compromise between many factors such as cost, suitability and resource requirements, we will also in that chapter review model and program development in a simpler and less resource demanding (but still powerful and easy to use) language called WIDES.

2. Programming

A simulation language is also a significant programming aid. This is because the language has affiliated with it a compiler or preprocessor that causes the model description to be translated into an executable program. This processor or compiler first checks for logical inconsistencies in the model, then it "blows" the model up into an executable model by adding code to perform most of the tasks required by a model utilizing the modeling philosophy of the language. Among program segments added to the model are segments to

(1)   include models of specific kinds of events,
(2)   perform event scheduling and control,
(3)   initialize and maintain data structure for entity, queue, and facility handling,
(4)   perform data collection,
(5)   perform report printing,
(6)   facilitate program begunning and checking.

To illustrate how some of these tasks are performed, we will in the next section review the design of a "minimal" simulation language.

D. A BASIC SIMULATION FACILITY

To illustrate key aspects of the internal design of most simulation programs (whether user written or processor generated), we will review the design of a simple "language" designed more for its simplicity, transparency, and ease of understanding than for its generality and flexibility. However, most of the principles utilized in this simple design do extrapolate to more general situations. For convenience we will refer to the language presented here by its acronym BSF.

1. Modeling Philosophy

The modeling philosophy employed in this language incorporates the concepts of entities, queues, and events discussed in Section B. Each entity is described by two user defined and one program assigned (time of insertion) attribute. The order of entities in a particular queue is established such that the values of the first attribute of the entities appear in increasing order. Two model operations are provided. INSERT places an entity in the proper place in a queue and REMOVE removes the entity at the head of the queue from the queue. Two auxiliary operations are also provided. INIT initializes the data base automatically maintained by the language, and REPORT calculates appropriate values and prints performance reports. Data is collected on the current size, average size, and total throughput for each file.

The language does not perform automatic event scheduling. However, one of the files in the data structure is reserved for the future event file. Future events are inserted into this file with the time of the event as the first attribute and the event code as the second attribute. The time and type of the next event is therefore always found by removing the head of this file.

2. The Data Base

The most important element of any simulation language or program is its internally generated and maintained data base. The purpose of this data base is at a minimum to

(a)   maintain a record of the status of the system at any time (such as the count of entries in a queue),

(b)   facilitate the implementation of changes in the system (such as removing an entity from a queue),

(c)   accumulate data required for performance reports (such as the total wait time in a queue),

(d)   maintain the future events file.

Thus, the design of the data base reflects both the modeling philosophy of the language and the kinds of model manipulation and data collection features that the language can accommodate.

a.   Data Records

The data base may conceptually be split into two parts. The first part contains sets of data items collected for each of the different modeling constructs (such as files) allowed by the system. It is convenient to refer to the set of data items collected for a particular construct as a *record* of data items. For example, a record containing performance data for a particular file may contain the following data items:

(1)   current file length,

(2)   count of all items inserted into the file,

(3)   total time spent in the file by all removed items,

(4) sum of the time spent in the file by all removed items,
(5) maximum file length,
(6) minimum file length,
(7) time of last activity involving the file.

Most simulation programs and languages are designed for a fixed number of different modeling elements. Thus the corresponding number of data records is fixed and this part of the data base can be maintained in an array with two dimensions (the first identifying the record (or file) number, and the second identifying the specific data item).

b. Entity Records

The second part of the data base is concerned with the maintenance of the content of the many changing files that the model may include. This content typically includes entities assigned to a given queue or events stored in the future events file. It is convenient to group all data related to a given event or entity into a single record. This record will for simplicity be referred to as the *entity record.*

Since the content of different files will be dynamically changing throughout the life of the simulation run, it is not practical to use physical adjacency as the method for maintaining the ordering relationship of a file. Instead we must employ the list processing techniques discussed in Chapter II. To do this we must expand the entity record to include the appropriate forward (and perhaps backward) pointer to the record describing the next (or perhaps previous) entity in the file.

c. The Structure of the Data Base

A few other details must be included before the data base becomes a viable foundation for the execution of a simulation program. Since space limitations will restrict the number of entity records that we may use, it will be necessary to string together into a *garbage file* (similar to the garbage list in Chapter II) all records not used elsewhere. The formation of this file is a straightforward matter since each entity record already contains a position for the required forward pointer. As in Chapter II, we will then take records from this file when needed, and we will return records back to this file when they no longer are needed.

In order to be able to retrieve specific items in a file, it is also necessary to include pointers to the heads (and perhaps tails) of each linked list in the data base. This is readily done for all real (i.e., nongarbage files) by expanding the corresponding data records to include the appropriate pointers. For consistency and to simplify our programming effort, we store the pointer to the head of the garbage list in a special entity record (the *garbage head* record) serving no other purpose than as the root of the garbage list.

The construction of the structure of the data base is now essentially complete. We only need to introduce appropriate conventions to indicate the facts that a list is empty and that the tail (and perhaps head) of a list is reached. We chose to flag all these cases by fixing the appropriate pointer to point to the garbage head record. For example, the pointer to the head of a file points to the garbage head if the file is empty. This choice of terminal pointer was made since (as we saw in Chapter II) it greatly simplifies the accompanying computer programs by eliminating all special cases requiring special algorithm treatment.

We have now defined the data base of the BSF to consist of three different kinds of interrelated records, the contents of which are summarized in Fig. X-5. To illustrate how these records are interrelated, we present in Fig. X-6 an overview of the structure of a typical BSF data base representing three different user defined files (one of which is empty) and one garbage list.

d. A FORTRAN Implementation

We have developed a data base utilizing three different kinds of data records, the layouts of which are represented in Fig. X-5. These records could be stored in three different arrays. However, since all records are of the same length (4 words), substantial flexibility and programming convenience result

Pointer to first entity record	Current file size	Count of entities inserted into files	Total time spent in file by all removed entities

File headed record

Pointer to first entity record in garbage file	not used	not used	not used

Garbage head record

Pointer to next entity record in same file	Time record was assigned to current file	User assigned attribute	User assigned attribute

Entity record

FIG. X-5   Layout of data record for basic simulation facility.

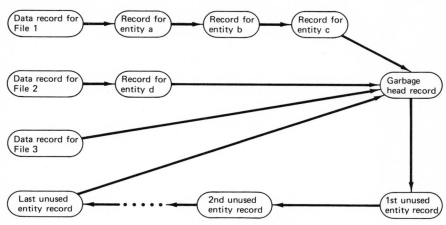

FIG. X-6 Structure of typical BSF data base.

if these records are all stored in a single array LIST, such that a column in LIST could be used either for a data record *or* an entity record. For additional flexibility we dimension the array to have 4 rows and *n* columns so that data items for a particular item are stored in physically adjacent locations. (Remember that the data in LIST is stored in the computer in a column-wise sequence in the following manner: LIST(1, 1), LIST(2, 1), LIST(3, 1), LIST(4, 1), LIST(2, 1), ...) This organization has the advantage of allowing a change in the size of LIST without changing the dimension statements in all subroutines. (A few compilers will not allow such changes if LIST is located in a common statement.)

Using this organization, the data base developed in this section can be stored in FORTRAN in the array LIST and the variable NFILES where

MAX number of columns in LIST.
NFILES Count of files in the system (excluding the garbage file).

and, if $I \leqslant$ NFILES

LIST(1, I) Pointer to column in LIST containing the data record for the entity at the head of file I. The value of this pointer is MAX if the file is empty.

LIST(2, I) Count of current number of entities in this file.
LIST(3, I) Count of total entities inserted into this file.
LIST(4, I) Accumulated total time spent by all items inserted into and removed from this file.

and, if NFILES $< I <$ MAX

```
      SUBROUTINE INIT(NFILE,MAXI)
      COMMON/LIST/NFILES,MAX,ITLAST,LIST(4,100)
      NFILES=NFILE
      MAX=MAXI
C
C
C         THIS SUBROUTINE INITIALIZES THE DATA STUCTURE FOR
C         THE 'BASIC SIMULATION FACILITY'.
C
C         FILE ORGANIZATION
C            HEAD OF I-TH FILE : LIST(1,I) = POINTER TO FIRST
C                                            ELEMENT IN FILE,
C                                LIST(2,I) = CURRENT FILE SIZE
C                                LIST(3,I) = COUNT OF INSERTIONS
C                                LIST(4,I) = AGGREGATED TIME
C                                            OF STAY IN FILE
C
C            FILE ELEMENTS     : LIST(1,I) = POINTER TO NEXT
C                                            ELEMENT IN FILE
C                                LIST(2,I) = TIME ELEMENT WAS
C                                            INSERTED
C                                LIST(3,I) = FIRST USER DEFINED
C                                            ATTRIBUTE (IA)
C                                LIST(4,I) = SECOND USER DEFINED
C                                            ATTRIBUTE (IB)
C            GARBAGE HEAD      :LIST(1,MAX)= POINTER TO FIRST
C                                            UNUSED LOCATION
C
C            NFILES            : COUNT OF FILES TO BE ACCOMODATED
C            MAX               : SECOND DIMENSION (I.E. CAPACITY)
C                                OF LIST
C            IT                : TIME SIMULATION STARTS
C
      DO 1000 I=1,MAX
      LIST(2,I)=0
      LIST(3,I)=0
      LIST(4,I)=0
 1000 CONTINUE
C
C         FLAG EMPTINESS OF FILES BY POINTING TO GARBAGE HEAD
C
      DO 1010 I=1,NFILES
      LIST(1,I)=MAX
 1010 CONTINUE
C
C         LINK GARBAGE LIST
C
      K=NFILES+1
      DO 1020 I=K,MAX
      LIST(1,I)=I+1
 1020 CONTINUE
      LIST(1,MAX)=K
C
C         SAVE START TIME
C
      ITLAST=0
      RETURN
      END
```

FIG. X-7   Program to initialize BSF data base.

LIST(1, I)   Pointer to column in LIST containing the next entity record belonging to the same file.

LIST(2, I)   Time entity described in this record was assigned to this file.

LIST(3, I)   User defined attribute. Entries in all files except the garbage file are ranked in increasing order on this attribute.

LIST(4, I)   User defined attribute.

Finally,

LIST(1, MAX)   Pointer to the head of the garbage list.

LIST(2, MAX) ⎫
LIST(3, MAX) ⎬ Undefined.
LIST(4, MAX) ⎭

In Fig. X-7 we present a FORTRAN subroutine that initializes the BSF data structure in the manner discussed here. The variables IT and ITLAST are used for data collection and error checking purposes. Their use will be discussed in the following section.

3. Instructions

BSF has four instructions, each of which takes the form of a FORTRAN subroutine call statement as follows:

CALL INIT(NFILES, MAX)   initializes the data structure as discussed in the previous section.

CALL INSERT(IQ, IT, IA, IB)   inserts an entity with attributes IA and IB into file IQ at time IT. The file is ranked in increasing order on attribute IA.

CALL REMOVE(IQ, IT, IA, IB)   removes the entity at the head of file IQ and returns its attributes in the variables IA and IB at time IT.

CALL REPORT(IT)   prints a summary report on file utilization at time IT.

Subroutine INSERT (Fig. X-8) was modeled after subroutine INSERT in Fig. II-8. However, the present subroutine handles many lists and performs several error checking and data collection features and is thus somewhat more complex. Two different error checks are made. First, the parameter IQ is checked for validity, then the parameter IT specifying the current simulated time is compared to the simulated time of the last BSF action. An error is detected if IT is not equal to or greater than this time.

If valid parameters are specified, a check is made to see if an unused entity record can be obtained from the garbage list. One is available unless the garbage head record points to itself.

```
      SUBROUTINE INSERT(IQ,IT,IA,IB)
      COMMON/LIST/NFILES,MAX,ITLAST,LIST(4,100)
C
C     THIS SUBROUTINE PERFORMS ALL LIST PROCESSING AND DATA
C     COLLECTION TASKS IN INSERTING AN ITEM INTO FILE IQ
C
C     CHECK IF A VALID FILE IS SPECIFIED
C
      IF(IQ.GT.0.AND.IQ.LE.NFILES) GO TO 1000
      WRITE(6,100) IQ,IT
  100 FORMAT(' CALL INSERT (',I3,') INVALID FILE AT T=',I5)
      RETURN
C
C     CHECK IF VALID TIME INCREMENT IS USED
C
 1000 IF(IT.GE.ITLAST) GO TO 1010
      WRITE(6,101)IQ,IT,ITLAST
  101 FORMAT(' CALL INSERT(',I3,')  NEW TIME LT OLD TIME' 2I5)
      RETURN
C
C     CHECK IF ENTITY RECORD IS AVAILABLE
C
 1010 ILOC=LIST(1,MAX)
      IF(ILOC.LT.MAX) GO TO 1015
      WRITE(6,102) IQ,IT
  102 FORMAT(' CALL INSERT (',I3,') LIST IS FULL AT T =',I5)
      RETURN
C
C     SCAN LIST TO FIND POSITION OF NEW ITEM
C
 1015 IPRED=IQ
      I=LIST(1,IQ)
 1020 IF(I.GE.MAX) GO TO 1030
      IF(LIST(3,I).GT.IA) GO TO 1030
      IPRED=I
      I=LIST(1,I)
      GO TO 1020
C
C     MOVE ELEMENT FROM HEAD OF GARBAGE LIST TO FILE IQ
C
 1030 LIST(1,MAX)=LIST(1,ILOC)
      LIST(1,IPRED)=ILOC
      LIST(1,ILOC)=I
C
C     SAVE ATTRIBUTE VALUES
C
      LIST(2,ILOC)=IT
      LIST(3,ILOC)=IA
      LIST(4,ILOC)=IB
C
C     COLLECT PERFORMANCE DATA
C
      LIST(2,IQ)=LIST(2,IQ)+1
      LIST(3,IQ)=LIST(3,IQ)+1
      ITLAST=IT
      RETURN
      END
```

FIG. X-8   BSF subroutine INSERT.

If an entity record is available, a scan is made of the linked list representing the specified file to determine the logical position of the new entry in the file. This position is determined by the requirement that the file be ordered in such a way that entity attribute one (IA) appear in increasing order. Pointers are then changed to reassign the new entity record from the head of the garbage list to the proper position in the specified file.

Finally, the attribute values are saved and performance data is collected. Saved attribute values include the user specified attributes IA and IB and the BSF assigned attribute "time of insertion" (IT).

Subroutine REMOVE (Fig. X-9) is modeled after subroutine REMOVE in Figure II-12. However the present subroutine is only able to remove the head of the list. On the other hand, the present subroutine includes error checking and data collection features not included in Fig. II-12 but similar to those in the above subroutine. The methods used in this subroutine are well-documented in Fig. X-9 and will not be repeated here.

Subroutine REPORT (Fig. X-10) prints a summary report on file utilization containing four items:

(a) file index, (IQ),
(b) current file size,
(c) total number of entities inserted into file,
(d) average length of stay in file.

Items (b) and (c) are copied from LIST$(2, IQ)$ and LIST$(3, IQ)$. To compute the average length of stay we first scan the file to compute the time spent in the file by the entities still there. To this quantity we add LIST$(4, IQ)$ (the length of stay of removed entities), then we divide this sum by LIST$(3, IQ)$ to get the average length of stay. Care is taken not to alter any of the data values in the data base (such as LIST$(4, IQ)$) in this operation since this data may be needed again later in the program.

4. An Example

We will now show how the data base and subroutines of the BSF may be used to develop and run a simulation model of the operation of the two chair barbershop discussed in Section B. The focus of this development will be the event based model of the barbershop presented in Fig. X-3. An overview of the model is given in Fig. X-11.

a. Events

Two model related events (customer arrival and customer departure) are recognized. Customer arrivals are modeled as recurrent events with a Poisson

```
      SUBROUTINE REMOVE(IQ,IT,IA,IB)
      COMMON/LIST/NFILES,MAX,ITLAST,LIST(4,100)
C
C        THIS SUBROUTINE PERFORMS ALL LIST PROCESSING AND DATA
C        COLLECTION TASKS WHEN REMOVING AN ITEM FROM FILE IQ
C
C        CHECK IF A VALID FILE IS SPECIFIED
C
      IF(IQ.GT.0.AND.IQ.LE.NFILES) GO TO 1000
      WRITE(6,100) IQ,IT
  100 FORMAT(I8,' IS INVALID FILE INDEX FOR REMOVAL REQUEST AT T =',I5)
      RETURN
C
C        CHECK FOR VALID TIME INCREMENT
C
 1000 IF(IT.GE.ITLAST) GO TO 1010
      WRITE(6,101)IQ,IT,ITLAST
  101 FORMAT(' CALL REMOVE(',I3,') NEGATIVE TIME INCREMENT',2I5)
      RETURN
C
C        IDENTIFY PHYSICAL LOCATION OF FILE HEAD
C
 1010 ILOC=LIST(1,IQ)
C
C        MAKE SURE FILE IS NOT EMPTY
C
      IF(ILOC.LT.MAX) GO TO 1020
      WRITE(6,102) IQ,IT
  102 FORMAT('  CALL REMOVE(',I3,') FILE IS EMPTY AT T =',I5)
      RETURN
C
C        RETURN ATTRIBUTE VALUES
C
 1020 IA=LIST(3,ILOC)
      IB=LIST(4,ILOC)
      ITLAST=IT
C
C        COLLECT PERFORMANCE STATISTICS
C
      LIST(2,IQ)=LIST(2,IQ)-1
      LIST(4,IQ)=LIST(4,IQ)=LIST(2,ILOC)+IT
C
C        MOVE ELEMENT FROM FILE TO GARBAGE LIST
C
      LIST(1,IQ)=LIST(1,ILOC)
      LIST(1,ILOC)=LIST(1,MAX)
      LIST(1,MAX)=ILOC
      RETURN
      END
```

FIG. X-9   BSF subroutine REMOVE.

distributed interarrival of 10 time units. End-of-service events are modeled as triggered events following the completion of a haircut with random length drawn from the Poisson distribution with a mean of 5. No other events are required to describe the steady state operation of the system. However, we chose to introduce a third event that causes the BSF to calculate and print a summary report and terminate the simulation run. This event is scheduled to occur after 100 time units.

```
      SUBROUTINE REPORT(IT)
      COMMON/LIST/NFILES,MAX,ITLAST,LIST(4,100)
C
C     THIS SUBROUTINE PRINTS A REPORT ON CURRENT AND AVERAGE
C     UTILIZATION OF FILES
C
C     CHECK FOR VALID TIME INCREMENT
C
      IF(IT.GE.ITLAST) GO TO 1000
      WRITE(6,100) IT,ITLAST
  100 FORMAT(' CALL REPORT(',I5,')  TIME LESS THAN TIME OF LAST ACTION
     *(',I5,')!')
      RETURN
 1000 ITLAST=IT
      WRITE(6,101) IT
  101 FORMAT(' SUMMARY REPORT AT T =',I8,//,' FILE    IN    OUT    NOW
     *AVG STAY  AVG LENGTH!')
      DO 1030 IQ=1,NFILES
      NIN=LIST(3,IQ)
      IF(NIN.LE.0) GO TO 1030
      NOUT=NIN-LIST(2,IQ)
      AVG=LIST(4,IQ)
C
C     ACCUMULATE WAIT TIMES FOR ITEMS CURRENTLY IN FILE
C
      J=LIST(1,IQ)
 1010 IF(J.GE.MAX) GO TO 1020
      AVG=AVG+IT-LIST(2,J)
      J=LIST(1,J)
      GO TO 1010
 1020 AN=AVG/IT
      AVG=AVG/NIN
      WRITE(6,102) IQ,NIN,NOUT,LIST(2,IQ),AVG,AN
  102 FORMAT(4I6,F9.2,F10.2)
 1030 CONTINUE
      RETURN
      END
      FUNCTION IPOISN(LAMBDA)
      REAL LAMBDA
C
C     THIS FUNCTION GENERATES POISSON DISTRIBUTED RANDOM
C     WITH MEAN LAMBDA
C
      IPOISN=0
      IF(LAMBDA.GT.0) GO TO 1000
      WRITE(6,100) LAMBDA
  100 FORMAT(' PARAMETER ERROR WHEN CALLING POISSON(LAMBDA),LAMBDA=',F1
     *0.2)
      RETURN
C
 1000 CONST=EXP(-LAMBDA)
      PROD=1.
 1010 PROD=PROD*RANU(0.,1.)
      IF(PROD.LT.CONST) RETURN
      IPOISN=IPOISN+1
      GO TO 1010
      END
```

FIG. X-10   BSF subroutine REPORT.

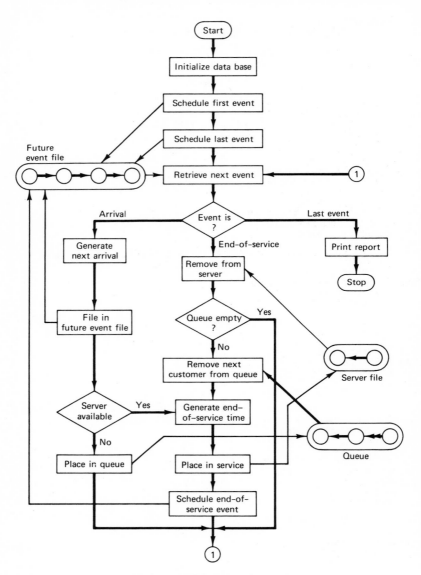

FIG. X-11   BSF simulation model.

b. Files

Three different files are used in this model. File 1 contains the queue of customers awaiting service. This queue is ranked FIFO. Since all files are ranked in increasing order on attribute 1 (IA), it is necessary to define the first attribute of all waiting customers equal to their time of arrival. The second attribute (IB) is not used for file 1.

File 2 contains the customers receiving service. Thus the average length of file 2 will give us the mean barber utilization, and the current length of file 2 (LIST(2, 2)) will yield the number of currently busy barbers. File 2 is ranked on the time of completion of service. (This is such that customers are removed from the file in the right order upon completion of service.)

File 3 is used to hold the file of future events. Events will be executed in the order in which they appear in this file. Thus, attribute 1 (IA) for file 3 is set equal to the time of the event.

c. The Program

The program implementing the two chair barbershop simulation model is shown in Fig. X-12. The initialization segment of the program includes the initialization of the clock to zero, the initialization of the data base to accommodate three files and 100 records, as well as the scheduling of the initial customer arrival event and the run termination event.

Events are removed from the future events file at statement 1000. If the event is a customer arrival (type 1) event, then the subsequent type 1 event is immediately scheduled by generating the time of the event as ITNEXT and by filing a record describing this event in the future events file. A check is then made to see if a barber is available. One is available if less than two entities are stored in file two. If one is available, then the end-of-service time is generated, the customer is inserted into file 2, and an end of service (type 2) event is scheduled at the appropriate time. If no barber is available, then the customer is inserted into the queue (file 1) at statement 1020. This completes this event for the customer arrival case and control as returned to statement 1000 for execution of the next event.

If the event is an end-of-service (type 2) event, then control is transferred to statement 1030 where the customer is removed from file 2. If customers are waiting in the queue (i.e., LIST(1, 2) > 0), then the customer at the head of the queue is removed from the queue and control is transferred to statement 1010. Here the end-of-service event is scheduled. Control is then transferred to statement 1000 for execution of subsequent events.

A type 3 event causes control to be transferred to statement 1040. Here subroutine REPORT is called and execution is terminated.

```
c
c
c          THIS PROGRAM SIMULATES A SIMPLE TWO-SERVERS QUEUING SYSTEM
c
c          EVENTS :  1   CUSTOMER ARRIVAL
c                    2   END OF SERVICE
c                    3   END OF SIMULATION RUN
c
c          FILES  :  1   QUEUE OF CUSTOMERS (RANKED ON TIME OF ARRIVAL)
c                    2   SERVERS (RANKED ON END-OF-SERVICE TIME)
c                    3   FUTURE EVENTS FILE (RANKED ON TIME OF EVENT)
c
      COMMON /LIST/NFILES,MAX,ITLAST,LIST(4,100)
c
c          INITIALIZE LISTS AND SIMULATION CLOCK
c
      ITIME=0
      CALL INIT(3,100)
c
c          SCHEDULE FIRST CUSTOMER ARRIVAL AT TIME = 0
c          SCHEDULE END-OF-RUN AT TIME = 200
c
      CALL INSERT(3,0,0,1)
c
      CALL INSERT(3,0,200,3)
c
c          DETERMINE IDENTITY OF NEXT EVENT
c
 1000 CALL REMOVE(3,ITIME,ITIME,ICODE)
      IF(ICODE.GT.1) GO TO 1030
c
c          CUSTOMER ARRIVAL,SCHEDULE NEXT ARRIVAL
c
      ITNEXT=IPOISN( 3,0) +ITIME
      CALL INSERT(3,ITIME,ITNEXT,1)
c
c          PLACE IN SERVICE IF SERVER IS AVAILABLE
c
      IF(LIST(2,2).GE.2) GO TO 1020
c
c          GENERATE END OF SERVICE TIME,PLACE IN SERVER
c          AND IN NEXT EVENT FILE
c
 1010 ISEND=ITIME+IPOISN(5,0)
      CALL INSERT(2,ITIME,ISEND,IB)
      CALL INSERT(3,ITIME,ISEND,2)
      GO TO 1000
c
c          PLACE IN QUEUE
c
 1020 CALL INSERT(1,ITIME,ITIME,IB)
      GO TO 1000
 1030 IF(ICODE.GT.2) GO TO 1040
c
c          END OF SERVICE,REMOVE FROM SERVER
c
      CALL REMOVE(2,ITIME,IA,IB)
c
c          SERVE WAITING CUSTOMER IF ANY
c
      IF(LIST(2,1).LE.0) GO TO 1000
      CALL REMOVE(1,ITIME,IA,IB)
      GO TO 1010
 1040 CALL REPORT(ITIME)
      STOP
      END
```

FIG. X-12   Main program for barbershop model.

This program uses integer variables throughout. This may seem unrealistic. In particular, clock increments, performance data, and user attributes may require a resolution higher than the one afforded by integer arithmetic. However, the choice of integer arithmetic is based on two important considerations. First, integer arithmetic is substantially faster on most computers than floating point arithmetic (for specific comparisons see Table I-3). Second, integer variables can usually be stored in half the space of floating point variables. Simulation programs usually have extensive core storage and computer time requirements. Thus substantial economic savings are obtained when integer arithmetic is used.

d. The Output

Execution of the program in Fig. X-12 results in the following summary report:

SUMMARY REPORT AT T = 200

FILE	IN	OUT	NOW	AVG STAY	AVG LENGTH
1	37	36	1	2.57	0.48
2	66	64	2	4.88	1.61
3	135	132	3	5.35	3.61

It is seen that the average wait for service is 2.57 time units while the average length of service is 4.88 (as compared to the theoretical mean of 5.0). On the average, 1.61 barbers are busy and the average queue length is about one half. The data for file 3 (the future event file) is less meaningful. However, we note that the average length of this file is close to its maximum value of 4 outstanding events.

PROBLEMS

1. What is the difference between a process and an event oriented modeling approach?

2. Write a simulation program of a single server queue using the list processing subroutines presented in Chapter II.

3. What are the advantages of using a simulation language in simulation modeling?

4. What key features should a discrete event simulation language possess?

5. Develop a BSF simulation model of an n-teller drive-up bank where cars line up in a single queue (Fig. X-13). Determine the optimal number of tellers for the case where interarrival times are exponentially distributed with a mean of 2 minutes and service times are exponentially distributed with a mean of 4 minutes.

FIG. X-13

6. Modify BSF such that an optional trace of each INSERT and REMOVE request is printed.

7. Expand the BSF data base and program to collect data for calculation of the variance of the length of stay in each file.

8. Write a simulation program for a single server queueing system with a LIFO queue utilizing a stack instead of a linked list for the queue and utilizing two separate variables (one for the time of next arrival and one for the time of next end-of-service event) instead of the conventional future events file. Compare the computational efficiency of this program with one utilizing the BSF. Explain the difference in performance levels.

BIBLIOGRAPHY

Chorafas, D. N., *Systems and Simulation.* Academic Press, New York, 1965.

Dahl, O. J., and **K. Nygaard,** "SIMULA-an ALGOL-based Simulation Language," *Comm. ACM,* **9,** No. 9, (September 1966), 671-678.

Fishman, G. S., *Concepts and Methods in Discrete Event Simulation.* Wiley, New York, 1976.

Gordon, G., *Systems Simulation.* Prentice-Hall, Englewood Cliffs, New Jersey, 1969.

Mize, J. H., and **J. G. Cox,** *Essentials of Simulation.* Prentice-Hall, Englewood Cliffs, New Jersey, 1968.

Pough, A. L., "DYNAMO User's Manual", 2nd ed. MIT Press, Cambridge, Massachusetts, 1963.

Pritsker, A. A. B., *The GASPIV Simulation Language.* Wiley, (Interscience), New York, 1974.

Pritsker, A. A. B., and **P. J. Kiviat,** *Simulation with GASPII.* Prentice-Hall, Englewood Cliffs, New Jersey, 1969.

Schmidt, J. W., and **R. E. Taylor,** *Simulation and Analysis of Industrial Systems.* Richard D. Irwin, Inc., Homewood, Illinois, 1970.

Shannon, R. E., *Systems Simulation: The Art and Science.* Prentice-Hall, Englewood Cliffs, New Jersey, 1975.

Tocher, K. D., *The Art of Simulation.* Van Nostren—Reinhold, Princeton, New Jersey, 1963.

CHAPTER XI

TWO SIMULATION LANGUAGES

In this chapter we shall review the use of two different simulation languages. The first language, GPSS, is included in this presentation as it is the main process oriented simulation language in use in the United States today. It is a major language of substantial complexity that is only implementable on fairly large computers. In the few pages available here we will not be able to give an in-depth treatment of the use of GPSS as a programming language. Instead, we opt to describe the use of the modeling aspects of the language. This discussion should enable the reader to ascertain the suitability of GPSS to his problem. He is then referred to one of the many GPSS texts cited in the references for further programming details.

The second language, WIDES, contrasts with GPSS in that it is a next-event type language and in that it is implementable even on many mini-computers with a FORTRAN compiler. Since WIDES is a substantially simpler and easier to use language, we are able to discuss several samples of WIDES computer programs. However, the reader is again referred to the users' guide cited in the bibliography for additional programming details. Copies of the WIDES language programs can be obtained for a nominal charge to cover reproduction cost from the Department of Industrial Engineering at the University of Wisconsin, Madison.

A. SIMULATION MODELING WITH GPSS

1. What is GPSS?

GPSS is a process flow oriented simulation language originally developed by Geoffrey Gordon at IBM. Many versions of GPSS have appeared over the years, including

GPSK	(Honeywell)
Flow Simulator	(RCA)
GPSS III	(IBM, 1965)
GPSS/360	(IBM, 1967)
GPSS V	(IBM, 1970)
GPSS/Norden	
GPSS/1100	(Univac)

with the earliest version being published as early as 1961 (Gordon, 1961). It is not our purpose in this chapter to develop an in-depth programming expertise in any of these versions, nor is it our intent to point out the differences between them. Rather, we aim to develop an appreciation for the capabilities of the language. With this appreciation and the appropriate users' manual, the reader should be able to design reasonably complex simulation models. For an in-depth treatment of GPSS, we refer the reader to any one of the recently published texts on the subject (Gordon, 1975; Greenberg, 1972; Schriber, 1974). The examples in this chapter are based on Gordon and are written in GPSS V.

GPSS is the "grand old dame" of discrete event simulation languages. The popularity of GPSS has increased over the years and few would dispute the claim that GPSS is the most widely used discrete event simulation language in the United States today. This popularity may be the result of the intrinsic properties of the language and/or the support of GPSS has received from the IBM Corporation.

GPSS can be studied on two levels: (1) as a modeling tool and (2) as a programming language. The strength of the language as a modeling tool lies in its provision of a large number of standard *blocks* that describe most functions found in process oriented systems. These blocks can be employed in a *block diagram* to conceptually describe the problem at hand. The strength of GPSS as a programming tool lies in the ease with which such block diagrams can be translated into an executable program. As for all simulation languages, an unfortunate drawback of GPSS is the large overhead in computer resources (in CPU time and core space) required to execute the program. For example, GPSS V requires from 52K to 178K bytes of storage depending upon which version is chosen. This means that GPSS V cannot run on most minicomputers.

2. Transactions

The design of simulation models using GPSS is a fairly simple task since all GPSS models employ the process flow view. This view considers the system to be simulated to be defined as a stationary set of storages or facilities through which a large number of transactions flow in some model-dependent manner, occasionally forming queues in front of a storage or facility. Based on this modeling premise, the GPSS modeling language provides functional blocks describing the generation, movement, queueing, and termination of transactions at proper times (the language processor provides the code necessary both to execute the resulting model and to collect the appropriate performance data). The main functions of the GPSS blocks used for systems modeling are shown in Tables XI-1 and XI-2. A key modeling feature in GPSS is the fact that each block is given a unique geometrical symbol. Hence, these symbols are also included in these figures.

Blocks for transaction control are presented in Table XI-1. To illustrate how these blocks are used for modeling, consider the flow of customers in a

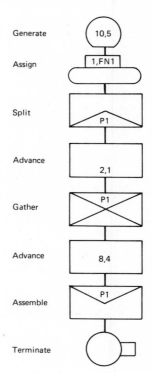

FIG. XI-1 Simplistic block diagram of group eating at fast food restaurant.

TABLE XI-1

GPSS MODELING BLOCKS FOR TRANSACTION CONTROL

Block	Action triggered by block	Transactions retained in block?	Symbol
GENERATE A, B	Transaction is generated and retained in block until departure time determined by A and B is reached. At this time the process is repeated (note many departure time options are available).	Yes	A,B
ADVANCE A, B	Transaction is retained in block until departure time specified by A and B is reached.	Yes	A,B
ASSIGN A, B	Transaction's Ath attribute parameter is assigned value B.	No	A,B
SPLIT A, B	A copies of entering transaction are created. Copies are sent to block B.	No	A (B)
GATHER A	Copies of a previously split transaction are retained until A transactions are accumulated: they are then all released.	Yes	A
ASSEMBLE A	Same as GATHER except only one copy is released. The remaining transactions are destroyed.	Yes	A
TERMINATE	Transaction is destroyed.	No	

TABLE XI-2

GPSS Modeling Blocks for Storage and Facility Control

Block	Actions triggered by entering transactions	Entry conditions	Symbol
SEIZE A	Transaction gets control of facility A.	A must be idle.	
RELEASE A	Control of A is relinquished, restoring A's idle state.	None	
PREEMPT A	Transaction gets control of Facility A. (More complex PREEMPT options are available.)	A must be idle or control must be SEIZEd.	
RETURN A	Transaction releases control of A. Control is restored to previously controlling transaction if any.	None	
ENTER A,B	B units of storage space A are occupied.	A must have B units available.	
LEAVE A,B	B units of storage space A are released.	None	

241

fast food restaurant. Customers enter in groups of random sizes, they then individually place their order at separate counters and then sit down as a group and eat. When the last member of the group is finished, they leave.

A GPSS block diagram for this situation is shown in Fig. XI-1. The GENERATE block specifies that transactions representing groups of people are to be generated every 10 ± 5 minutes. As the transaction leaves this block, it enters an ASSIGN block. In this block, the size of the group represented by the transaction is computed by a function FN1 and assigned to the first attribute parameter of the transaction. GPSS is designed such that when we want to retrieve the value of this parameter we reference the variable P1. The transaction is now SPLIT into P1 transactions such that each member of the group is represented by a separate transaction. Since alternate paths for the new copies are not provided, all transactions are immediately forwarded to the ADVANCE block. This block represents the 2 ± 1 minutes that are required to place an order at the counter at this time of the day. Here each transaction will be assigned an individual "process" time in the range of 1–3 minutes, and when this process time is up, the transaction is forwarded to the next block. Members of all groups are assumed to be polite, waiting for their slowest friend before they sit down. This is reflected by the GATHER block. Here the transactions that were SPLIT earlier are held until all P1 members of the group have received their food. Note that several different groups could be waiting at the GATHER block at one time. (GPSS knows how to distinguish between members of different groups.) The collected group then sits down to eat. Different members require from 4–12 minutes to finish their lunch. This is represented by the subsequent ADVANCE block. Finally, the group leaves when all members have finished their lunch. This is represented by the ASSEMBLE and TERMINATE blocks. As members finish their lunch, they are released from the ADVANCE block and collected by the ASSEMBLE block. There they are retained until all group members are released from the ADVANCE block. At this point, a single transaction representing the original group is released. This transaction is then destroyed in the TERMINATE block.

There are no restrictions on entry into a transaction control block. Hence, it is possible for a transaction to traverse a large number of transaction control blocks in zero simulated time. Transactions are retained in a transaction control block either because of intrinsic properties of the block (such as for an ADVANCE) or because conditions are such that in the subsequent block entry is presently denied (such as for a SEIZE block). In this simple example, we assumed that a sufficient number of servers and tables were available. Thus, we did not need to include such queueing features in the corresponding model.

3. Facility and Storage Management

The previously discussed model of a fast food restaurant is somewhat simplistic due to the assumption that both servers and tables are immediately available. This is frequently not the case as servers may already be busy and tables may be occupied. To model such queueing situations, GPSS introduces the concept of facility and storage.

A facility is a logical entity that is able to accommodate one transaction at a time. A queue of transactions will emerge in front of the facility if more than one transaction wishes to use the facility at one time. The GPSS modeling blocks relating to the use of facilities by a transaction are summarized in Table XI-2. The transaction obtains control of a facility through a SEIZE block. A queue results if the desired facility is already busy. This queue is not formed in the SEIZE block, rather it is formed one block prior. Entry into the SEIZE block is not permitted until the facility is in its idle state. (Transactions are normally released from the previous block in a FIFO discipline.) The transaction immediately leaves the SEIZE block after having gained control of the facility. (It may even procede to SEIZE control of some other facility if desired.) Control of the facility is not relinquished until the transaction reaches a RELEASE block specifying the return of this particular facility to its idle state. In some cases, high priority transactions may have to interrupt the control that another transaction may have over a facility. This is accomplished by a PREEMPT block. The return of a PREEMPTed facility to its previous activity is accomplished by a RETURN block.

A storage is similar to a facility except that (1) it may accommodate many different transactions at one time, and (2) transactions removing units from a storage need not previously have inserted units into the storage. As shown in Table IX-2, units are inserted into a storage in an ENTER block, and they are removed in a LEAVE block. Transactions are allowed entry into an ENTER block whenever the storage has sufficient room for the additional units. (The capacity of a storage is easily defined elsewhere by a GPSS control block.) Transactions with small space requests may bypass the queue of those with larger requests waiting for additional storage to be released. Storages are used to model both inventory situations where the stored units represent some "goods" and any multiserver queueing situations where the stored units represent customers (i.e., transactions) and departure is requested by the same transactions that requested entry.

We illustrate the use of storages in Fig. XI-2 where the previous fast food example has been extended to allow for both queueing at the service counter and congestion at the tables. Queueing at the counter has been introduced

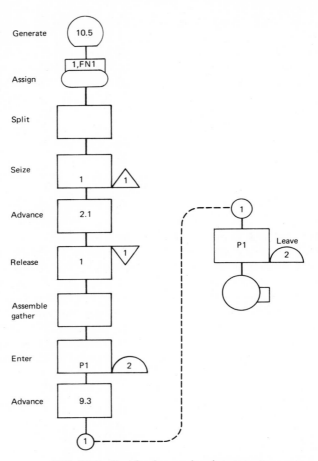

FIG. XI-2   Fast food example using storage.

by the first SEIZE–RELEASE pair of blocks. Entry is into facility one and each transaction requests one unit of storage. The capacity of the servers (i.e., the number of servers) is defined elsewhere by a storage control block. Entry into the SEIZE block is only permitted when a server is idle. Transactions queue up in the SPLIT block waiting for such capacity to be available. Transactions are retained in the ADVANCE block. Upon departure of this block, they now relinquish control of a server in the RELEASE block. To illustrate the use of a storage, we now ASSEMBLE the group such that it is only represented by one transaction. When the group has been assembled, we ENTER the eating area (Storage 2) with a request for P1 seats. If the request cannot be met at this time, the transaction is kept waiting in the ASSEMBLE block until sufficient space is relinquished by departing customers. Upon entry, the group is retained by between 6 and 12 minutes to simulate their joint eating time (i.e., the time of the slowest eater). Use of the P1 chairs is then relinquished in the LEAVE block and the group is destroyed in the TERMINATE block.

B. SIMULATION MODELING WITH WIDES

1. What is WIDES?

WIDES is a FORTRAN based collection of subroutines that performs all the routine model manipulation and data base maintenance tasks normally encountered in discrete event simulation programs. WIDES is designed with the inexperienced FORTRAN programmer in mind. Thus no understanding of list processing is required to use WIDES and the average user has no need to understand how the WIDES data base is designed, initialized, or maintained. In fact, a WIDES user may not even be aware of the existence of the rather extensive WIDES maintained data base. (WIDES is a substantial extension of the GASP language, but without the ability of GASPIV to simulate continuous time systems (Pritsker and Kiviat, 1969; Pritsker, 1974).)

Among the tasks performed automatically by WIDES are
(1) initialization of the data base,
(2) generation of recurrent events at proper intervals,
(3) scheduling of events as required,
(4) updating of the clock,
(5) collection of throughput and utilization data for files, facilities, and storages.

In addition, to reduce program development time, the following features are incorporated:

(1) Simple free format control statements.
(2) WIDES is completely isolated from the user. Accidental changes of WIDES data or pointers are not possible.
(3) All input parameters to WIDES are screened for validity.
(4) Specific error messages are generated whenever user errors are detected.
(5) Informative trace eases debugging.

TABLE XI-3

WIDES INPUT COMMANDS

I. MODEL INITIALIZATION
    A. Facilities
        QORDER($i$fac, $i$que) = DECR, $i$col Defines queue ranking method
        QORDER($i$fac, $i$que) = INCR, $i$col Defines queue ranking method
        QORDER($i$fac, $i$que) = FIFO   Defines queue ranking method
        QORDER($i$fac, $i$que) = LIFO   Defines queue ranking method
        SERVE($i$fac) = $t$serv, $i$end, $a1$, $a2$, $a3$ Assigns entity to facility
        SERVERS($i$fac) = $i$value   Defines facility server capacity
    B. Sets
        FILE($i$event) = $a1$, $a2$, $a3$, $a4$ Places entity in set
        ORDER($i$set) = DECR, $i$col Defines set ranking method
        ORDER($i$set) = INCR, $i$col Defines set ranking method
        ORDER($i$set) = FIFO   Defines set ranking method
        ORDER($i$set) = LIFO   Defines set ranking method
    C. Storages
        SLEVEL($i$store) = value   Initializes storage level
II. EVENT SCHEDULING
        CLEAR = time   Clears all data collection arrays
        FUTURE($i$event) = time, $a1$, $a2$, $a3$, $a4$ Initializes future event file
        RECURRENT($i$event) = $t$mean, k $i$seed Defines recurrent event
        SUMARY = time   Prints summary at specified time
III. RUN CONTROL
        DUMPQS   Content of all nonempty queues
                 included in summary report
        ERRMAX = $i$value   Allows errors before abort
        EVENTS($i$type) = $i$max   Fixes upper limit of events
        TBEG = time   Defines initial value of clock
        TFIN = time   Defines end of simulation run
        TRACE = t_{on}, t_{off} Prints detailed trace
IV. OTHER
        ENTITIES = $i$count   Expands core storage allocation
        FACILITIES = $i$count   Expands core storage allocation
        FILES = $i$count   Expands core storage allocation
        STORAGES = $i$count   Expands core storage allocation
        SEED(i) = $i$seed   Redefines initial random number
                 seed

The language has two elements: (a) a set of control cards (Table XI-3) initializes the model and defines the run conditions, and (b) a collection of FORTRAN subroutines (Table XI-4) executes the operational aspects of the model. The use of these elements to construct simulation models and programs are discussed in the following section. An example program is presented in Section C. Detailed programming information is provided in the WIDES Users' Guide (Thesen, 1976).

TABLE XI-4

WIDES Subroutine Commands

I. MODELING		
A. FACILITIES		
	CALL CREATE(ATTRIB)	Defines entity attributes
	CALL PARAMS(ATTRIB)	Returns entity attributes
	CALL SERVE(IFAC, IQ, TSERV, IEND)	Assigns entity to facility
	IBUSY(IFAC)	Returns count of busy servers
	IQUE(IFAC, IQ)	Returns queue length
B. SETS		
	CALL FILE(ISET, ATTRIB)	Places entity in set
	CALL FINDEQ(ISET, ICOL, IPOS, VAL)	Finds specific entity
	CALL FINDMN(ISET, ICOL, IPOS)	Finds specific entity
	CALL MINDMX(ISET, ICOL, IPOS)	Finds specific entity
	CALL FMAXLT(ISET, ICOL, IPOS, VAL)	Finds specific entity
	CALL FMINGT(ISET, ICOL, IPOS, VAL)	Finds specific entity
	CALL HIFRST(ISET)	Ranks set in decreasing order
	CALL LOFRST(ISET)	Ranks set in increasing order
	CALL LOOKAT(ISET, IPOS, ATTRIB)	Returns attributes of entity in specified position
	CALL UNFILE(ISET, IPOS, ATTRIB)	Removes item in given position
	LENGTH(ISET)	Returns length of set
C. STORAGES		
	CALL REDUCE(ISTORE, AMOUNT)	Withdraws from storage unit
	CALL STORE(ISTORE, AMOUNT)	Inserts into storage unit
	SLEVEL(ISTORE)	Returns current storage level
D. EVENTS		
	CALL CREATE(ATTRIB)	Defines event attributes
	CALL FUTURE(IEVENT, TINTER)	Schedules a future event
	CALL PARAMS(ATTRIB)	Returns event attributes
II. DEBUGGING		
	CALL ERROR(IVALUE, VALUE)	Prints TNOW, IVALUE, and VALUE
	CALL IERROR(IVALUE)	Prints TNOW and IVALUE
	CALL PRINTF(IFAC)	Prints facility content
	CALL PRINTQ(IFILE)	Prints file content
	CALL SUMARY	Prints summary report
	CALL TRACE	Turns on trace
III. DATA COLLECTION		
	CALL CLEAR	Clears all data collection arrays

Table XI-4 (continued)

CALL COLCT(ICLCT, VALUE)	Collects data; mean, var, max, and min printed at end
CALL HISTO(IHIST, VALUE)	Collects data for histogram
CALL SUMARY	Prints summary report
IV. RUN CONTROL	
CALL WIDES	Assigns control to WIDES
CALL WSTOP	Stops simulation run
V. RANDOM NUMBER GENERATORS	
ANORM(AMEAN, VAR, ISTRM)	Normal distribution
CHISQ(N, ISTRM)	Chi-square distribution
ERLANG(AMEAN, K, ISTRM)	Erlang distribution
EXPON(AMEAN, ISTRM)	Exponential distribution
IPOISN(AMEAN, ISTRM)	Poisson distribution
PNORM(AMEAN, VAR, ISTRM)	Positive distribution
UNIF(A, B, ISTRM)	Uniform distribution

2. WIDES Modeling Elements

a. Events

Two different classes of events are recognized. *Recurrent* events have the property that the interval between two recurrent events of the same type is a stationary random variable completely independent of the state of the system being simulated. Systems inputs (such as customer arrivals) are usually described by recurrent events. WIDES automatically schedules perpetual sequences of recurrent events at proper random intervals. *Triggered* events are events that are triggered by some external or internal systems conditions (end-of-service is a typical triggered event). Triggered events must be individually scheduled in the user program.

Events are inserted into the future event file by a "FUTURE = type, time, attributes" control card, a "RECURRENT(type) = $t$mean, k" or a CALL FUTURE statement. In the latter case, if the event has attributes affiliated with it, these are defined by a CALL CREATE statement. When the time of a scheduled event occurs, WIDES calls the user written subroutine EVENT. Any previously defined event attributes are retrieved in this routine by a CALL PARAMS statement. The EVENT routine transfers control to the appropriate user written subroutine describing the event.

Data is automatically collected on the count of and interval between different events. An upper limit on the number of different types of events that may be scheduled prior to termination of the simulation can be specified through an "EVENTS(type) = limit" parameter card.

The following illustrates a typical WIDES summary report on event frequencies:

```
************COUNT OF EVENTS***********
EVENT   COUNT MEANINTERvAL MAX-ALLOWED
    2     19      5.26            100
    1     51      1.96        8360000
 97o1     19      5.26        8360000
    3      1    100.00        8360000
```

b. Storages

A WIDES *storage* is a logical unit into which "matter" of any kind can be inserted for later withdrawals. A storage differs from a file/queue in that the storage does not recognize the individual identities of the different units of "matter" in the store. WIDES collects substantial performance data on each storage unit and prints a summary report such as the following at the end of each run:

```
*************************
*                       *
*  STORAGE UTILIZATION  *
*                       *
*************************
```

STORE	TRANSACTIONS		SIZE-OF-INSERTIONS			SIZE-OF-WITHDRAWALS		
NO	INSRT	WITHDR	AVG	MIN	MAX	AVG	MIN	MAX
1	1	19	4C.00	40.00	40.00	1.86	1.C4	2.90
2	1	1	40.00	40.00	40.00	40.00	4C.C0	40.00

STORE	********INVENTORY-LEVEL********					*****STOCKOUT-DATA******			LOST-
NO	START	NOW	AVG	MIN	MAX	AVG-LENGTH	PERCENT	COUNT	SALES
1	32.00	36.72	45.64	23.87	69.87	0.00	0.00	0	0.00
2	0.00	0.00	6.76	0.00	40.00	83.11	83.11	1	0.00

Each storage unit is assumed to be empty at the start of the simulation run. To initialize the storage to some other level, the following control card is required:

SLEVEL(unit) = level

To insert units into the storage, subroutine STORE is called:

CALL STORE(IUNIT, QUANT)

with IUNIT specifying the storage unit used and QUANT being a positive *real* number specifying the amount inserted. To withdraw units, subroutine REDUCE is called:

CALL REDUCE(IUNIT, QUANT)

where QUANT now is the number of units withdrawn.

The current level in storage unit is obtained through the function

SLEVEL(IUNIT).

c. Entities

An entity is a tangible object described in WIDES by up to 20 different user defined attributes. Entities may be used to describe customers, requests, automobiles, or whatever other objects are of interest in a simulation study. In addition to the user defined attributes, WIDES automatically affiliates the following three descriptors with each entity:

(1) a unique sequence number,
(2) the time of creation,
(3) the time of insertion into most recent file or queue.

Entities are created by FILE or SERVE parameter cards or subroutine calls. Entities are destroyed by a CALL UNFILE statement or by failing to transfer an entity to another facility upon completion of service. Data is automatically collected on the length of stay of entities in the system and in individual queues and sets.

d. Sets

1. *Background* A set is a storage unit for entities where the identity of individual units in the set is maintained (Figure XI-3). Items are usually ordered in the set in a strict chronological order; however, other ranking methods are available.

The WIDES set manager collects substantial performance data and prints the summary reports such as the following at the end of the simulation run:

SET NO	***SET SIZE***			THRUPUT		**LENGTH OF STAY**		
	NOW	MEAN	MAX	IN	OUT	MEAN	STDV	MAX
1	26	13.00	26	26	0	25.00	15.30	50.00
7	1	1.00	1	1	0	50.00	0.00	50.00

2. *Using Sets* Each set is initially assumed to be empty. To load entities into the sets at the start of the simulation run, the following control card is required:

FILE(file) = attrib 1, attrib 2, ..., abbrib 5

To initialize the ranking method to some other method than FIFO, one of the following control cards may be used:

FORDER(set) = INCR column
FORDER(set) = DECR column
FORDER(set) = LIFO

where INCR, DECR, and LIFO represent the ranking methods and "column"

FIG. XI-3 Set.

is the index of the attribute on which the set is to be ranked in increasing or decreasing order.

To insert an item into a set during the simulation run, the subroutine FILE is called:

CALL FILE(file, attrib)

where attrib is a real array of five user assigned attributes. (This array must be provided even if it is not used.) WIDES will automatically insert the entity into its proper location in the file.

An item is removed from a set by the subroutine CALL UNFILE(file, position, attributes). An attempt to remove an item from an empty file results in an error message and a possible program termination.

Five subroutines for finding the logical position of specific items in a file are available:

CALL FINDEQ(set, column, position, value)
CALL FINDMN(set, column, position)
CALL FINDMX(set, column, position)
CALL FINDLT(set, column, position, value)
CALL FIRSTG(set, column, position, value)
CALL FMINGT(set, column, position, value)

FINDEQ finds an item with a specific attribute value. FINDMN finds the item with the smallest attribute value while FINDMX finds the item with the largest value. FMAXLT finds the item with the largest attribute value less than a ceiling value while FMINGT finds the item with the smallest value greater than a floor value. FIRSTG and FIRSTG finds the *first* item with an attribute value greater than or equal to, or less than or equal to the specified value.

The function LENGTH(file) returns the current length of a file.

e. Facilities

A WIDES *facility* is a collection of one or more identical servers drawing customers from one or more queues. Queues cannot be shared by different facilities. A 3 server 2 queue facility is illustrated in Fig. XI-4.

When inserted into a facility, an entity will immediately be assigned to a server if one is idle. The entity will be placed in the specified queue if all servers are busy. In this case, WIDES will place it in service as soon as the server does become available. Upon completion of service, an idle server will scan the facility queues *in increasing order* until a waiting entity is found. Thus queue 1 has priority over queue 2, queue 2 over queue 3, etc.

Extensive performance data is collected. The following illustrates the report that is printed at the end of a run:

```
*************************
*                       *
*  FACILITY UTILIZATION *
*                       *
*************************
```

FACI LITY	SER VRS	QUE UES	THRUPUT IN	THRUPUT OUT	**LENGTH OF STAY** MEAN	**LENGTH OF STAY** STDV	**LENGTH OF STAY** MAX	*BUSY SERVERS* NOW	*BUSY SERVERS* MEAN	*BUSY SERVERS* MAX
1	1	1	51	19	28.97	18.14	57.63	1	.94	1

```
*************************
*                       *
*  QUEUE UTILIZATION    *
*                       *
*************************
```

FACI LITY	QUEUE NO	TOTAL INPUT	THRUPUT IN	THRUPUT OUT	QUEUE SIZE NOW	QUEUE SIZE MEAN	**LENGTH OF STAY** MEAN	**LENGTH OF STAY** STDV	**LENGTH OF STAY** MAX
1	1	51	50	19	31	5.12	10.24	17.08	55.80

The capacity of a WIDES facility is defined by the following control cards:

SERVERS(facility) = count

Default value is one server per facility.

To load initial entities into a facility, the following parameter card is used:

SERVE(facility) = service, time, end-of-service event, attributes

Here "attributes" is a list of up to 8 attribute values that upon request will be returned unchanged when the end of the service for this event is reached.

The entity will immediately be assigned to a server if one is idle. The entity will be placed in the queue if all servers are busy. In this case, WIDES will place it in service as soon as a server does become available.

The end-of-service event for an entity in a facility may be important in the systems being studied. WIDES gives control to a user written subroutine describing actions that take place at this time, if a positive end-of-service event code is provided in the SERVE statement. Entities are assigned to a

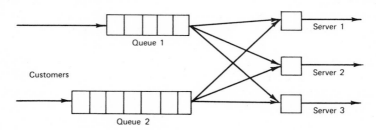

FIG. XI-4   Facility with three servers and two queues.

facility during a run through a CALL SERVE statement:

CALL SERVE(facility, queue, service time, end-of-service event)

The effect of this is equivalent to a SERVE parameter card except that entity attributes cannot be accommodated. However, a CALL CREATE statement immediately preceding the SERVE statement will affiliate up to three attribute values with the entity.

The facility queue is normally FIFO. Other ranking schemes are defined through one of the following parameter cards:

QORDER(facility, queue) = INCR column
QORDER(facility, queue) = DECR column
QORDER(facility, queue) = LIFO

The effect is similar to the ORDER commands for sets. The current length of a facility queue is returned through an IQUE(facility, queue) function call. The number of busy servers is returned through an IBUSY(facility) function call.

3. Controlling a Run

At least one initial event must be provided on a "FUTURE" or "RE-CURRENT" control card. (Without this event, WIDES would not know what to do.) The simulation process is then started by transferring control to WIDES by a CALL WIDES statement in the main program. WIDES will then start the clock and return control to the user written SUBROUTINE EVENTS at the proper time to execute the first externally specified event.

It is frequently desirable to let a model run for some time until a steady state is reached before data collection is started. This is achieved by using a "CLEAR = time" control card or a CALL CLEAR statement to erase all past data at the point where data collection is to begin.

The normal way to terminate a simulation run is to use a "TFIN = time" control card to specify the simulated clock time at which termination is to occur. Simulation may also be terminated by using one or more "EVENTS(type) = count" control cards to specify the maximum number of specific events that are to be simulated. This event count is initialized by WIDES to 2^{23} for each event.

C. PROGRAMMING WITH WIDES

1. A Single Server Queueing System

One of the simplest WIDES simulation programs is one that simulates the operations of a simple queueing system with recurrent customer arrivals

and no end-of-service events. For example, the following program describes the dynamic operation of a single server queueing system with exponentially distributed service time with a mean of 2.0:

```
CALL WIDES
END
SUBROUTINE EVENTS(ICODE,TNOW)
STIM = EXPON(2,0,1)
CALL SERVE(1,1,STIM,0)
RETURN
END
```

Here subroutine EVENTS emulates the customer arrival event by generating the appropriate service time for the customer and by inserting the customer
into facility number one. The end of service event is not of interest in this
model. Thus, WIDES is told through the fourth parameter in SERVE not
to call EVENTS when these events take place.

The customer arrival events are modeled as recurrent events with an interarrival time following the Erlang distribution with a mean of 3 and k equal
to 2. A sequence of such an event is generated by the parameter card:

RECURRENT(1) = 3., 2

For this example, simulation is to be terminated after the arrival of 100
customers or after 200 time units, whichever comes first. This is achieved by
the parameter cards

EVENTS(1) = 100
TFIN = 200

These control cards together with the above programs and the WIDES language processor form a complete simulation program. This program is illustrated in the flowchart in Figure XI-5.

2. An Inventory/Queueing System with Back Orders

We will now review a slightly more complex system utilizing several different WIDES modeling elements. The system now under study is a simple,
one queue serving system where the service involves the delivery of some
product from an inventory. An example of such a system is a one vendor
hot dog stand. As shown in Fig. IX-6, arriving customers enter a single
queue, single server facility. Customers are served in a FIFO manner and
upon end-of-service the inventory level is (if possible) reduced by the amount
of the customer's purchase. At this time, an order for additional inventory
items to be delivered after a certain lead time is placed if the on-hand plus
on-order inventory level falls below a predefined order point. Back orders
are placed if there is insufficient merchandise to meet a demand. In this case,

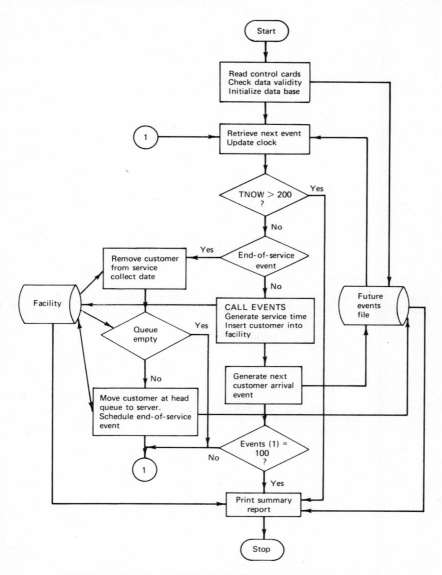

FIG. XI-5   Flowchart of WIDES single server queueing program.

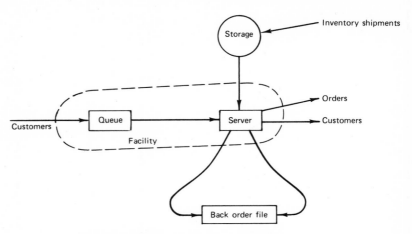

FIG. XI-6   Simple inventory queueing system.

```
      COMMON EOQ,ORDRPT
c
c   SIMULATION MODEL OF INVENTORY SITUATON WITH BACKORDERS.
c   CUSTOMERS QUEUE UP TO PLACE ORDERS. INVENTORY REDUCTION TAKES PLACE AT
c   END OF SERVICE
c
c   SET(1)    = CUSTOMERS AWAITING BACKORDESR
c   SET(1)    = CUSTOMERS AWAITING BACKORDERS
c
c   STORE(1) = ON HAND INVENTORY
c   STORE(2) = OUTSTANDING ORDERS
c   STORE(3) = BACKORDERED ITEMS
c
c   EVENT(1) = CUSTOMER ARRIVAL (RECURRENT EVENT)
c   EVENT(2) = END OF SERVICE
c   EVENT(3) = ARRIVAL OF ORDERS
c
      EOQ=40.
      ORDRPT=30.
      CALL WIDES
      STOP
      END
```

FIG. XI-7   Main program for inventory queueing model.

the customer is moved to a separate back order queue. Back orders are satisfied as soon as a shipment is received.

The main program for the WIDES model is shown in Fig. XI-7. The purpose of this program is to (a) initialize the order point and order quantity,
(b) transfer control to WIDES, and (c) document the design of the model.
The dynamics of the model are described in the event routine in Fig. XI-8.

This program was executed using the WIDES parameter cards shown in
Fig. XI-9. Most of these cards are self-explanatory. However, we point out

```
            SUBROUTINE EVENT(ITYPE,TNOW)
            DIMENSION ATTRIB(6),DATA(4)
            COMMON EOQ,ORDRPT
            IF(ITYPE.NE.1)GOTO 1000
     C
     C  CUSTOMER ARRIVAL. PLACE IN FACILITY QUEUE
     C
            STIME=ERLANG(1.5,1 ,1)
            CALL SERVE(1,1,STIME,2)
            RETURN
     C
     C  END OF SERVICE. REDUCE INVENTORY IF POSSIBLE
     C
      1000 IF(ITYPE.NE.2)GOTO 1020
            DEMAND=UNIF(1.0,3.0,2)
            ATTRIB(1)=DEMAND
            IF(SLEVEL(1).GT.DEMAND)GOTO 1010
     C
     C  BACKORDER
     C
            CALL FILE(1,ATTRIB)
            CALL STORE(3,ATTRIB)
            RETURN
     C
     C FILL DEMAND. ORDER MORE IF NECESSARY
     C
      1010 CALL REDUCE(1,DEMAND)
            IF(SLEVEL(1)+SLEVEL(2).GT.ORDRPT)RETURN
            TLEAD=PNORM(20.,4.,3)
            CALL FUTURE(3,TLEAD)
            CALL STORE(2,EOQ)
            RETURN
     C
     C  ORDER ARRIVAL
     C
      1020 CALL STORE(1,EOQ)
            CALL REDUCE(2,EOQ)
     C
     C FILL BACKORDERS
     C
      1030 CALL FIRSTL(1,1,IPOS,SLEVEL(1))
            IF(IPOS.LE.0)RETURN
            CALL UNFILE(1,IPOS,ATTRIB,DATA)
            CALL REDUCE(3,ATTRIB(1) )
            GOTO 1030
            END
```

FIG. XI-8   Event subroutine for inventory queueing model.

```
            RECURRENT(1)=2. 2
            EVENTS(2)=100
            SLEVEL(1)=32
            TFIN=400
            SUMARY=100
            DUMPQS
            FORDER(1)=INCR(1)
            ERRMAX=10
            TRACE=0,4
            TRACE=20.,20.5
```

FIG. XI-9   Echo of parameter cards.

that event 1 (customer arrival) was defined as a recurrent event with an inter-arrival time following the Erlang distribution with a mean of 2 and $k = 2$. The simulation was to be terminated after 400 time units or 200 end-of-service events, whichever came first. Finally, the set of customersa waiting back ordered items was ranked in increasing order on attribute one (the size of the purchase).

After the successful execution of the program, summary reports for the facility, the storages, and the events were generated. The specific reports generated by this run have already been presented as sample reports in the section of this work on modeling elements. (Event 9701 is a WIDES generated end-of-service event.) No set performance reports were generated since no back orders were placed. A WIDES generated trace showing all activities for the first four units of time is displayed in Table XI-5.

PROBLEMS

1. Develop a WIDES model of the hamburger restaurant example discussed in Section A.

2. Develop a GPSS model of the inventory queueing system with back orders discussed in Section C.

3. Discuss the relative advantages of GPSS and WIDES. Develop two contrasting examples where one language is an obvious choice over the other one.

4. John Smith operates a barbershop. Customers arrive at the rate of 3 customers per hour, while John gives haircuts at the rate of four haircuts per hour.

  (a) If both the service times and the interarrival times are exponentially distributed, how many chairs should Mr. Smith provide under the following policies:
    (1) no waiting customer is ever going to lack a chair,
    (2) most customers will be provided with a chair; however, in some cases, there will be an insufficient supply of chairs.
  (b) After some time, Mr. Smith's barbershop has become more popular. Now customers arrive at a rate of four customers per hour. How many chairs are now needed under the policies indicated above?
  (c) Modify your program so that when there are four customers waiting, arriving customers leave immediately without receiving a haircut. Set up your program so that you count the number of balking customers.
  (d) To meet the increased demand, Mr. Smith desires to hire another

TABLE XI-5

PARTIAL TRACE OF SIMULATION PROGRAM

SIMULATION STARTED AT TIME = 0.00

TNOW	ACTION	TYPE	UNIT	SEQUEN	T-THEN	VALUE	POS	COL
1.12[a]	EVENT	1		−10000[b]				
1.12[c]	SERVE	2[d]	1 1	1		0.21[e]		
1.12[f]	FUTURE 9701[f]			10005	1.33[f]	0.21		
1.12 ₂	FUTURE	1		−10006	1.21	0.09		
1.21	EVENT	1		−10006				
1.21	SERVE	2	1 1	2		2.04		
1.21	FUTURE	1		−10007	3.36	2.15		
1.33[f]	ENDSRV		1	1				
1.33[g]	QMOVE		1 1	2	1.21	2.04		
1.33	FUTURE 9701			10008	3.37	2.04		
1.33	EVENT	2		10005				
1.33	SLEVEL		1			32.00		
1.33	REDUCE		1			1.05	30.96	
1.33	SLEVEL		2			0.00		
1.33	SLEVEL		1			30.96		
3.36	EVENT	1		−10007				
3.36	SERVE	2	1 1	3		5.41		
3.36	FUTURE	1		−10009	5.21	1.85		
3.37	ENDSRV		1	2				
3.37	QMOVE		1 1	3	3.36	5.41		
3.37	FUTURE 9701			10010	8.78	5.41		
3.37	EVENT	2		10008				
3.37	SLEVEL		1			30.96		
3.37	REDUCE		1			1.33	29.64	
3.37	SLEVEL		2			0.00		
3.37	SLEVEL		1			29.64		
3.37[h]	FUTURE	3		10011	20.26	16.89		
3.37	STORE		2			40.00	40.00	
4.00	TRACE OFF							
20.00	TRACE ON							
20.26[h]	EVENT	3		10011				
20.26	STORE		1			40.00	63.87	
20.26	REDUCE		2			40.00	0.00	
20.26[i]	SLEVEL		1			63.87		
20.26	FIRSTL		1			63.87	0[j]	1
20.50	TRACE OFF							

[a] An event of type 1 is scheduled at $t = 1.12$.

[b] Recurrent events have negative sequence numbers.

[c] A call serve is executed at $t = 1.12$.

[d] End-of-service event is a type 2 event.

[e] Service time is 0.21 time units.

[f] End-of-service for customer at facility I is scheduled for $t = 1.33$.

[g] Customer number 2 is moved from queue 1 to get service in facility 1 at $t = 1.33$. Service time is 1.21.

[h] An order arrived event occurs at $t = 20.26$.

[i] The level of storage unit 1 is at 63.87 at $t = 20.26$.

[j] No customer with a back order of less than 63.87 can be found.

barber. Two alternatives are available:
(1)   hire an apprentice at $3.00 per hour,
(2)   hire a journeyman barber.
The apprentice can give haircuts at a rate of two per hour. The journeyman gives haircuts at a rate of three per hour. Mr. Smith will receive a commission of $1.50 per haircut from the journeyman barber. If haircuts cost $3.00 each, which of the two alternatives should he choose?

(e)   At what arrival rate does the other alternative become more attractive?

(f)   How much must he charge for haircuts to make the other alternative more attractive?

5. An architect has completed his initial design of a four floor office building. He now wishes to explore the effects of installing either two or three elevators in the building. Preliminary analysis indicates that the following traffic pattern may be expected:

$$P(i,j) \begin{bmatrix} 0.6 & 0.2 & 0.2 & 0 \\ 0.4 & 0.4 & 0 & 0.2 \\ 0.3 & 0 & 0.3 & 0.4 \\ 0 & 0.2 & 0.4 & 0.4 \end{bmatrix},$$

where $P(i,j)$ is the probability that a passenger originating at the ith floor wishes to go to the jth floor. Furthermore, the mean interarrival time between the passengers is exponentially distributed with a mean of 0.05 minutes on the first floor and a mean of 0.1 minutes on the other floors. Alternative

Alternative	Car capacity Min	Car capacity Max	Travel speed (minutes/floor)	Relative cost per car for capacity of n
1	5	10	0.1	$0.7n + 0.25n^2$
2	6	12	0.2	$n + 0.1n^2$

elevators are considered as shown in the tabulation. You are requested to suggest the best elevator design for this building.

(a)   Determine a reasonable criterion for elevator selection (be sure to include cost and waiting time).

(b)   Build a simulation model capable of measuring the performance of any feasible elevator configuration.

(c) Develop a strategy for locating the best elevator configuration.

(d) Determine the number and type of elevators.

6. A local supermarket is reviewing its current inventory control policies for left handed rubber widgets. To facilitate an educated decision on this matter, the following data has been collected:

(A) Demands

    (1) An average of 10 units are sold each day.

    (2) The interval between demands follow the exponential distribution.

    (3) Demands during a stockout period are lost.

(B) Orders

    (1) Lead time is exponentially distributed with mean of ten days.

    (2) Items can only be ordered in case lots containing 24 units each.

(C) Costs

    (1) Cost of placing an order is $25 per order.

    (2) Holding cost is four cents per unit per day.

    (3) Each lost sale is equivalent to a five dollar loss in profit.

(D) Operating Policies

    (1) All orders are placed at the end of the day.

    (2) All shipments are made available for sale on the morning of the day following their arrival.

    (3) For costing purposes all sales are assumed to take place in one operation in the middle of the day.

Perform a simulation study to determine the optimal order point and quantity.

7. A machine shop performs custom work of a highly technical nature, each order involving the use of each of the shops four uniquely different machining centers. However, the sequence in which these operations is performed a random variable differing from order to order. All machine service times are uniformly distributed between 5 and 15 time units.

Determine the average overall service time if orders appear in a random fashion with an exponentially distributed interarrival time with a mean of 8 time units.

8. Modify the situation described in Problem 7 to include two randomly occurring order classes, regular and priority, such that priority orders have priority over regular orders at all machine centers. What is the average service time for the two order classes if 25% of the orders are priority orders?

BIBLIOGRAPHY

Gordon, G., *The Application of GPSSV to Discrete System Simulation.* Prentice-Hall, Englewood Cliffs, New Jersey, 1975.

Gordon, G., "A General Purpose Systems Simulation Program," *Proc., ECJJ, Washington, D.C..* pp. 87–104. MacMillan, New York, 1961.

Greenbert, S., *GPSS Primer.* Wiley (Interscience), New York, 1972.

Pritsker, A. A. B., *The GASPIV Simulation Language.* Wiley (Interscience), New York, 1974.

Pritsker, A. A., and **P. J. Kiviat,** *Simulation with GASPII.* Prentice-Hall, Englewood Cliffs, New Jersey, 1969.

Schriber, T. J., *Simulation Using GPSS.* Wiley, New York, 1974.

Thesen, A., "WIDES Users Guide," Tech. Rep. 76–1, Department of Industrial Engineering, University of Wisconsin-Madison, May 1976.

INDEX

A
B
C
D
E
F
G
H
I
J